Suicide and Euthanasia in Older Adults: A Transcultu

Dedication

To my parents, with deep love

Diego De Leo
(Editor)

Suicide and Euthanasia in Older Adults

A Transcultural Journey

Hogrefe & Huber Publishers
Seattle · Toronto · Bern · Göttingen

Library of Congress Cataloging-in-Publication Data

is available via the Library of Congress Marc Database under the
LC Catalog Card Number 2001093389.

National Library of Canada Cataloguing in Publication Data

Main entry under title:

Suicide and euthanasia in older adults : A transcultural journey
Includes bibliographical references.
ISBN 0-88937-251-9

1. Aged—Suicidal behavior—Cross-cultural studies. 2. Euthanasia—Cross-cultural studies.
I. De Leo, Diego, 1951–

HV6545.2.S83 2001 362.28'084'6 C2001-901872-X

USA:	P.O. Box 2487, Kirkland, WA 98083-2487 Phone (425) 820-1500, Fax (425) 823-8324
CANADA:	12 Bruce Park Avenue, Toronto, Ontario M4P 2S3 Phone (416) 482-6339
SWITZERLAND:	Länggass-Strasse 76, CH-3000 Bern 9 Phone (031) 300-4500, Fax (031) 300-4590
GERMANY:	Rohnsweg 25, D-37085 Göttingen Phone (0551) 49609-0, Fax (0551) 49609-88

Printed in Germany
ISBN 0-88937-251-9

Foreword

Suicide is a subject known in almost every culture, in every continent. In many of cultures there is usually some mythical hero or forefather who committed suicide, making it part of the eschatology of many peoples. The interpretation of that mythical suicidal behaviour is always to be taken in its special context and symbolic meaning. Accounts of godly or mythical behaviours carry a lesson and, because of the very nature of the characters involved, they are not part of the everyday life of ordinary human beings, even though in many instances they were created precisely as examples to be followed. Or avoided.

An important distinction, however, should be made between the mythical, symbolic suicide of immemorial times and the actual self-inflicted death of a real person who, generally speaking, has many interpersonal relationships which are left in disarray after a sudden, unexpected, violent and, in most cases, avoidable death.

Demographic and cultural changes have made people more distant from myths, even more distant from each other. From isolated, exceptional cases of heroic and sometimes commendable death we reach a situation of about one million miserable, anonymous deaths every year around the world. Beyond, or in addition to, its cultural and symbolic meanings, suicide has become a major public health problem, with clear psychopathological dimensions.

Secularization of life, which has occurred in most of the world, with a few important exceptions nonetheless, seems to have contributed to the vulgarization of suicide. The strengthening of individualism coupled with a much greater tolerance of deviant behavior, also seems to have an impact in the different perception and meanings suicide has acquired more recently. We are witnessing a movement in the perception of suicide as an exceptional event, referred to with awe, fear and respect in the days of yore, to a not infrequent front page headline, an easily acceptable at-hand "solution" to sometimes trivial problems and difficulties. One could quite reasonably add another category to the typology of suicide proposed by Durkheim more than a century ago (i. e., altruistic, egoistic, anomic and fatalistic suicides): that of the "trivial" suicide.

Although the overall picture of suicide in a global perspective is rapidly changing, the fact remains that suicide still holds very strong links with cultural factors. Almost every "truth" about suicide in a given place or culture can be more or less easily contradicted in another one. Basic, accepted knowledge in suicidology, for example, the predominance of suicide in men, in the elderly, in countries in socio-economic transition, and in people with depression, is constantly challenged by data from countries and cultures heretofore not yet studied with due attention (WHO: *Facts and Figures about Suicide,*

1999). For example, in rural China female suicides predominate over male's; in New Zealand the suicide rates of people aged 15–24 years are higher than in any other age group; in spite of an ongoing transition, suicide rates are going down in Sri Lanka; in some studies, which used psychological autopsies in cases of suicide, schizophrenia and alcohol abuse are more frequently found than depression, to name just a few.

The greatest interest and importance of a good understanding of cultural aspects of suicide lies in its potential for prevention. There is now a general understanding that controversies around some dichotomies such as nature vs nurture, biological vs psychosocial and cultural determinants are less and less fruitful. Unless some flexible approach is adopted, taking into account a diversity of factors such as genes, physical and psychological environment, cultural background and social dispositions and limitations, we will witness a sharp increase in suicide rates.

This book is remarkable in that it addresses cultural aspects of suicide of the elderly, a particular group that is more often than not left aside. If indeed it is true that when suicide rates were clearly higher among the elderly than in any other age group the issue was not taken seriously enough, there is now a great risk that with the already observed shift of higher suicide rates towards younger age groups, suicide of the elderly will receive even less attention. In fact, it is known that in some places where successful suicide prevention programs have been implemented, suicide rates were reduced among younger people, who were targeted more aggressively and efficiently, whereas suicide rates among the elderly have continued to increase, probably due to a lack of specific preventive strategies.

Most of the examples in this book come from the Northern hemisphere, something which can be explained by demographic reasons: currently the proportion of the population 65 years old and over elderly in that part of the world is around 17% of the total population, whereas in the majority of countries in the Southern hemisphere that proportion is about 6%. However, projections made by demographers indicated that in the year 2020, those percentages will increase to 21% and 13%, respectively; in other words, an increase of 25% in developed countries, against an increase of more than 100% in developing countries. Other projections forecast that with the improvement in telecommunications and the increase of geographical displacements, leaps across cultural boundaries will become more and more frequent. People will be rapidly exposed to other cultural norms and patterns, not infrequently quite distinct from their own, without the necessary time to develop adaptative mechanisms and strategies.

We must develop strategies for the integration of the rapidly expanding knowledge in the area of suicidology, and be smart enough to transform it into efficient interventions for the prevention of suicidal behaviour, if we want to avert an explosion of suicide rates in the near future. Important lessons are in front of us and we had better learn them quickly; ignoring them can result in massive, untimely and unnecessary deaths.

Dr J. M. Bertolote
Coordinator, Mental and Brain Disorders
Department of Mental Health and Substance Dependence
World Health Organization

Preface

The suicide of an older adult is a dreadful event, every bit as dreadful as the suicide of any individual, whether young or old. And if we can, for a moment, leave aside cynical, quantitative calculations – such as those concerning years of life lost – it should be clear to us all that the suicide of an older person is associated with just the same amount of suffering, and with the same consequences, as the suicide of a younger person. Like other suicides, it may also have a modeling effect for peers, as well as for younger relatives or acquaintances. The death by suicide of an older person also means that, for that particular individual, life has become so unbearable as to push him or her to try and escape from it, even after accumulating so many years of experiences and knowledge. But the step of suicide is rarely taken, even in older adults, after a reasoned stock-taking of the pros and cons: most of the time it is the outcome of an altered state of mind, just as it appears to be in other periods of life.

This volume talks about suicide in old age and in different countries and cultures, a phenomenon that has been somewhat neglected in recent years. It also reports on other forms of unnatural death that are rapidly increasing in prevalence in today's world (and particularly among the elderly), namely assisted suicide and euthanasia. The book does not pretend to provide a complete, worldwide overview of these phenomena. It is intended more to promote reflection (and hopefully to urge intervention) on topics that so far have been rather neglected: How widespread is suicide among the elderly? What trends can we expect in the future? What role is played by culture and traditions? And what is the status of disquieting "new" phenomena such as active/passive euthanasia and physician-assisted suicide in this particular age group? Discussion of these themes will be found inside this collection of experiences, written by well-known suicidologists and experts in euthanasia from four continents.

It would have been extremely interesting to add some contribution from African countries but unfortunately, this has not been possible. Of the 184 countries belonging to the United Nations, only 97 report mortality data on suicide to the World Health Organization, and for several of these countries data are not divided according to traditional age groups, especially as far as older individuals are concerned. No data are provided by the vast majority of African countries, from the Middle East, or from Central and South America.

Elderly people deserve more consideration and respect. It is they who have constructed the society in which we now live, they who have provided us with the means to study and learn, and to do research to improve our world. But the current and previous generations have changed the way we live to such an extent that there is no meaningful place left for the elderly anymore. And that leads me to another thing this book intends to do, beyond calling attention to the neglected tragedy of elderly suicide, and perhaps the most important thing: to claim more attention for our fathers and mothers, especially if they have been left lonely and isolated.

Prof. Diego De Leo
Director, Australian Institute for Suicide Research and Prevention
President, International Association for Suicide Prevention

Contributors

Karin Andersen
Centre for Suicidological Research
WHO Collaborating Centre for
Prevention of Suicide
Odense, Denmark

Ella Arensman
Department of Clinical and
Health Psychology
University of Leiden
Leiden, The Netherlands

Cigdem Aydemir
Department of Psychiatry
Faculty of Medicine
University of Ankara
Ankara, Turkey

Margaret P Battin
Division of Medical Ethics
University of Utah
Salt Lake City, Utah
USA

José Manoel Bertolote
Mental and Brain Disorders
Department of Mental Health and
Substance Dependence
WHO
Geneva, Switzerland

Unni Bille-Brahe
Centre for Suicidological Research
WHO Collaborating Centre for
Prevention of Suicide
Odense, Denmark

Vincent Camus
Psychogeriatric Service
Department of Psychiatry
University of Lausanne
Lausanne, Switzerland

Iris Chi
Medical and Health Research Network
Department of Social Work and
Social Administration
University of Hong Kong
Hong Kong, PR China

Diego De Leo
Australian Institute for Suicide Research
and Prevention
Griffith University, Brisbane
Brisbane, QLD, Australia

Robert Goldney
Department of Psychiatry
Adelaide University
Adelaide, SA, Australia

Onja T Grad
Department of Psychiatry
University of Ljubljana
Ljubljana, Slovenia

Christian Haring
Regional Neurological Hospital
Hall, Austria

Keith Hawton
Department of Psychiatry
University of Oxford
Oxford, UK

Heidi Hjelmeland
Department of Psychology
Norwegian University of Science and
Technology
Trondheim, Norway

Brian Kelly
Department of Psychiatry
University of Queensland
Brisbane, QLD, Australia

Aleš Kogoj
Department of Psychiatry
University of Ljubljana
Ljubljana, Slovenia

Antoon Leenaars
Windsor, Ontario, Canada, and
University of Leiden
Leiden, The Netherlands

Robyn Leigh
Department of Psychiatry
University of Queensland
Brisbane, QLD, Australia

David Lester
Richard Stockton College of New Jersey
Pomona, NJ, USA

Carlos Augusto De Mendonca Lima
Psychogeriatric Service
Department of Psychiatry
University of Lausanne
Lausanne, Switzerland

Jouko Lonnqvist
National Public Health Institute
Mental Health Department
Helsinki, Finland

Konrad Michel
Psychiatric Department
University of Bern
Bern, Switzerland

Kerryn Neulinger
Australian Institute for Suicide Research and Prevention
Griffith University
Brisbane, QLD, Australia

Susanne Ringskog
National Institute for
Psychosocial Medicine
Karolinska Institute
Stockholm, Sweden

Ellinor Salander-Renberg
Department of Psychology
Umea University
Umea, Sweden

Isik Sayil
Department of Psychiatry
Faculty of Medicine
University of Ankara
Ankara, Turkey

Armin Schmidtke
Department of Psychiatry
University of Würzburg
Würzburg, Germany

Willem J Schudel
Department of Psychiatry
University of Rotterdam
Rotterdam, The Netherlands

Italo Simeone
Psychogeriatric Service
Department of Psychiatry
University of Lausanne
Lausanne, Switzerland

Jože Trontelj
National Medical Ethics Committee
Ljubljana, Slovenia

Johanna M Vroom-Jorgerden
Department of Psychiatry
University of Rotterdam
Rotterdam, The Netherlands

Danuta Wasserman
Centre for Suicide Research and
Prevention of Mental Ill-Health
Karolinska Institute
Stockholm, Sweden

Naoki Watanabe
Department of Psychiatry
Saint Marianna University
School of Medicine
Kawasaki, Japan

Paul S F Yip
Department of Statistics and Actuarial
Science and Medical and Health Research
Network
University of Hong Kong
Hong Kong, PR China

Contents

Suicide Among the Elderly in the World: Covariation with Psychological and Socio-Economic Factors

David Lester

The Richard Stockton College of New Jersey, Pomona, NJ, USA

The prevention and treatment of suicidal behavior requires that we understand the causes and correlates of it. Since this book is focussed on suicidal behavior in the elderly, the group which in many countries has the highest suicide rate, the question arises, therefore, of not only what causes suicidal behavior in general but whether there are special factors which have an influence in the etiology of suicide in the elderly.

Epidemiological Trends

The most striking epidemiological feature of suicide rates in many nations is the increasing rate of both male and female suicide with age, but this pattern is not found in every nation. Fusé (1980) described and labeled three patterns for the variation of suicide rates with age. The Hungarian pattern is one in which the suicide rate increases regularly with age. The Japanese pattern is one with two peaks, a lesser peak in young adulthood and a major peak in old age. The Scandinavian pattern is one which peaks in middle age and is an inverted U-shaped curve.

Lester (1982) examined the validity of Fusé's hypothesis for suicide rates of nations of the world in 1975. The patterns Lester identified are shown in Table 1. Lester concluded that Fusé's patterns were useful for describing the variation of suicide rates with age, but that his labels for them were not the best since, for example, Japanese males had the Hungarian pattern rather than the Japanese pattern. Furthermore, not all patterns could be fitted to one of the three proposed by Fusé. (For example, Danish and Swedish males fell into none of the three patterns.)

Lester also divided the nations into four groups on the basis of their gross national product per capita. In general, male suicide rates increased with age for all four groups of nations. For females, the peak age for suicide rose (from the age group 55–64 to 75+) with decreasing gross national product per capita from the first to the third quartile and then dropped dramatically to the 15–24-year-old group for the poorest nations (those in the fourth quartile).

Table 1. Patterns of Suicide in Males and Females

	Males	Females
Hungarian (peak in old age)	Austria Bulgaria Chile Cuba Czechoslovakia England & Wales France Hong Kong Italy Japan Portugal Spain West Germany	Austria Czechoslovakia Germany Hungary Italy Singapore West Germany
Scandinavian (peak for age 45-54 or 55-64)	Canada Norway Poland	Australia Canada Demark Netherlands Poland Sweden USA
Japanese (minor peak for age 15–24, 25–34 or 35–44)	Belgium Greece Puerto Rico Singapore Uruguay Venezuela USA	Bulgaria Hong Kong Japan Portugal Spain

Source: Lester. (1982)

Changes in Suicide Rates since 1980

The suicide rates by age for some nations of the world who have reported suicide rates to the World Health Organization for 1990 are shown in Table 2a and 2b.

In some of these nations, the peak in old age is striking. For example, in Hungary the suicide rate for men aged 75+ in 1990 was 196.6 per 100,000 per year compared to 20.1 for men aged 15–24. The rate for the elderly men in Hungary was almost double that found in Austria, Bulgaria and France, the nations with the next highest suicides for elderly men.

Table 2a. Male Suicide Rates by age in Countries of the World in 1990

Males	Age						
	15–24	**25–34**	**35–44**	**45–54**	**55–64**	**65–74**	**75+**
Argentina	6.6	7.9	9.9	15.1	19.7	29.6	55.0
Armenia	3.7	5.2	9.9	4.3	7.1	2.3	7.4
Australia	26.6	29.5	26.2	22.6	26.1	25.0	31.4
Austria	25.0	32.7	37.3	47.7	44.0	66.8	107.6
Bulgaria	13.9	17.2	17.6	24.2	27.6	43.5	97.1
Canada	24.6	29.6	26.7	23.4	22.6	20.7	32.4
Costa Rica	11.9	11.6	22.1	10.6	13.9	12.2	26.3
Czechoslovakia	12.2	25.4	36.0	48.9	41.1	54.3	98.6
Czech Rep.	12.6	24.7	36.8	45.0	39.2	62.2	110.5
Denmark	14.1	26.7	44.5	53.0	43.7	47.3	76.7
Estonia	25.9	52.5	66.5	61.9	64.4	61.4	81.0
Finland	50.9	64.1	68.1	63.7	56.3	49.6	90.1
France	14.1	30.6	37.2	41.1	38.3	47.1	105.9
Germany	14.4	22.1	25.2	33.8	35.6	38.1	88.3
E Germany	11.8	25.7	37.5	57.0	54.6	55.0	161.8
W Germany	15.0	21.3	22.2	28.2	31.0	34.6	72.2
Greece	5.2	6.3	5.5	5.3	7.1	7.1	17.4
Hong Kong	7.1	13.6	15.3	13.8	21.5	35.0	66.5
Hungary	20.1	56.0	79.5	99.6	90.2	97.3	196.6
Ireland	14.2	21.5	19.2	23.3	28.2	18.2	14.8
Israel	6.7	14.3	11.2	15.2	15.1	27.1	36.3
Italy	5.9	9.9	10.3	11.5	15.6	23.3	50.3
Japan	9.2	18.4	21.5	32.0	32.5	36.6	62.9
Kazakhstan	26.3	41.4	48.1	60.7	53.0	43.4	80.2
Latvia	20.7	58.4	62.7	69.1	59.2	72.7	104.9
Lithuania	18.2	49.0	71.9	94.1	71.4	74.9	56.0
Mexico	5.0	6.1	6.7	6.0	7.4	10.0	17.8
Netherlands	8.2	15.8	16.2	14.8	16.1	15.4	34.0
New Zealand	38.0	26.1	24.0	24.5	27.4	18.9	38.6
Norway	22.1	28.0	29.7	28.3	34.1	34.3	30.9
Poland	16.2	30.4	33.0	38.4	36.3	28.0	27.3
Portugal	7.4	14.0	11.9	15.9	22.0	30.2	57.8
Romania	9.0	13.3	17.8	25.1	22.5	21.9	25.7
Singapore	13.3	16.0	15.1	22.7	22.1	38.2	79.2
Spain	7.1	10.6	9.5	12.0	16.8	23.4	51.5

Table 2a. Male Suicide Rates by age in Countries of the World in 1990 (cont)

Males	Age						
	15–24	25–34	35–44	45–54	55–64	65–74	75+
Sweden	14.7	25.9	27.2	31.1	32.8	39.3	55.1
Switzerland	24.8	33.2	32.2	39.0	42.7	51.6	86.8
Trinidad & Tobago	26.1	40.2	37.7	18.2	45.2	9.5	10.0
UK	12.2	17.2	17.5	17.1	14.2	14.1	19.4
England & Wales	11.7	16.0	17.1	16.4	13.3	13.6	19.4
N Ireland	12.7	25.2	21.2	16.1	32.2	20.6	10.8
Scotland	16.5	26.1	20.5	24.4	18.5	18.2	21.5
Uruguay	13.4	12.5	19.8	24.8	30.2	29.9	71.2
USA	22.0	24.8	23.9	23.2	25.7	32.2	57.9
USSR	21.3	43.6	54.2	63.4	57.2	54.5	77.7
Russia	28.6	55.0	64.0	72.8	67.0	66.3	98.8
Byelorussia	18.8	42.5	53.4	70.1	54.3	42.4	47.8
Ukraine	17.3	38.8	49.2	62.1	55.5	49.7	71.8
Yugolsavia	9.6	17.2	23.2	34.1	40.3	56.5	97.3
Slovenia	18.9	41.5	48.1	82.3	82.7	75.6	127.1

Source: WHO. (1990).

Table 2b. Female Suicide Rates by age in Countries of the World in 1990

Females	Age						
	15–24	25–34	35–44	45–54	55–64	65–74	75+
Argentina	3.5	3.4	3.4	5.8	6.9	8.7	9.5
Armenia	1.2	1.2	2.9	5.9	1.3	5.8	2.0
Australia	4.7	7.8	5.6	7.3	6.6	8.1	7.9
Austria	5.5	8.4	13.9	16.5	20.8	22.0	35.5
Bulgaria	4.2	4.9	6.4	8.1	11.7	23.1	38.9
Canada	5.0	6.4	9.0	7.4	5.4	5.9	4.2
Costa Rica	1.8	1.2	3.6	0.0	1.4	2.2	4.2
Czechoslo-vakia	4.3	6.4	8.8	11.3	13.8	19.7	29.4
Czech Rep.	4.5	7.7	9.5	11.9	15.9	23.7	35.4
Denmark	4.0	6.9	18.4	27.3	31.5	30.0	32.2
Estonia	5.8	10.2	9.7	25.8	19.7	26.2	42.7
Finland	11.0	12.9	17.7	17.4	19.8	16.6	10.2

Table 2b. Female Suicide Rates by age in Countries of the World in 1990 (cont)

Females	Age						
	15–24	**25–34**	**35–44**	**45–54**	**55–64**	**65–74**	**75+**
France	4.4	9.1	11.8	16.4	18.1	18.5	25.6
Germany	4.3	6.9	7.9	12.9	14.4	19.3	29.5
E Germany	3.4	6.9	8.9	18.7	20.2	28.5	54.6
W Germany	4.5	6.9	7.6	11.4	12.8	17.1	23.7
Greece	1.1	1.5	0.9	3.0	2.1	2.6	2.4
Hong Kong	6.7	11.1	10.7	10.5	13.8	23.7	45.6
Hungary	8.2	11.8	20.3	29.9	28.8	37.1	75.6
Ireland	4.1	8.4	7.1	7.8	7.9	6.9	2.0
Israel	3.3	4.2	3.5	5.9	5.3	10.4	12.2
Italy	2.0	3.0	3.8	4.7	7.0	7.5	9.5
Japan	4.7	9.0	9.2	15.0	17.6	25.3	48.6
Kazakhstan	12.7	7.2	9.7	15.5	17.6	18.0	29.2
Latvia	6.2	5.4	9.4	13.6	14.1	22.3	35.2
Lithuania	4.1	7.4	12.3	12.7	18.6	15.7	24.8
Mexico	1.2	0.9	0.8	0.8	1.2	0.9	0.8
Netherlands	3.6	7.2	8.7	10.1	12.1	9.4	14.9
New Zealand	6.7	7.4	8.0	5.9	5.7	7.6	6.3
Norway	6.3	6.1	10.3	14.1	12.8	13.9	7.9
Poland	2.8	4.3	6.0	7.4	8.7	7.2	7.4
Portugal	3.1	3.6	3.5	5.8	5.7	8.3	15.9
Romania	3.7	3.7	4.4	7.3	8.1	10.3	11.3
Singapore	7.7	15.2	11.6	13.1	14.1	25.5	65.2
Spain	1.7	3.0	3.2	4.3	6.8	9.1	12.9
Sweden	5.3	11.0	12.9	14.9	17.1	14.2	14.9
Switzerland	6.3	10.9	12.8	19.6	16.3	23.1	23.5
Trinidad & Tobago	14.9	7.3	11.3	6.3	2.9	17.4	6.1
UK	2.1	4.1	4.6	5.5	5.5	6.3	5.9
England & Wales	2.0	3.8	4.5	5.1	5.3	6.1	6.2
N Ireland	4.7	2.6	9.3	15.5	6.8	7.8	3.7
Scotland	1.8	8.1	3.8	6.8	7.0	8.5	3.2
Uruguay	2.9	3.6	3.7	4.1	3.0	16.8	10.0
USA	3.9	5.6	6.8	6.9	7.3	6.7	6.0

Table 2b. Female Suicide Rates by age in Countries of the World in 1990 (cont)

Females	Age						
	15–24	**25–34**	**35–44**	**45–54**	**55–64**	**65–74**	**75+**
USSR	6.2	6.2	8.7	13.9	15.5	19.4	28.2
Russia	6.6	7.5	10.0	15.6	17.9	22.6	33.2
Byelorussia	3.4	5.4	9.3	13.3	14.1	14.8	18.0
Ukraine	4.8	5.2	7.6	12.1	13.5	17.3	23.1
Yugoslavia	3.6	5.1	8.6	13.3	16.9	23.7	32.3
Slovenia	4.8	5.7	13.9	20.6	21.1	25.4	36.6

Source: WHO. (1990).

As can be seen in Table 3, the 1980s have been a time of increasing suicide rates in the elderly for some nations: in particular, Finland, Ireland and Spain for males and Northern Ireland, Norway and Spain for females. In contrast, other nations have witnessed a decrease in elderly suicide rates: in particular, Canada, Japan and the Netherlands for males and Greece, New Zealand, Puerto Rico and Scotland for females. It would be useful if we could ascertain why some nations have witnessed a decrease in the suicide rate of the elderly during a period while others have experienced an increase.

Table 3. Percentage change in Youth (15–24) and Elderly (75+) Suicide Rates, 1980–1990

	Males			Females		
	Total	**Youth**	**Elderly**	**Total**	**Youth**	**Elderly**
Australia	+26%	+51%	-2%	-7%	+4%	-13%
Austria	-8%	-13%	+26%	-10%	-18%	+5%
Bulgaria	+8%	+25%	-11%	+7%	-43%	+22%
Canada	-4%	-1%	-15%	-24%	-7%	-29%
Costa Rica	-45%	-6%	+14%	+14%	-65%	+infinity
Denmark	-12%	-13%	-6%	-27%	-87%	+2%
England/Wales	+10%	+83%	-10%	-45%	-33%	-44%
Finland	+19%	+36%	+50%	+16%	+21%	+5%
France	+6%	-10%	+6%	0%	-19%	+5%
Greece	+17%	+73%	+5%	-21%	+83%	-61%
Hong Kong	-12%	-10%	+6%	-14%	-12%	-29%
Hungary	-7%	-36%	-3%	-19%	+2%	-17%
Ireland	+73%	+154%	+289%	+9%	+21%	-47%
Israel	+17%	-38%	-1%	-5%	+175%	-47
Italy	+13%	+11%	+34%	-11%	-17%	-8%
Japan	-8%	-45%	-14%	-5%	-43%	-19%

Table 3. Percentage Change in Youth (15–24) and Elderly (75+) Suicide Rates, 1980–1990 (cont)

	Males			Females		
	Total	**Youth**	**Elderly**	**Total**	**Youth**	**Elderly**
Netherlands	-4%	-1%	-17%	-3%	-3%	+24%
New Zealand	+51%	+95%	+8%	-24%	-17%	-65%
N Ireland	+107%	+87%	+20%	+56%	+213%	+61%
Norway	+27%	+8%	+29%	+21%	+91%	+68%
Portugal	+21%	+42%	+8%	+15%	-24%	+45%
Puerto Rico	+24%	-19%	+39%	-25%	-24%	-100%
Scotland	+30%	+72%	-7%	-37%	-42%	-60%
Singapore	+19%	+48%	-26%	+15%	-34%	+14%
Spain	+67%	+65%	+81%	+86%	+55%	+102%
Sweden	-13%	-13%	+13%	-8%	-9%	+31%
Switzerland	-14%	-27%	+8%	-16%	-49%	+1%
USA	+10%	+9%	+33%	-11%	-9%	+11%
USSR	-24%	-24%	+6%	-16%	+5%	+6%
W Germany	-21%	-21%	-1%	-32%	-20%	-8%
Yugoslavia	+4%	-5%	+22%	+6%	-36%	+28%

Why Is the Elderly Suicide Rate Low in Some Societies?

Looking at American suicide rates, Seiden (1981) noted that American Indian suicide rates decline in older American Indians, similar to the pattern found in African Americans and Hispanics, and different from that found in whites and Chinese Americans whose suicide rates continue to rise with age. Seiden suggested six reasons why American Indian suicide rates might peak at a young age, and the reasons he proposed may be applicable to nations whose elderly have relatively low suicide rates.

1. American Indians have a lesser life expectancy than whites, and perhaps only the strongest (physically and psychologically) American Indians survive into old age?
2. If suicide can validly be conceptualized in the oppressed as anger felt toward others directed inward onto the self (Henry and Short, 1954), then this aggressive behavior should, like other aggressive and criminal behaviors decline with age – a form of the "burn-out" which is found for alcohol abuse, drug abuse, traffic accidents, and crime.
3. In particular, those prone to violence (directed inward or outward) might have been killed early in life, either through murder or accidental deaths with a self-destructive component, such as motor vehicle deaths.

4. American Indian culture may provide more of a role for the elderly, thereby increasing their social integration above and beyond that found for whites who typically place a greater emphasis on the nuclear family and a lesser emphasis on the extended family.
5. Along with this, American Indians may accord the elderly more prestige in the community as well as condemning suicide more.
6. The precipitants for elderly suicide may differ from those for the young, and perhaps American Indian elderly experience fewer stressors than elderly whites? For example, elderly whites may experience much greater downward mobility (or fall from status) than American Indian elderly who were already at a relatively low status.

Explaining the Societal Suicide Rate

Although it is extremely difficult to predict individual acts of suicide (primarily because suicide occurs so infrequently), the suicide rates of societies remain remarkably stable over time. For example, the American suicide rate has stayed at about 12 per 100,000 per year for the last couple of decades.

The major theory still used to explain societal suicide rates is that of Durkheim (1897). Durkheim proposed that suicide would be more common when the level of social integration (that is, the number and strength of the social relationships of the people in the society) was weaker and when the level of social regulation (that is, the extent to which social norms and rules controlled the people's desires and emotions) was weaker.[1] As a result, social and economic variables in the society, such as the divorce rate and the economy, affect the suicide rate of the society by changing the levels of social integration and social regulation. Divorce, for example, breaks social ties and so weakens social integration while it also implies a reduced level of social regulation in those who divorce.

Lester and Yang (1992) reviewed their own research and that of others on the social correlates of the elderly suicide rate and found that the regional correlates of suicide rates in the United States were similar in the elderly and in younger adults. The strongest correlates were measures of social integration. The suicide rates of all age groups were higher in places where divorce and migration were more common and church attendance less common.

Over time, at least in the United States, there were differences by age. The suicide rate of the elderly decreased during times of economic prosperity in America whereas the suicide rate of younger adults increased during such times. This has important implications for the mental health of the elderly during economic depressions, and it also identifies a way in which the causes of suicide in the elderly might be

---

[1] Durkheim actually proposed a U-shaped function and hypothesizied that suicide might also be more common when the levels of social integration and social regulation were extremely high, but modern sociologists have rejected this part of Durkheim's theory (Johnson, 1965).

determined rather differently from suicide in other age groups. These studies need to be replicated in other nations before we consider them to be generally valid.

The Causes of Individual Elderly Suicides: Are there really Differences in Suicidal Behavior by Age?

This question must be addressed because some scholars stress the commonalities of suicide. Shneidman (1985), for example, has listed the ten commonalities of suicide which he feels apply to every suicidal person: the purpose of seeking a solution, the goal of cessation of consciousness, the stimulus of intolerable psychological pain, the stressor of frustrated psychological needs, the emotion of hopelessness-helplessness, the cognitive state of ambivalence, the perceptual state of constriction, the action of egression, the interpersonal act of communicating intent, and the consistency of lifelong coping patterns.

Other scholars, however, have identified differences in suicidal behavior by age. Before reviewing these studies, however, it must be noted that most suicidologists have not studied suicidal behavior across the life span, but rather they have studied suicidal behavior in people of a particular age group, be it adolescence, adulthood or old-age. Only a few researchers have included suicidal persons of all ages, and this section reviews briefly some of these studies.

Physiological Causes

There has been great interest in recent years with the physiological causes of human behavior, and this has extended to suicidal behavior (Lester, 1988a). The major finding has been that defects in the serotonin-mediated neural pathways in the brain may lie behind suicidal behavior and depression in general. However, there is much research which disputes this conclusion, and much more research is needed before we can make a definitive statement about the physiological basis for suicide. There is as yet no research which explores whether the physiological basis for suicide differs for the young and the old.

Childhood Experiences

A good deal of research has documented that particular childhood experiences increase the likelihood of suicide. Parents who are psychiatrically disturbed, who abuse drugs and alcohol, who are depressed and suicidal themselves, who physically and sexually abuse their children and who abandon the children (either through divorce or death) are more likely to have children who eventually become suicidal than parents who do not show these traits and behaviors. For example, Kosky (1983) compared a group of adolescent suicide attempters with a group of nonsuicidal adolescent psychiatric inpatients and found that the suicidal adolescents had more experience of violence between the parents, loss (of any kind, whether through death or separation and of people, pets or possessions), parents with both medical and psychiatric illnesses, and physical abuse from their parents.

This study raises two important questions. The first concerns the direct linkage of suicide with these childhood experiences. It may be that trauma such as physical abuse or the loss of parents through death directly increases the risk of suicide. It is more likely, however, that these experiences increase the likelihood of psychiatric or psychological disturbance which then increases the risk of suicide. Thus, such studies may simply be telling us about the risk factors for psychiatric disturbance and little or nothing about the risk factors for suicide. Be that as it may, such childhood experiences are worth noting in a comprehensive evaluation of a suicidal individual.

The second issue raised by research such as Kosky's is whether these possible etiological factors are more often found in the backgrounds of young suicidal people than of elderly suicidal people. For example, Lester (1991a) examined the lives of the suicides in the sample of 1528 gifted children first studied by Lewis Terman at Stanford University in the 1920s and followed-up carefully ever since. Lester found that those suicides who killed themselves at a younger age were more likely to have experienced the loss of their father by death than were those suicides who killed themselves later in life.

Recent Stressors

Research has documented that suicides have experienced a great deal of recent stress, sometimes escalating in the months and weeks prior to the suicide (Litman, 1989). However, the kinds of stressors experienced by older suicides differ from those experienced by younger suicides. For example, Eisele, et al. (1987) found that psychiatric illness and medical illness were more common precipitants of elderly suicides whereas interpersonal and school/work problems were more common precipitants of young suicides. Similarly, Rich, et al. (1986) found that elderly suicides were precipitated more by medical illness whereas young suicides were precipitated more by legal problems, employment problems and interpersonal separations.

This has led many scholars to comment on the particular losses which characterize the elderly. Stillion, et al. (1989) mentioned the experience of cumulative recent losses, in which the person loses many people in rapid succession, often including the spouse, without adequate time to resolve the grief of any of the losses. There is loss of physical and mental capabilities (often in association with medical illness), retirement, inadequate income, and social isolation and loneliness. These stressors often have a secondary affect on the elderly person by injuring their body-image and their self-esteem (Achté, 1988).

These stressors are common to many, if not most, elderly people. What is missing in the discussion of suicide in the elderly is why some elderly people can cope with these stressors whereas others cannot.[1] For, even though suicide is more common in the elderly than in other age groups, it is still a very rare event.

Psychiatric Disorder

Suicide is more common in those who are psychiatrically disturbed, in particular in those who have an affective disorder and in those who are substance abusers. Suicide is more common in those who have a psychiatric diagnosis of depression, who show the syndrome of depressive symptoms and who have a depressed mood. For example, Barraclough and Hughes (1987) found that 93 percent of a sample of suicides in England were judged to be psychiatrically ill, with 70 percent diagnosed as having an affective disorder.

Beck, et al. (1974) have argued that one component of depression, namely feeling hopeless about the future, is an especially powerful predictor of suicide. Although a great deal of research has supported this assertion (Lester, 1992), the association seems to be weaker, if it exists at all, in the elderly (Hill, et al., 1988; Trenteseau, et al., 1989).

The most common psychiatric illness in suicides differs with age. For example, Rich, et al. (1986) found that elderly suicides were more often diagnosed as having affective disorders and organic brain disorders while young suicides were more often diagnosed as having an antisocial personality disorder or substance abuse.

However, in order to show that psychiatric disorder is more relevant to elderly suicides than to young suicides, it would be necessary first to have data on the incidence of psychiatric disorder by age (to show that the incidence was greater in the elderly than in the young) and second to show that a greater proportion of elderly suicides were psychiatrically disturbed than expected and that fewer younger suicides were psychiatrically ill than expected. This has not been done.

Medical Illness

Many elderly suicides are medically ill at the time they kill themselves. Miller (1979) found that about 60 percent of elderly suicides had extreme health problems, while Dorpat, et al. (1968) found that 85 percent of elderly suicides were ill and that, in 69 percent of the cases, the illness contributed to the suicide.

Barraclough and Hughes (1987) found that 59 percent of suicides in England were medically ill at the time of death, but this percentage did not differ from that found in nonsuicidal people matched for age. Although some studies report more medical illnesses in elderly suicides as compared to those dying of accidental deaths (Barraclough, 1971), more recent research has failed to replicate this (Cattell, 1988).

---

[1] The same question is relevant to the suicides of younger people, namely, why a very few young people commit suicide in response to interpersonal problems whereas the vast majority do not.

On the other hand, suicide is reported to be more common in those suffering from AIDS, epilepsy, peptic and gastric ulcer (though possibly because many of these patients are alcohol abusers), lupus, kidney disease, multiple sclerosis, Huntington's chorea and spinal cord injury (Lester, 1992). The findings for cancer are inconsistent, though some studies do report a high suicide rate especially among the elderly (Olafsen, 1983).

However, the existence of a medical illness does not mean that it is a precipitating factor for the suicide. Vogel and Wolfersdorf (1989) studied elderly psychiatric inpatients who committed suicide and found that only 7.5 percent were motivated by an acute illness and 20 percent by a chronic incurable illness.

The question arises, as before, why, if medical problems are more common in the elderly, both in suicides and in nonsuicides, does medical illness provoke suicide in only a very small minority of the elderly?

One noteworthy trend is the growing number of double suicides and euthanasia deaths among the elderly. Especially with the rise in the incidence of long-term degenerative diseases (of both the body and the mind), more elderly are turning to suicide as a way of avoiding prolonged suffering. This trend is evident in the books being written about children helping aged parents commit suicide (Rollin, 1985) and the recent publicity given to physician-assisted suicide.

Wickett (1989) examined almost a hundred cases of double suicides and found that two-thirds were mercy killings followed by suicide and one-third double suicides. In the typical case, the wife or both partners were suffering, and the husband was the instigator. The couple was usually living alone, and frequently killed their pets too. The couple felt exhausted and helpless and had a fear of being institutionalized and parted. Usually the husband could not bear his wife's suffering or the prospect of life without her.

These issues have resulted in increased discussion in recent years about whether suicide can be rational, whether suicide should be assisted (by physicians, significant others or counselors), and whether there may be social pressure exerted on some (such as the terminally ill elderly) to kill themselves.

The Motives for Suicide

We have seen that, though the elderly in some nations do have higher suicide rates than younger adults, the etiological factors seem similar to those for younger suicides. Analyses of the suicide notes left by the elderly do, however, suggest different motives for their suicide.

Farberow and Shneidman (1957) found that the suicide notes of the elderly reflected more of a wish to escape from suffering and less of a wish to punish themselves or to punish others. Capstick (1960) similarly noted that the suicide notes of the elderly more often referred to illness, the hereafter, management of affairs, and directions intended to protect the survivors from distress or danger, and these notes were less wounding and malicious toward others. In line with these findings, Leenaars (1989) found a lesser emphasis in the suicide notes of the elderly on interpersonal relationships and ties to others, less ambivalence or anger toward others, and less discussion of their inability to overcome personal difficulties.

Also, like the young, but unlike middle-aged adults, the elderly show an imitation response to media news of famous suicides. The elderly show an increase in the suicide rate in the weeks after a famous suicide (Stack, 1991).

There is clinical opinion, not yet substantiated by research, that the suicidal behavior of younger people is more impulsive and, especially in children and adolescents, caused in part by the unconscious hostile desires of their parents. There is also the belief among some that suicide by the elderly can be more rational, but this may be a reflection of the ageist biases of our society. We appear to "approve" of suicide in the elderly, yet view the suicide of a youth as a "tragic waste."

Less Lethal Suicidal Behavior

It has long been held that the elderly use more lethal methods for suicide and are less likely to attempt suicide than younger adults (for example, Templer & Cappelletty, 1986). In the United States, elderly male suicides use guns and hanging (the relatively more lethal methods) more often than do young male suicides, while elderly females use medications for suicide more often than do young female suicides (McIntosh and Santos, 1985-1986). However, since all of these suicides died, all of their methods were lethal!

What then of the lower incidence of suicide attempts in the elderly? Although this is widely believed, recently Osgood, et al. (1991) have documented a high incidence of self-destructive behavior by the elderly in nursing homes. The completed suicide rate was 16 per 100,000 per year, the attempted suicide rate 63, the rate of death from indirect self-destructive behavior 79, and the rate of non-lethal indirect self-destructive behavior 228! Indirectly self-destructive behavior was defined as "repetitive acts by individuals directed toward themselves, which result in physical harm or tissue damage and which could bring about a premature end of life, and included active methods such as self-mutilation and ingesting foreign substances and passive behaviors such as refusing to eat or drink or refusing to follow the medical regime. Those over the age of 75 were more likely to use the passive forms of indirect self-destructive behavior, but they were also more likely to die as a result.

It seems very likely that Osgood's research will cause others to revise their opinion about non-lethal suicidal behavior in the elderly. Perhaps the elderly who act in a suicidal manner but who survive are less likely to be brought to medical emergency rooms or to the attention of authorities who could count the incidence? The acts are taken care by the family caretakers or nursing home staff who do not typically report such behaviors (unless especially asked to do so, as Osgood did).

Do Theories of Suicide Apply to All Ages?

Some theories of suicide may apply better to some groups than to others. As we have seen, investigators have noted that the precipitants of suicide appear to differ for the young and the elderly, with the younger suicides responding more to interpersonal crises. Younger individuals also make many more nonfatal attempts at suicide than do the elderly. Thus, it seems likely that not all theories of suicide apply equally well to both the young and the elderly.

To explore this, Lester (1991b) took ten theories of suicide which Leenaars (1988) had summarized in ten propositions: Alfred Adler, Ludwig Binswanger, Sigmund Freud, Carl Jung, George Kelly, Karl Menninger, Henry Murray, Edwin Shneidman, Harry Sullivan and Gregory Zilboorg. Lester applied these statements to the lives of thirty famous suicides for whom a biography was available and found that some theories were more successful in describing the suicidal lives than others.

Looking at the success of the theories based on the age of the suicides, the lives of the teenagers in the sample were not well described by the theories. Lester found that the theory of Binswanger was more appropriate for the older suicides than the younger suicides, while the theories of Jung, Murray, and Sullivan were less appropriate. Five of the suicides were over the age of sixty. For Binswanger's theory, four of these (80 percent) received a score of 6 or more (out of ten) as compared to only 16 percent of the younger suicides.

Looking at the items which correlated with age, the indications were that suicide for the elderly was more often a liberation from the effects of trauma, while for the younger suicides it was a response to interpersonal problems and intrapsychic problems.

The Relevance of a Developmental Perspective to Prevention

An important question to ask is whether a developmental perspective has implications for preventing suicide. If the suicidal act occurs in different circumstances, is predicted by different variables, and has a different meaning in the elderly as compared with the young, then efforts to prevent suicide might well differ depending upon the age of the target group.

The major strategies utilized in efforts to prevent suicide are: (1) suicide prevention centers, (2) psychiatric treatment, including medication and psychotherapy, and (3) educational programs, supplemented in recent years by (4) restricting availability to lethal methods for suicide. Let us examine each of these in turn.

Suicide Prevention Centers

Suicide prevention centers typically consist of 24-hour telephone counseling services which provide crisis counseling, supplemented in some centers by walk-in clinics which also provide crisis counseling. Who uses these centers?

A study at the suicide prevention center in Buffalo (Lester and Brockopp, 1973) showed that the modal caller was aged 20 to 29 (27%), female (70%), and single (38%). The modal person dying from suicide was, however, elderly and male. Thus, it is clear that telephone services attract a younger (and female) clientele and, therefore, are going to be more effective in preventing suicide in those groups. Suicide prevention centers are aware of this fact, and some do make extra efforts to advertise their services to those groups at high risk for suicide.

Psychiatric Treatment

Psychiatric treatment for suicidal people involves treatment for the underlying psychiatric disorder and the personal and interpersonal problems contributing to the suicidal crisis. This treatment can be given only to those who seek help, and medications, of course, can be prescribed only to patients of physicians and psychiatrists. Thus, it is of interest to ask which types of patients seek help from such resources.

In addition, it was noted above that depressive disorders are more common in older suicides than in younger suicides, suggesting that detection and treatment of depressive disorders might be more effective for preventing suicide in the elderly. Rutz, et al. (1989) found that a program to educate physicians in Gotland, Sweden, in the detection, evaluation and appropriate treatment of depression and suicide led to a reduction in the suicide rate in that region. It would of interest to see whether this reduction was obtained in all age groups.

Education Programs

Education programs are almost always directed toward school children, a group where nonfatal suicidal behavior and ideation is common, but for whom fatal suicidal behavior is infrequent in many nations (Lester, 1988b). Suicidologists should give some thought as to how education programs about suicide could be designed to focus on other groups, such as working adults and the retired.

Restricting Access to Means

In institutions such as hospitals and prisons, inmates thought to be at risk for suicide are placed in "suicide-proof" rooms and monitored continually to minimize their opportunities for self-harm. Easy access to lethal methods for killing is often found to characterize the homes of children who engage in fatal and nonfatal suicidal behavior, especially through overdosing or use of the parents' firearms. The same strategy has been explored at the societal level.

In recent years, much research has documented that restricting access to lethal methods for suicide reduces the use of those methods for suicide and may, in some cases, reduce the total suicide rate. The switch in the United Kingdom from toxic coal gas to less toxic natural gas led to a reduction in the total suicide rate by about thirty percent (Clarke and Lester, 1989).

These changes are usually introduced for reasons other than preventing suicide. Natural gas became cheaper than coal gas in the United Kingdom; emission controls for car exhaust (which reduces the carbon monoxide content) are introduced to reduce pollution; gun control laws are tightened to prevent their use in crime. However, controls over the number and size of prescriptions of medications, medications which are intended for treatment of psychiatric disorders, but which can also be used for suicide, are specifically intended to reduce the risk of suicide.

The question in the present context is whether these methods work better for the young or for the elderly. Again, there is little research on this particular issue. Clarke and Lester (1989) noted that the detoxification of domestic gas in England and Wales had the greatest impact on the total suicide rate of men over the age of 45 and least impact on the total suicide rate of those younger than 24. Furthermore, for men over the age of 45, there was no evidence for switching to alternative methods for suicide. For younger males, there appeared to be some switching to alternative methods for suicide.

In contrast, in a time-series study of the impact of gun control legislation in Canada, Leenaars and Lester (1998) found that imposing stricter controls had an impact on the suicidal behavior of young adults, but no impact on the suicidal behavior of elderly Canadians. On the other hand, in a cross-sectional study over the states of America Lester (1984) found that stricter state handgun control laws had similar beneficial effects on the suicide rates of the young and the old.

Thus, the relevance of age in the success of preventing suicide by restricting access to lethal methods for suicide needs to be explored in much greater depth, especially with regard to the particular method for suicide under study and the nation in which access to the method is restricted.

Conclusions

The elderly suffer from major losses – the loss of physical and mental capacities as a result of aging and illness, the loss of employment and meaningful activity, and the loss of social interaction. It makes sense, therefore, that in many nations the elderly have a very high suicide rate.

What is remarkable, therefore, is that the suicide rate in the elderly, though high, is not even higher. The vast majority of the elderly suffer these losses but do not turn to suicide. This is puzzling, and it is important for scholars to ascertain what prevents so many elderly people with the risk factors for suicide from killing themselves.

Our conclusion from this review concurs with that of others (for example, Carney, et al., 1991), namely that the general determinants of suicide among the elderly are similar to those for younger adults, even though the specific psychiatric disorders and stressors differ. Much more research is needed to identify the ways in which suicide differs for those of different ages.

It can be seen from this review that there is a paucity of research and theorizing on the *unique* features of suicide in those of different ages. All too often, the variables thought to be important in determining the appearance of suicidal behavior in those in one age group (such as depression or alcoholism) are demonstrated to be important for explaining the suicidal behavior of those in other age groups. Though such research findings are useful, we also need to ascertain what etiological factors apply specifically to each age group. The lack of information of this kind prevents us from devising and directing suicide prevention efforts specifically directed toward those of different ages.

Furthermore, most of the research studies cited in this chapter have come from the United States, with occasional studies from Europe. The results of these studies need to be replicated in other nations for it is unlikely that all of the suicidal phenomena reported in this chapter are invariant with respect to culture.

Finally, although it might seem that we have a wide variety of strategies for preventing suicide, we have seen that each strategy in fact is more useful for one age group than others,[1] and so we are less well equipped to prevent suicide than it might appear.

References

Achté, K. (1988). Suicidal tendencies in the elderly. *Socijalna Psyhijatrija, 13,* 57–66.

Barracolough, B. M. (1971) Suicide in the elderly. In D. W. P. Kay & A. Walk (Eds.) *Recent Developments in Psychogeriatrics.* London: RMPA, pp. 87–97.

Barraclough, B. M., & Hughes, J. (1987). *Suicide.* London: Croom Helm.

Beck, A. T., Weissman, A., Lester, D., & Trexler, L. (1974). The measurement of pessimism. *Journal of Consulting & Clinical Psychology, 42,* 861–865.

Capstick, A. (1960) The recognition of emotional disturbance and the prevention of suicide. *British Medical Journal, 1,* 1179–1182.

Carney, S. S., Rich, C. L., & Burke, P. A. (1991). Suicide over 60. In D. Lester (Ed.), *Suicide '91* (p. 14). Denver: American Association of Suicidology.

Cattell, H. R. (1988). Elderly suicide in London. *International Journal of Geriatric Psychiatry, 3,* 252–261.

Clarke, R. V., & Lester, D. (1989). *Suicide: closing the exits.* New York: Springer-Verlag.

Dorpat, T. L., Anderson, W. F., & Ripley, N. S. (1968). The relationship of physical illness to suicide. In H. L. P. Resnik (Ed.), *Suicidal behaviors* (pp. 209–219). Boston: Little Brown.

Durkheim, E. (1897). *Le suicide.* Paris: Felix Alcan.

Eisele, J. W., Frisino, J., Haglund, W., & Reay, D. T. (1987). Teenage suicide in King County, Washington. *American Journal of Forensic Medicine & Pathology, 8,* 208–216.

[1] And we might add, more useful for one sex than for the other.

Farberow, N. L., & Shneidman, E. S. (1957). Suicide and age. In E. S. Shneidman & N. L. Farberow (Eds.), *Clues to suicide* (pp. 41-49). New York: McGraw-Hill.
Fusé, T. (1980). To be or not to be. *Stress, 1(3),* 18–25.
Henry, A. F., & Short, J. F. (1954) *Suicide and homicide. New York: Free Press,*
Hill, R. D., Gallagher, D., Thompson, L. W., & Ishida, T. (1988). Hopelessness as a measure of suicidal intent in the depressed elderly. *Psychology & Aging, 3,* 230–232.
Johnson, B. D. (1965) Durkheim's one cause of suicide. *American Sociological Review, 30,* 875–886.
Kosky, R. (1983). Childhood suicidal behavior. *Journal of Child Psychology & Psychiatry, 24,* 457–468.
Leenaars, A. A. (1988). *Suicide notes*. New York: Human Sciences.
Leenaars, A. A. (1989). Suicide across the adult life-span. *Crisis, 10,* 132–146.
Leenaars, A. A., & Lester, D. (1998). The impact of gun control on suicide. *Archives of Suicide Research, 4,* 25–40.
Leenaars, A. A., & Wenckstern, S. (Eds.). (1991). *Suicide prevention in schools*. New York: Hemisphere.
Lester, D. (1982). The distribution of sex and age among completed suicides. *International Journal of Social Psychiatry, 28*, 256–260.
Lester, D. (1984). *Gun control*. Springfield, IL: Charles Thomas.
Lester, D. (1988a). *The biochemical basis of suicide*. Springfield, IL: Charles Thomas.
Lester, D. (1988b). Youth suicide in cross-cultural perspective. *Adolescence, 23,* 955–958.
Lester, D. (1991a). Childhood predictors of later suicide. *Stress Medicine, 7*, 129–131.
Lester, D. (1991b). The study of suicidal lives. *Suicide & Life-Threatening Behavior, 21,* 164–173.
Lester, D. (1992). *Why people kill themselves*. Springfield, IL: Charles Thomas.
Lester, D., & Brockopp, G. W. (1973). *Crisis intervention and counseling by telephone*. Springfield, IL: Charles Thomas.
Lester, D., & Yang, B. (1992). Social and economic correlates of the elderly suicide rate. *Suicide & Life-Threatening Behavior, 22*, 36–47.
Litman, R. E. (1989). 500 psychological autopsies. *Journal of Forensic Sciences, 34,* 638–646.
McIntosh, J. L., & Santos, J. F. (1985-1986). Methods of suicide by age. *International Journal of Aging & Human Development, 22*, 123–139.
Miller, M. (1979). *Suicide after sixty*. New York: Springer.
Olafsen, O. (1983). Suicide among cancer patients in Norway. In J. P. Soubrier & J. Vedrinne (Eds.), *Depression and suicide* (pp. 587–591). Paris: Pergamon.
Osgood, N. J., Brant, B. A., & Lipman, A. (1991). *Suicide among the elderly in long-term care facilities.* New York: Greenwood.
Rich, C. L., Young, D., & Fowler, R. C. (1986). San Diego suicide study. *Archives of General Psychiatry, 43*, 577–582.
Rollin, B. (1985). *Last wish*. New York: Simon & Schuster.
Rutz, W., van Knorring, L., & Walinder, J. (1989). Frequency of suicide in Gotland after systematic postgraduate education of general practitioners. *Acta Psychiatrica Scandinavica, 80*, 151–154.
Seiden, R. H. (1981). Mellowing with age. *International Journal of Aging & Human Development, 13*, 265–284.
Shaffer, D., Garland, A., Gould, M., Fisher, P., & Trautman, P. (1988). Preventing teenage suicide. *Journal of the American Academy of Child & Adolescent Psychiatry, 27,* 675–687.
Shneidman, E. S. (1985). *Definition of suicide*. New York: Wiley.
Stack, S. (1991). Social correlates of suicide by age. In A. A. Leenaars (Ed.), *Life span perspectives of suicide* (pp. 187–213.). New York: Plenum.

Stillion, J. M., McDowell, E. E., & May, J. H. (1989). *Suicide across the life span*. New York: Hemisphere.
Templer, D. I., & Cappelletty, G. G. (1986). Suicide in the elderly. *Clinical Gerontologist, 5*, 475–487.
Trenteseau, J. A., Hyer, L., Verenes, D., & Warsaw, J. (1989). Hopelessness among later-life patients. *Journal of Applied Gerontology, 8*, 355–364.
Vogel, R., & Wolfersdorf, M. (1989). Suicide and mental illness in the elderly. *Psychopathology, 22*, 202–207.
Wickett, A. (1989). *Double exit.* Eugene, OR: Hemlock Society.
World Health Organization. (1990) Statistics Annual. Geneva: WHO.

Suicidal Behavior in Elderly Europeans

Diego De Leo[1], Unni Bille-Brahe[2], Ella Arensman[3], Heidi Hjelmeland[4], Christian Haring[5], Keith Hawton[6], Jouko Lonnqvist[7], Konrad Michel[8], Ellinor Salander-Renberg[9], Armin Schmidtke[10], Danuta Wasserman[11,*]

[1]*Australian Institute for Suicide Research and Prevention, Brisbane, Australia*
[2]*Centre for Suicidological Research, Denmark*
[3]*Free University of Amsterdam, The Netherlands*
[4]*Norwegian University of Science and Technology, Trondheim, Norway*
[5]*Regional Neurological Hospital, Hall, Austria*
[6]*University of Oxford, Oxford UK*
[7]*National Public Health Institute, Finland*
[8]*Department of Psychiatry, University of Bern, Switzerland*
[9]*Umea University, Umea, Sweden*
[10]*University of Würzburg, Germany*
[11]*Centre for Suicide Research and Prevention, Stockholm, Sweden*

Introduction

Attempted and completed suicide incidence rates exhibit opposing tendencies with respect to age: whilst the incidence of suicide rises as age increases, attempted suicide tends to decrease with age reaching lowest levels among the elderly (De Leo & Diekstra, 1990). The ratio between attempts and completions in elderly people has been approximated as 4:1 versus somewhere between 8:1 and 15:1 for the population in general and 200:1 for the young (McIntosh, 1992).

As with all age groups there are problems in ascertaining the true extent of self-destructive acts. Many cases of attempted suicide in older people go unobserved, as they are not reported to health authorities. Others are of dubious interpretation, such as the suspected intentional overdoses in people with cognitive impairment or cases related to passive self-destructive forms of behavior, such as refusing food or medical care, and whose import is extremely difficult to gauge.

---

*This chapter represents a revised and adapted version of a paper appeared in *the International Journal of Geriatric Psychiatry*. As such, it reports only the names of principal investigators of each center currently involved in the referred study. We wish to express our gratitude to co-workers [W.Padoani & P.Scocco (Italy), D.Lie (Australia), E.Arensman (The Netherlands), S.Fricke & B.Weinacker (Germany)] and previous principal investigators from centers not any longer contributing to the study [P.Crepet (Italy), X.Pommereau & J.Philippe (France), I.Querejeta (Spain), B.Temesvary (Hungary), J.Sampaio Faria (WHO/EURO)].

Comparison of suicide and attempted suicide rates according to age suggests that manipulative or demonstrative self-destructive behaviors occur less often in the elderly than in older age groups: those engaging in such acts seem determined to die as a result. This is also suggested by their choice of more lethal methods (Frierson, 1991), the content of suicide notes (Miller, 1979), psychiatric evaluations (Lonnqvist & Achtè, 1985) and the higher rate of completed suicides following one or more previous attempts, compared with younger groups (Gardner et al., 1964).

These observations have led some to assert that elderly suicide attempts may very often be classified as "failed suicide" especially in men (Busse & Pfeiffer, 1969). Moreover, Kreitman (1976) and Nowers (1993) stressed that the affinity between suicide and attempted suicide is far more marked in this age group than in the younger populace. Lindesay (1986) and Draper (1996) strongly emphasized this observation, suggesting that the study of suicide attempts in the elderly might allow a clearer understanding of suicide and its prevention than in other age groups.

The data presented in this chapter derive from the WHO/EURO Multicentre Study on Parasuicide, which began in 1989 and is still in progress (Bille-Brahe et al., 1996, 1997; Schmidtke et al., 1996). The study arose as a European response to rising suicide and attempted suicide rates, whose reduction was a WHO target for the region (WHO, 1992). The study of suicidal acts in the elderly was considered of particular relevance in realising this goal.

Method

Instruments and Data Sources

This report is based on data collected by 16 centers from 13 European countries participating in the above mentioned study in the years 1989–1993: Odense (Denmark), Padua and Emilia-Romagna (Italy), Sor-Trondelag (Norway), Helsinki (Finland), Stockholm and Umea (Sweden), Oxford (UK), Leiden (The Netherlands), Pontoise and Bordeaux (France), Wuerzburg (Germany), Bern (Switzerland), Innsbruck (Austria), Guipuzcoa (Spain), and Szeged (Hungary).

The study collected data on attempted suicide and used the term parasuicide by defining it as "an act with non-fatal outcome, in which an individual deliberately initiates a non-habitual behavior that, without intervention from others, will cause self-harm, or deliberately ingests a substance in excess of the prescribed or generally recognized therapeutic dosage and which is aimed at realizing changes which the subject desired via the actual or expected physical consequences" (WHO, 1986). The title of the study was changed in 1999 to "WHO/EURO Multicentre Study of Suicidal Behavior."

Information relating to parasuicidal episodes was collected using a standard monitoring form, which recorded sociodemographic variables, specific clinical characteristics, psychiatric diagnosis and any referrals to health facilities following parasuicide. Data were obtained from admissions to health facilities or from other sources assessing parasuicides in the same catchment area (eg., general practitioners, private doctors, residential institutions, etc.). For a complete description of sources see Schmidtke et al. (1996).

It was presumed that attempted suicides were registered in all health facilities in which parasuicidal subjects could be received (and/or registered) by health professionals. As some centers were unable to monitor health facilities seven days a week, day and night, "estimation factors" were calculated (Platt et al., 1992; Schmidtke et al., 1996). Suicide data for each center were taken from official health statistics for the district.

Unfortunately, not all sixteen centers were able to collaborate for a full five years of data collection, largely due to a lack of renewed annual funding. For some analyses therefore, not all centers are considered and these details are indicated where relevant.

Statistical Analysis

Within the data, repeat attempters were identified and considered once only. A distinction was made between "first evers" (subjects who attempted suicide for the first time ever within the study period) and "repeaters" (subjects who reported at least one other attempted suicide at the start of the study or who had multiple attempts within the study period).

Increases and decreases in rates for each center were calculated by considering percentage differences between rates for the last available year and rates for the first year of observation. Since the available data were particularly heterogeneous, we restricted calculations for all centers to a mean rate over the total period of data collection, for both suicides and parasuicides, rather than, for example, each year.

To assess global trends for suicide and parasuicide over the five year period the total number of cases was divided by the sum of the total study population (i.e., combined populations of individual reference groups) and the first year's data compared with the last.

Eight centers provided complete parasuicide data for the five year period (Wuerzburg, Umea, Padua, Odense, Stockholm, Sor-Trondelag, Oxford and Helsinki) and six centers (Wuerzburg, Umea, Padua, Odense, Stockholm and Bern) had complete suicide data for those five years. Trends for suicide and parasuicide and analysis of data across age groups were conducted for these combinations of centers only.

Similarly, to correlate parasuicide with suicide only the five centers with five years' complete data for both suicides and parasuicides (Wuerzburg, Umea, Padua, Odense, Stockholm) were used.

Year rates, for total sample and by gender, were used (by calculating Pearson's auto-correlation coefficients) to look for any relationship between time and rates of suicide/parasuicide.

Sociodemographic and Clinical Characteristics

The sociodemographic and clinical data relate to 1518 parasuicidal subjects in 15 out of 16 centers (these data and those relating to absolute parasuicide for 1993 are missing for Pontoise). Generally such data were available for 1989–93 but Leiden, Emilia-Romagna and Innsbruck provided data for 1989–92, Szeged and Guipuzcoa for 1989–91, Bern for the years 1989, 1990 and 1993 and Bordeaux for 1989 only.

As stated previously, six centers had five years of official suicide statistics but for other analyses, suicide data was also available from four (Szeged and Innsbruck 1989–92, Oxford and Helsinki 1989–91).

Many of the variables have missing data but at relatively low levels: parasuicidal method (2%), marital status (18%), household composition (16%), referral to health facility (23%), past history of parasuicide (28%) with one case of unrecorded gender. Incomplete data were more significant an issue for educational and religious belief (50%) and professional qualification (64%). Data concerning the variables “marital status”, “household composition”, “referral to health facility”, “religious belief” and “professional qualification” will not be commented upon further. Psychiatric diagnosis was only recorded in Padua, Wuerzburg, Sor-Trondelag, Innsbruck and Emilia (638 subjects, 42% of total sample).

As noted earlier, incompleteness of data is not so much related to differences in methodology or accuracy of collection, as to lack of funding renewal for some centers who were then unable to continue collaboration for this part of the WHO/EURO Study.

Results

Age and Gender

A total of 1734 parasuicidal events were considered related to the actions of 1518 subjects over 65 (Gender details were unavailable for one subject): 35.5% males (n = 538) and 64.5% females (n = 979). Women committed 65.1% (n = 1129) of parasuicides and men 34.9% (n = 604) with a F/M ratio = 1.9. An event/person ratio of 1.1 emerged, with 1.1 for males and 1.2 for females. The mean age of the total parasuicide sample was 74.7, SD 6.9 years. There were no significant differences in terms of gender (74.7, SD 6.9 for males and 74.6, SD 6.9 for the females). No statistical differences emerged between the individual centers for mean age. The center with the highest mean age was Wuerzburg (77.0, SD 7.1); the center with the “youngest” mean age was Sor-Trondelag (72.3, SD 5.4).

Incidence of Parasuicide

The mean parasuicidal rate for the over 65-year-old population was 61.4/100,000 inhabitants in the total sample, 57.7/100,000 for males and 64.0/100,000 for females (see Table 1). The ratio between these rates for both sexes slightly favours *women (F/M = 1.1).*

Table 1. Mean suicide and parasuicide rates in the elderly of 15 European centers, 1989–1993

Rates	Males	Females	Total	F/M
Suicide	49.48	19.29	29.28	0.39
Parasuicide	57.73	64.02	61.43	1.11
Parasuicide/ Suicide	1.17	3.32	2.09	

Stockholm was the center with the highest parasuicide rate, in both the total sample (116.9) and by gender (101.1 for males and 127.6 for females). Guipuzcoa reported the lowest parasuicide rates both for the total sample (32.3) and for the female sample (26.6), while the lowest incidence of parasuicide among males was reported for Umea (30.6) (see Figure 1).

Figure 1. Elderly suicide attempt rates in 15 European centers, 1989–1993

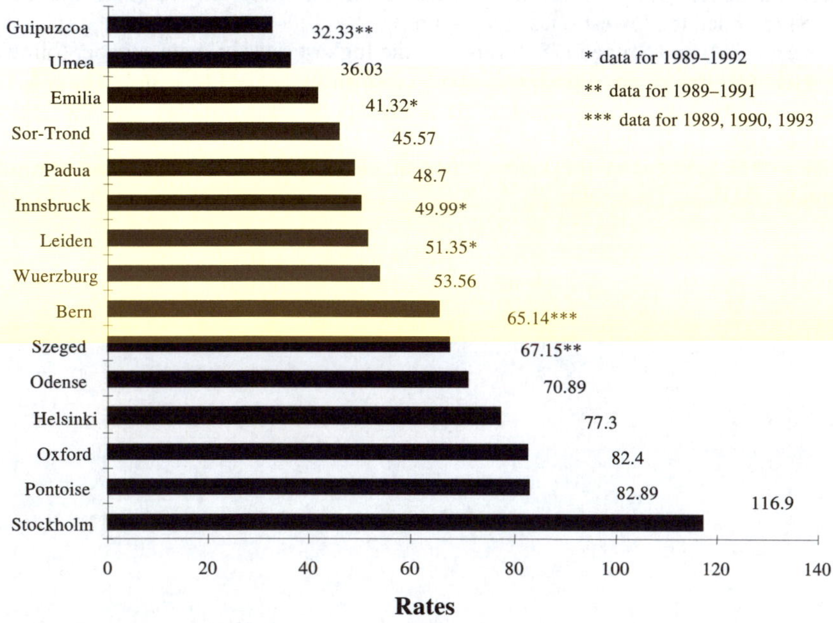

Parasuicide rates decreased across the five years both in the total sample (fall of –4.9%) and among females (drop of –9.3%), while there was a slight increase for males (+3.1%). The rates/years auto-correlation series was not statistically significant.

Parasuicide rates decreased in eleven centers. The greatest fall was reported in Pontoise (-85.7%), followed by Umea (-35%) and Bern (-34.2%). Conversely, increases were reported in Wuerzburg (+42.1%), Leiden (+40.8%), Sor-Trondelag (+23.4%) and Emilia-Romagna (+15.1%).

Nine out of 15 centers reported a decrease for males, with the highest rates in Guipuzcoa (-68.1%), Oxford (-24.1%) and Bern (-23%). The highest increase was observed in Sor-Trondelag (+588%), with a rise in incidence from 6.0 in 1989 to 41.3 in 1993, in Helsinki (+27.1%) and in Emilia-Romagna (+19.5%). In nine centers there was a decrease in female parasuicide, particularly in Pontoise (-85.7%), Helsinki (-68.9%) and Innsbruk (-45%), in six centers, female parasuicide proved to be on the increase from 1989 to 1993, with the highest increases emerging in Guipuzcoa (+150%), Wuerzburg (+62.5%) and Leiden (+68.8%). It should be noted that in most cases big differences in percentage resided in small number fluctuation.

Incidence of Suicide

In the ten centers providing suicide rates for the period 1989–1993, the population aged 65 and over showed a mean suicide rate of 29.3 for the total sample, 49.5 for males and 19.3 for females (ratio F/M = .39) (Table 1). Bern reported the highest mean incidence (45.6), followed by Odense (42.9), while Oxford (9.2) and Umea (15.8) recorded the lowest rates (see Figure2).

Bern (83.0) and Szeged (78.0) reported the highest rates of male suicide, followed by Helsinki (64.9) and Innsbruck (63.8), while Oxford (11.7) and Umea (24.3) exhibited the lowest rates. As for the female population, Odense had the highest suicide rate (31.4), followed by Szeged (27.7) and Bern (25.0). Oxford (7.4) and Umea (9.2) maintained the lowest rates of all centers, in terms of both the total sample and males (see Table 2).

Figure 2. Elderly suicide rates from 10 European centers, 1989–1993

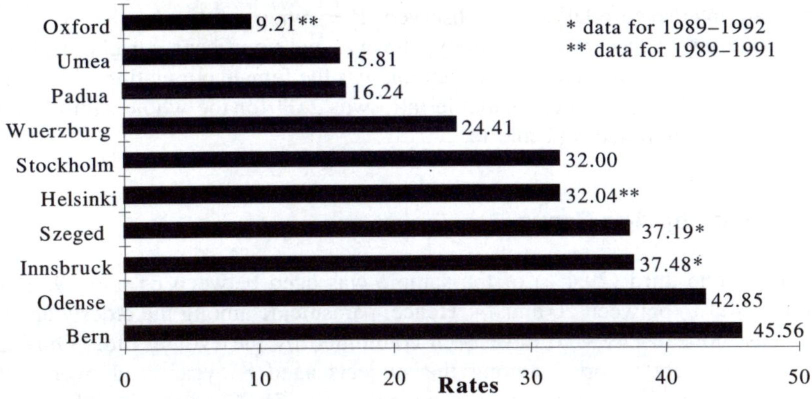

Table 2. Mean suicide rates by gender in the elderly of 10 European centers, 1989–1993

Centers	Males	Females
Umea	24.25	9.15
Padua	24.59	11.31
Innsbruck*	63.83	23.15
Wuerzburg	40.08	16.11
Bern	**82.99**	25.04
Szeged*	78.02	27.67
Odense	59.9	**31.44**
Helsinki**	64.86	18.12
Oxford**	**11.71**	**7.44**
Stockholm	44.5	23.46

Lowest and highest rates in bold. Data for 1989–1992(*), 1989–1997(*)

Suicide rates showed a total decrease of -14.6% (-25.3% in males and -1.4% in females) and no significant decrease emerged on computation of the rates/ years auto-correlation series.

The highest increase was reported in Umea (+290.9%) and Innsbruck (+27.3%), while the greatest decrease emerged in Bern (-56.0%), Stockholm (-51.6%) and Oxford (-42.7%). In males, the highest decreases were observed in Bern (70.0%), Padua (-53.8%) and Oxford (-47.2); only Umea (+198.2%) and Wuerzburg (+63.0%) reported an increase in suicide incidence. In the female population, Szeged (-62.4%) and Stockholm (-56.8%) reported the highest decrease, while the highest increase in the phenomenon was recorded in Padua (+180.4%) and Innsbruck (+40.0%).

The correlation between suicide and parasuicide rates (five centers only) was not statistically significant in the total and female samples. In males, however, a significant inverse correlation was observed ($R = -.96$, $p < .01$).

Considering each center separately, the was no significant correlation between suicide and parasuicide. The only exception was the female population of Umea ($R = -.94$, $p < .05$). The parasuicide/suicide ratio was 2.09 for the whole sample, 1.17 in males and 3.32 in females (Table 1).

Distribution by Age Group

Just under one third (29.4%) of the sample was aged between 65 and 69, and one quarter (24.3%) between 70 and 74. Hence, parasuicide among the elderly appeared, in at least 50% of cases, to have been committed by the "young old." Only a few parasuicides were reported among the subjects aged 85 years and over (<10%). Taking account of repeaters, the percentage rose to 55.9% in the 65–74 age group. The largest group was concentrated in the 65–69 age band in 10 of the 15 centers and in the 70–74-year-old age group in three centers. There was a significant difference in frequency distribution among the various centers (chi-square = 91.4, df = 70, $p < .05$).

The parasuicide rate for the eight centers providing complete data over the entire study period was highest in the 70–74-year-old age group for both the total and male samples (67.0 and 61.0/100,000 respectively). In the 65–69-year-old age group there was a preponderance of women (82.7/100,000).

The trend in inter-sex differences was not, however, statistically significant (see Figure 3). While rates for women always remained higher, rates for men and women converge in the 70–74 and 75–79 age groups (F/M ratio 1.18 and 1.15, respectively).

Parasuicide Method

On comparison of the various centers, a high prevalence (57.2% of all parasuicides) of drug overdoses emerged (especially benzodiazepines and hypnotics). The second method, in most centers, in order of frequency, was self-injury with sharp objects (especially wrist cutting)(11.2%), followed by poisoning with non-steroid anti-inflammatory agents (6.4%) and other unspecified drugs (5.5%). The exception was Guipuzcoa, where the most widely adopted method for the 16 reported cases proved to be jumping from high places (29.4%), with a similar incidence of drug overdoses and use of sharp objects (23.5%). Interestingly, the third most frequently used method in Umea and Wuerzburg was hanging, strangling and suffocation. In Szeged the second most common method was poisoning with chemicals such as pesticides, solvents, and so forth (24.1%). The differences between the centers appeared to be statistically significant (chi-square = 72.23, df = 14, $p < .000$).

On distinction by gender, women more frequently used overdose with benzodiazepines and hypnotics than men (F = 63.3% vs M = 45.5%). By contrast, a slightly higher percentage of men than women injured themselves with sharp objects (13.8% vs 9.8%). Overdose with other drugs was the third method for men (7.5% vs 4.5%) and the fourth for women (who appeared to prefer non-steroid anti-inflammatory agents). Hanging was also more widely adopted by men (6.6%) than women (2.3%). Gender differences were statistically significant (chi-square = 85.42, df = 1, $p < .000$). In the sample as a whole, 15% used more than one method (18% of males and 14% of females). The most commonly adopted method used in association was overdose with anti-inflammatory drugs and pain killers (25.3%) or with other types of drugs (22.3%).

Figure 3. Parasuicide rates by age groups in the elderly, 1989–1993*

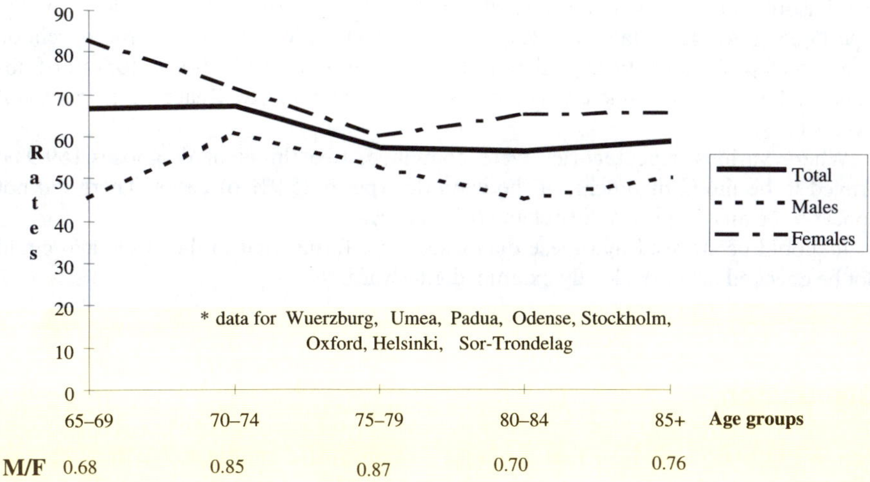

On further subdivision of suicidal methods into two additional categories, according to level of violence (hard and soft), where "soft" methods include voluntary ingestion of drugs or superficial self-injury with sharp or blunt objects, and "hard" ones include all other methods, less violent methods were adopted in 89.1% of cases. Significant gender differences emerged, with males adopting "hard" methods (16.1%) more frequently than women (8.1%) (chi-square = 22.0%, df = 1, $p < .000$). The over 75 age group also exhibited a higher prevalence of hard methods than the younger groups.

Previous Parasuicides

In the sample as a whole, 66.4 % of subjects had never attempted suicide prior to the index event. In 11.9% of those who repeated parasuicide, the penultimate event had occurred during the previous year. The mean age of the repeaters (72.7, SD 6.2) was lower than the "first evers" (74.8, SD 6.9%) (t = 3.7; p = .000).

Psychiatric Diagnosis

Six centers (Emilia, Padua, Wuerzburg, Stockholm, Sor-Trondelag, Innsbruck) provided data on psychiatric diagnosis formulated according to ICD-9 criteria (638 subjects) (WHO, 1977). In 247 subjects (38.7% of the total sample; 31.6% males, 68.4% females) a psychiatric disorder meeting ICD-9 diagnostic criteria was present.

The most frequently observed diagnosis was Manic-Depressive Psychosis, depressive type (17.8% of cases), followed by Neurotic Depression (15.8%), Depressive Disorders not classified elsewhere (10.1%), Manic-Depressive Psychosis, manic type (9.3%), Anxiety states (9.3%), Adjustment Disorders (8%), Organic psychotic states (5.6%), Personality Disorders (3.6%), Schizophrenia (3.2%), Alcohol or Substance Abuse or Dependency Disorders (2.8%) and Acute Reaction to Stressful Events (2%).

Where various subcategories were combined, two thirds of diagnoses (69.9%) proved to be mood disorders, of the neurotic type in 25.9% of cases. There did not appear to be any major gender-related differences.

It should be stressed that these diagnoses were formulated in the clinic and could not be checked or more closely examined afterward.

Discussion

The WHO/EURO study offers a unique example of a multinational but regional effort to accumulate data on parasuicide (and to a lesser extent suicide). This focus on its findings in respect to older subjects can be explored in terms of significant demographic and clinical correlates of parasuicidal behavior, trends for attempted and completed suicide across Europe in the 1989–93 period and parasuicide and its relationship to suicide. Some observations as to the value of studying elderly parasuicide in order to prevent elderly suicide conclude the discussion.

Correlates of Parasuicidal Behavior

Parasuicide is a phenomenon more common among the young and this study confirms a fact that has been well-known for some time. In the pool of 22,665 cases of parasuicide recorded between 1989 and 1993, elderly subjects accounted for 9% of all parasuicides (the 15–34 age group accounted for 50%). Considering the centers and all ages globally, parasuicide was four times less frequent among elderly women than young women, while the elderly/young ratio in males was 1 to 3 (Schmidtke et al., 1996).

The various collaborating centers did, however, report very different rates. Stockholm had an overall incidence of elderly parasuicides 3.6 times higher than the Spanish center of Guipuzcoa, which was lowest in ranking. The difference was even more marked between these two centers for females, where the ratio was 4.8:1.

The ratio between number of recorded parasuicidal events and persons was lower in elderly subjects than in the total sample described by Schmidtke et al. (1996): 1.14 vs 1.29, without noticeable gender differences.

An interesting pattern emerges for parasuicidal behavior as a function of gender and increasing age. While in the sample considered as a whole (15 years of age and upwards), the F/M ratio was 1.5 (Schmidtke et al., 1996), male and female parasuicide rates among elderly Europeans tend to level up, albeit with a slight female bias (=1.1). Thus, as age increases, the difference in parasuicide rates between the sexes tends to converge considerably. Unlike the parasuicide phenomenon, completed suicides by elderly males are twofold those of females and the male/ female ratio increases with age.

The subjects in our sample most frequently employed voluntary poisoning by drugs and self-injury with sharp objects. Male individuals more frequently adopted more lethal means. Parasuicidal method also differed significantly between the various centers, for example, peculiar features in Guipuzcoa (where jumping was most frequently used) and Szeged (where the second most common method was poisoning with chemicals such as pesticides and herbicides). Unfortunately lack of data precludes similar considerations being addressed to methods employed in completed suicide.

In terms of diagnosis, although there are missing data and most of the available data were collected after routine consultation in hospital, there was evidence of a preponderance of depressive disorders (two thirds of all diagnoses) with a relatively low number of personality, substance abuse and schizophrenia-spectrum illnesses.

Suicidal Behavior and Temporal Trends

Over the five year study period, parasuicide rates in Europe remained practically constant with only a slight fall in older groups as a whole (-4.9%). In the WHO/ EURO study, ten countries were able to provide local data for suicide and a slight fall in rates was observed.

Parasuicide and its Relationship to Suicide

The parasuicide/suicide ratio was 2:1 for the ten centers presenting local figures for suicide but parasuicide as a behavior was not particularly linked to completed suicide and some centers recorded very important differences. Stockholm, for example, reported the highest suicide rate with a ratio of 3.6:1 between the two. Bern, on the other hand, presented very similar parasuicide to suicide rates (1.4:1) with a 1:1 ratio in males. Oxford, by contrast, had a ratio of 9:1 with one of the highest rankings for parasuicide and one of the lowest positions for completed suicide.

As previously stated, there was no significant correlation between parasuicide and suicide in the total sample where both phenomena were recorded across the full five years and none for each center separately with the exception of females in Umea.

Implications for the Prevention of Suicide

The group of parasuicides aged 75 and over exhibited a greater tendency towards the use of more violent methods compared with younger age bands, providing some support to the notion that with advancing age, parasuicide is increasingly likely to assume connotations of failed suicide. However our inability to demonstrate wide-spread correlation between the two phenomena does not suggest this and an inverse correlation for males in the group of five centers (Wuerzburg, Umea, Padua, Odense and Stockholm) may indicate that the group of attempters is not overlapping to a great degree with those who complete suicide.

Moreover, as their age increased, parasuicidal subjects displayed only a limited tendency to repeat self-destructive acts over the five years. This makes it unclear what role specific interventions might play if older patients with parasuicidal behavior were selected out. However, in generalising the above considerations much caution has to be adopted. First of all, the examination of the correlation between fatal and non-fatal suicidal behavior has been performed on a limited number of centers (5 out of 16, approximately one third of the collaborating centers). Secondly, hidden suicide behavior (rather frequent in the elderly) was not investigated. Hypothetically, it could be that a number of deaths might have been recorded as "undetermined" (or due to other causes) instead of suicide (De Leo & Carollo, 1996), thus influencing the resulting lack of association between parasuicide and suicide. Lack of completeness in data collection within centers may also have affected some of the results.

Limitations of the Study

A large mass of data from different national centers allows for the abstraction of patterns which are probably common to the species whilst differences between sites underline the impact of cultural factors. A disappointing aspect, however, in terms of our ability to look at cultural influences, was inconstant participation (due to funding problems) which limited the availability of educational and occupational data.

Regarding assessment of suicidal behavior within the various countries, there are obviously variations in coverage, reliability and definition (Lonnqvist & Achtè, 1985), with the phenomenon of underreporting further complicating epidemiological assessment. Certain features, in particular, strongly influence data collection among the elderly, namely the high frequency of chronic disease states and prescribed drugs, the higher incidence of accidents, the influence of insurance benefits, the social status of the person and, more recently, increasing issues surrounding euthanasia and assisted suicide. Despite these considerations, we feel the reported trends can still be considered valid.

Conclusions

In spite of the heterogeneity recorded by various centers, this study confirms that there is a lower parasuicidal tendency among the elderly compared with the young. Among elderly Europeans, the female/male parasuicide ratio tends to level out, although a slight female bias remains. While parasuicidal rates were almost the same for men and women, the number of suicides committed by elderly European males was almost twofold.

The period during which this work was undertaken testified to essentially stable parasuicide rates and a slight fall in suicide rates in the elderly European population, without any significant correlation between the two trends over those years.

With advancing age, suicidal behavior appears to be more determined and only a limited tendency to repeat self-destructive acts emerged from our sample.

Regarding the assumption that attempts in the elderly can be treated conceptually as failed suicides, the paper demonstrates that there is not a direct correlation between parasuicidal and suicidal behavior in the elderly. Furthermore, in contrast to the finding by Hawton et al. (1998) (in the context of the same WHO/EURO study) of a direct correlation between parasuicidal and suicidal behavior in young males, the reverse appears to be true for elderly male subjects. This may be relevant for the prediction of suicidal behavior in this age group in that the two phenomena correlate inversely.

In addition, even if it's probably true that studying parasuicide in older people would provide more insight into suicidal behavior in this age band, the low repetition rate observed in the elderly limits the impact of specific intervention for this group. This lower repetition rate does not allow them to be considered as a high risk group in the same way as younger subjects.

Increasing our understanding of suicidal behaviors has specific challenges at different stages across the lifespan. In some ways, this process is most difficult for the elderly, due to reduced access to both the behaviors themselves (less attempts, less repeats, masked intent) and an increasing attitudinal divide between them and their youth. If this paper illustrates the limitations of parasuicide as a focus of this undertaking, it should not diminish our perseverance, as our efforts are, in some ways, part of a process that seeks to reconcile the young with the old.

References

Bille-Brahe, U., Kerkhof, A., De Leo, D., Schmidtke, A., Crepet, P., Lonnqvist, J., Michel, K., Salander-Renberg, E., Stiles, T. C., Wasserman, D., Aagaard, B., Egebo, H., & Jensen, B. (1997). A repetition-prediction study on European parasuicide populations. A summary of the first report from Part II of the WHO/EURO Multicentre Study on Parasuicide in cooperation with the EC Concerted Action on Attempted Suicide. *Acta Psychiatrica Scandinavica, 95* (2), 81–86.

Busse, E. W., & Pfeiffer, E. (1969). *Behaviour and Adaptation in Late Life*. Boston: Little Brown & Co.

De Leo, D., & Carollo, G. (1996). Relationship between suicide and undetermined causes of death among the elderly – analysis of Italian data from 1951 to 1988. *Omega, 33*, 215–231.

De Leo, D., & Diekstra, R. F. W. (1990). *Depression and Suicide in Late Life.* Toronto/Bern: Hogrefe & Huber.

Draper, B. (1996). Attempted suicide in old age. *International Journal of Geriatric Psychiatry, 11,* 577–587.

Frierson, R. L. (1991). Suicide attempts by the old and the very old. *Archives of Internal Medicine, 151*, 141–144.

Gardner, E. A., Bohn, A., & Mack, M. (1964). Suicide and psychiatric care in the ageing. *Archives of General Psychiatry, 10*, 547–553.

Hawton, K., Arensman, E., Wasserman, D., Hultén, A., Bille-Brahe, U., Bjerke, T., Crepet, P., Deisenhammer, E., Kerkhof, A., De Leo, D., Michel, K., Ostamo, A., Philippe, I., Querejeta, I., Salander-Renberg, E., Schmidtke, A., & Temesváry, B. (1998). Relation between attempted suicide and suicide rates among young people in Europe. *Journal of Epidemiology and Community Health, 52,* 191–194.

Kreitman, N. (1976). Age and parasuicide (attempted suicide). *Psychological Medicine, 6*, 113–121.

Lindesay, J. (1986). Trends in self-poisoning in the elderly 1974–1983. *International Journal of Geriatric Psychiatry, 1*, 37–43.

Lonnqvist, J., & Achté, K. (1985). Follow-up study on the attempted suicides among the elderly in Helsinki in 1973–1979. *Crisis, 6*, 10–17.

McIntosh, J. L. (1992). Suicide of the elderly. In B. Bongar (Ed.), *Suicide Guidelines for Assessment, Management and Treatment.* New York: Oxford University Press.

Miller, M. (1979). *Suicide after sixty*. New York: Springer.

Nowers, M. (1993). Deliberate self-harm in the elderly: a survey on one London Borough. *International Journal of Geriatric Psychiatry, 8*, 609–614.

Platt, S., Bille-Brahe, U., Kerkhof, A., Schmidtke, A., Bjerke, T., Crepet, P., De Leo, D., Haring, C., Lonnqvist, J., Michel, K., Philippe, A., Pommereau, X., Querejeta, I., Salander-Renberg, E., Temesváry, B., Wasserman, D., & Sampaio-Faria, J. (1992). Parasuicide in Europe: the WHO/EURO Multicentre Study on Parasuicide. Introduction and preliminary analysis for 1989. *Acta Psychiatrica Scandinavica, 85*, 97–104.

Schmidtke, A., Bille-Brahe, U., De Leo, D., Kerkhof, A., Bjerke, T., Crepet, P., Haring, C., Hawton, K., Lonnqvist, J., Michel, K., Pommereau, X., Querejeta, I., Philippe, I., Salander-Renberg, E., Temesvary, B., Wasserman, D., Fricke, S., Weinacker, B., & Sampaio-Faria, J. G. (1996). Attempted suicide in Europe: rates, trends and sociodemographic characteristics of suicide attempters during the period 1989–1992. Results of the WHO/EURO Multicentre Study on Parasuicide. *Acta Psychiatrica Scandinavica, 93*, 237–338.

WHO. (1977). *Manual of the International Statistical Classification of Diseases, Injuries and Causes of Death* (9th revision). Geneva: WHO.

WHO. (1986). *Working Group on Prevention Practices in Suicide and Attempted Suicide.* York, 22–26th September 1986 ICP/PSF 017 (s) 6526V.

WHO. (1992). *Health-for-all Targets. The Health Policy for Europe. Summary of the Updated Edition* (EUR ICP/HSC 013). Copenhagen: WHO.

Suicide Among the Elderly in Sweden

Danuta Wasserman[1] and Susanne Ringskog[2]

[1]National Centre for Suicide Research and Prevention of Mental Ill-Health,
[2]National Institute for Psychosocial Medicine, Karolinska Institute, Sweden

Attitudes

Sweden, Denmark and Norway are countries with great similarities – historical, cultural and linguistic. Today, all three are prosperous, modern economies. These countries' prevailing Protestant Christian faith has largely lost its everyday significance in people's lives and been superseded by materialist values. In this context, youth, vigour and health are idealised, while the elderly, past their productive time of life, receive less and less respect. This is also an effect of industrialisation, with younger people leaving the countryside to work in urban areas, thus breaking up traditional family structures and alienating the generations from one another.

Another factor contributing to the problem of ageing in modern industrialised society is the growing proportion of elderly in the population. In Sweden in 1997, the over-65s made up some 17 percent of the population – a figure that, by the year 2010, is expected to rise to almost 20 percent. Supporting the growing elderly population represents, of course, a heavier burden on the diminishing segment of the population that is employed. Is this demographic trend reflected in changing attitudes towards the elderly?

One interesting study (Hagberg, 1993) compared attitudes towards the elderly in Sweden as shown in literary fiction between 1830 and 1950, on the one hand, with the image reflected in newspaper headlines in 1981 and 1991 on the other. Hagberg found that, historically, the elderly were seen as religious, mature, and enjoying life, but also as costly and a burden. The same attitudes recurred in both 1981 and 1991, but in these later years certain new opinions had surfaced: the elderly were looked upon as exposed to crime, as complaining and as requiring care. In 1981, the elderly were perceived as active, competent and fighting for their rights, but ageing was also looked upon as frightening. Unique attitudes found in 1981, but not in 1991, were that ageing is attractive, that the elderly are resourceful and show ego strength, and that they have equal rights to common resources. In 1991, again, the most common attitudes were that the elderly are active and that they cost money. One possible interpretation of this finding is that the elderly should be allowed to work. These attitude changes may possibly mirror economic trends in Sweden: in 1991, Swedish society was undergoing a sharp economic recession in the course of which its ranking in the global welfare league plummeted from second to 17th.

Society has a relatively high disposition to prevent its citizens from completing suicide, irrespective of whether these citizens are young or middle-aged. In practice, however, attitudes towards the elderly are divergent – and seem to have diverged over a long period, as Birgitta Odén points out in a historical study (Odén, 2000). In the 18th century, the proportion of suicides in Sweden was already highest among the elderly, as it remains today. Nonetheless, most suicide-preventive efforts are focused on younger generations.

Epidemiology of Suicide in Sweden

A myth still exists that Sweden is among the countries that have very high suicide rates. One contribution to the myth of Sweden as a country with high suicide figures was made by Ingmar Bergman's films, shown worldwide, depicting in poetic terms such ordinary human problems as marital conflict, various crises, loneliness and depression. These types of human conflict and depression occur throughout the world, but became associated with Sweden since they were shown in Bergman's films. This obviously fostered retention of the myth of Sweden as a "high-suicide country."

The fact is that suicide rates in Sweden showed a decrease from 27 per 100,000 inhabitants in 1980 to 19 per 100,000 inhabitants in 1996. Unfortunately, despite the favourable trend for the adult population, suicide among the youngest and oldest age groups in Sweden is not declining to the same extent (Figure 1).

When suicide rates for the entire population of Europe are divided into four categories – classified as "very high", "high", "low" and "very low" – Sweden comes into the category with "low suicide rates" for both men and women. The same is true of men and women aged 65 and over (Figures 2 and 3). However, suicide remains a major problem area in Sweden since suicide is still the most common cause of death in the 15–44 age group. In terms of gender differences, suicide retains its lead in this age group as the foremost cause of death among men, and comes second after cancer for women aged 15–44.

Epidemiology of Suicide among the Elderly in Sweden

The longitudinal trend of suicide from 1970 to 1996 among men and women aged 65 and over (Figure 4) shows that suicide rates are relatively stable in this age group. The suicide rate for men aged 65 and over was 52.5 per 100,000 men in 1970 and 41.5 per 100,000 in 1996. The corresponding figures for women aged 65 and over were 17.5 per 100,000 in 1970 and 15.5 per 100,000 in 1996.

Comparison of these suicide rates with the corresponding figures for the entire Swedish population shows that the overall male suicide rate of 26/100,000 is well below that of men aged 65 and over. The suicide rate for women in the general population is 11.5 per 100,000 – also well below that of women in the 65 and over age group.

Figure 1. Suicide in Sweden, 1980-1989 and 1990-1996, by age group

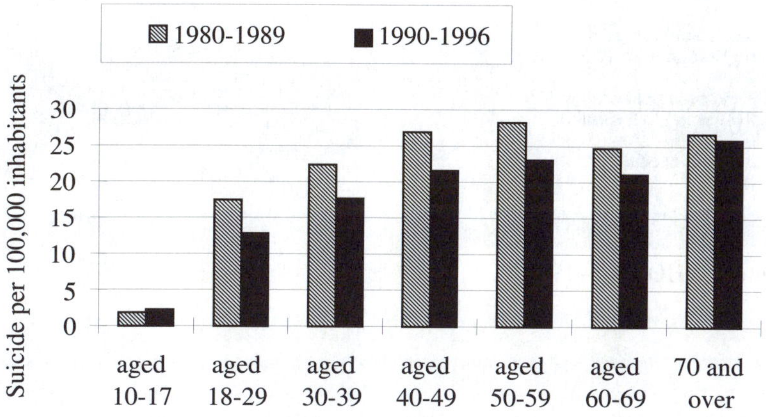

Figure 2. Suicide among elderly men (65 and over) in 33 European countries. Data from 1990 to the latest year of availability

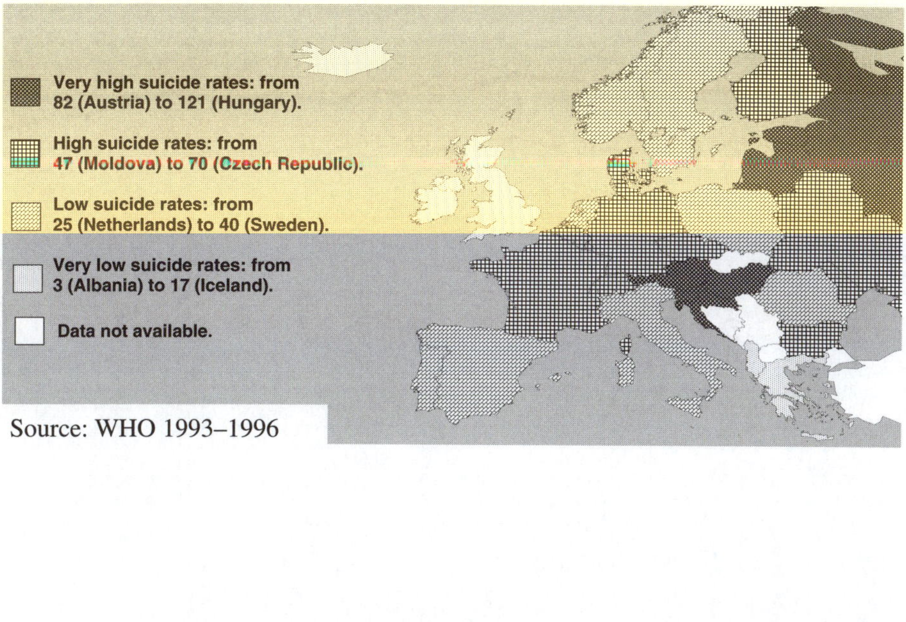

Source: WHO 1993–1996

Figure 3. Suicide among elderly women (65 and over) in 33 European countries. Data from 1990 to the latest year of availability

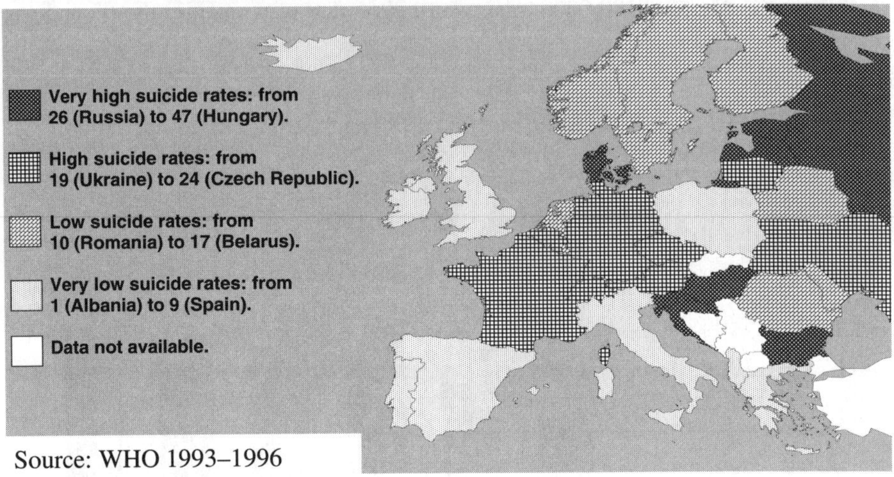

Source: WHO 1993–1996

Figure 4. Suicide among elderly people aged 65 and over in Sweden 1970-1996, by gender

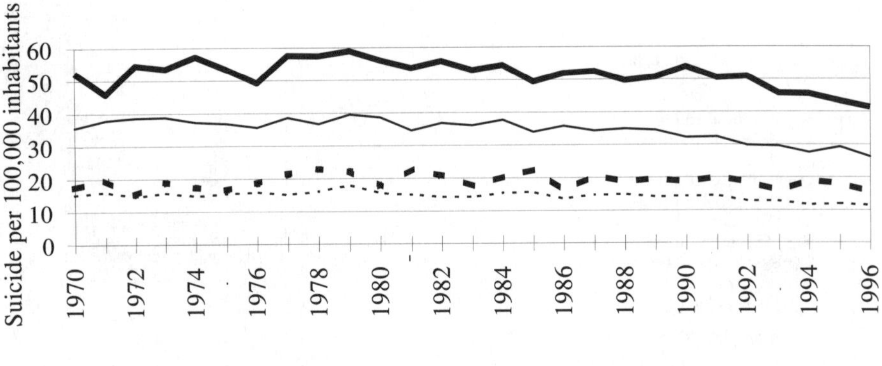

This fact has been noted by the National Council for Suicide Prevention in Sweden, and prevention of suicide in these groups is one of the priority areas in this country.

In 1996, 1,663 people took their own lives in Sweden: 1,150 men and 513 women (Table 1). These figures include both certain and uncertain suicides. Undetermined deaths constitute about a quarter of the aggregate total of certain suicides and undetermined deaths. The 1,663 suicides included 408 deaths of people aged 65 and over (270 men and 138 women). This means that roughly a quarter of suicides in Sweden are committed by elderly people.

Table 1. Numbers of Suicide among Elderly people in Sweden, 1996

	Men	Women	Total
Aged 65–74	270	138	408
75 and over	129	80	209
Whole population	1150	513	1663

Suicide Methods Used by the Elderly

The suicide method used most frequently by elderly people in Sweden is hanging. Among men poisoning using drugs ranks second, while among women poisoning using drugs is the most frequent method used. The drugs used most often for suicidal purposes among the elderly are benzodiazepines. Reduced sale of benzodiazepines in Sweden over the past ten years has, unfortunately, not been reflected in a decrease in suicide among elderly people who use these drugs for this purpose.

Attempted Suicide among the Elderly in Sweden

Elderly people who attempt suicide are known to be at higher risk of subsequent suicide (Nordentoft et al, 1993; Conwell et al, 1998). The attempted-suicide rates found among people aged 65 and over in Huddinge, south of Stockholm, the catchment area in Sweden that forms part of a WHO multicentre study on attempted suicide/parasuicide (Schmidtke, 1993) are 74 per 100,000 for men and 93 per 100,000 for women.

Suicidal Thoughts among the Elderly in Sweden

In questionnaire surveys, 10.8% of Stockholm residents aged 75 and over have reported "fleeting suicidal thoughts" and 2.5% reported "frequent suicidal thoughts" (Forsell et al, 1997). A study from Gothenburg (Sweden's second-largest city) reports that 4% of mentally healthy (non-demented) people aged 85 and over had thoughts that life was not worth living, against 29% among mentally ill members of this age group. Among the mentally ill, 9.2% have been found to have suicidal thoughts, compared with 0.9% among mentally healthy 85-year-olds (Skoog et al, 1996). The incidence of suicidal thoughts and feelings was gauged by instruments designed by Paykel et al (1974).

Suicidal thoughts in the above-mentioned Stockholm study (Forsell et al, 1997) characterised elderly people who were depressed, lived in institutions and suffered from functional disabilities in everyday life, and also those who used more psychotropic drugs than their mentally healthy counterparts who had no suicidal thoughts.

Why Do Elderly People Take Their Own Lives?

The above-mentioned findings show that suicidal thoughts are fairly rare among elderly people who are in a mentally stable state, and indicate that mental illnesses are not a feature of ordinary ageing. It is, perhaps, time to discard the common myth or misunderstanding that such mental troubles as despondency, worry and anxiety are part and parcel of the normal ageing process. Today, vitality is retained up to an advanced age. Most old people find a new role and a new way of life.

Unfortunately, for some people ageing is a lonely wait for nothing. Some elderly people may have no relatives, or the relatives they have are too busy to visit them. Expectations may be dashed, in some individuals physical health fails, and institutional care is the outcome.

Elderly people are also relatively stress-intolerant, and adjust more slowly to new circumstances. In old age, one needs much more time both for various tasks and for mental activity. Some elderly people are plagued by aches and pains, and troubled by the deterioration in how their bodies function. Nor, perhaps – owing to age-related changes in the neurotransmittors' function in the brain – is their mental functioning what it was. One major risk factor for suicide, among elderly and younger people alike, is depression (Wasserman, 1999/2000).

Depression in the Elderly

Of all suicides in Sweden, 70–75% are triggered by a depressive illness (Beskow, 1979). Other major risk factors include advanced age and male gender. Thus, the risk of suicide rises with age; and the highest suicide rates are in men over 65.

A depressive illness is caused partly by a person's psychosocial situation and partly by disturbances in the brain's neurotransmitters. Psychosocial and social changes undergone by elderly people can frequently impact upon their emotional life and mood. Such changes may include the situation where their skills and knowledge are no longer in demand, and age-related changes in the central nervous system causes reduced activity in the noradrenergic, serotonergic and dopaminergic systems. From here a relapse into depression is not far off (Katona, 1997). Dementia illnesses, such as vascular dementia and Alzheimer's, also cause disturbances in noradrenaline and serotonin metabolism in the brain.

Deteriorating bodily functions, and also physical illnesses such as stroke, cancer, cardiac illness, Parkinson's disease, epilepsy and multiple sclerosis, may also contribute to the emergence of depression in an elderly person. Certain drugs used by the elderly to treat their somatic ill-health can also, as a side-effect, cause depression.

Summing up, depression in the elderly – as among younger people – may be said to be multifactorial in origin. Undiagnosed and untreated depression is a major risk factor for suicidal acts, i.e. attempted and completed suicide (Isacsson et al, 1999). Manifestations of depression in the elderly differ somewhat from those in other age groups. This is why learning how to diagnose depression among elderly people and treat it adequately is important. It is commonly estimated that 15% of people aged 65 and over suffer from depression (Katona, 1994). However, the incidence of depression is not evenly spread. Depression is much more widespread, for example, among elderly residents of institutions than among elderly people living in their own homes: as many as 30–40% of the former, against well under 10% of the latter, suffer from depression.

Other Risk Factors for Suicide among the Elderly

Previous and current suicide attempts are a major risk factor for completed suicide. Substance and alcohol abuse are fairly rare among elderly people who commit suicide in Sweden. On the other hand, the incidence of anxiety disorders among elderly suicides is underestimated, and more attention should be paid to this factor.

Treatment of Depression: An Important Measure of Suicide Prevention among the Elderly

Carefully devised strategies for treating depression are required. Strategies for depression in the elderly must be closely tailored to their needs. A study from Sweden (Waern, 1996) has shown that treating depression with antidepressant drugs alone fails to prevent suicide. Although 52% (139/275 patients) of those studied aged 65 and over who took their own lives had been receiving antidepressant or lithium treatment, this medication did not suffice to prevent their suicides.

Another interesting finding of the same study (Waern, 1996) was that for people aged 65 and over suffering their first episodes of depression, the median interval between the first suicidal communication and the final act was only one month. This finding should focus further attention on the importance of very prompt provision of adequate depression treatment, with frequent medical checks and social support. This is especially so in view of the fact that the impact of antidepressants – especially the newer drugs – becomes apparent only after prolonged treatment, while during the initial stages of treatment anxiety increases. This exacerbation of anxiety may, in a despondent person who has previously entertained fleeting suicidal ideation, prompt more intense suicidal thoughts while, at the same time, he/she may experience utter hopelessness, be inundated with anxiety and, eventually, opt for suicide as the final way out.

Clearly, antidepressant treatment alone is insufficient. Treatment of depression in the elderly, as in other groups, needs to be reinforced with psychological treatment methods and social support. Underlying somatic illnesses must also be treated adequately (Wasserman, 2001).

Euthanasia and Physician-Assisted Suicide in Nordic Countries

In Denmark, Norway and Sweden alike, both physician-assisted suicide and euthanasia are illegal. However, in Denmark, the notion of a "living will" has been sanctioned by law. Writing such a will means that, on a special form, a person chooses one, two or three options for the care he/she wishes to receive in the event of terminal illness, senile decrepitude or severe pain. The living will is then centrally registered in a special unit of the National Hospital in Copenhagen, and physicians are obliged to comply with the wishes expressed therein if the life-or-death circumstances it refers to arise for the individual concerned.

In the Nordic countries, physician practice regarding euthanasia has been investigated in Denmark, Norway and Sweden. In Denmark in 1995, Folker et al. investigated attitudes towards and the practice, if any, of euthanasia among 500 physicians (Folker, 1996). The doctors formed a random sample from the register of the Danish Medical Association, covering all medical specialities. The rate of response to a questionnaire sent by post was 64 percent.

This survey showed that 74 percent of the respondent Danish physicians had been asked by their patients to administer pain-relieving morphine in lethal doses. Moreover, with the patients' informed consent, 80 percent of the doctors had done so. Fifty-three percent of the physicians stated they had done so on occasion without the informed consent of the patient.

Twelve percent of the Danish doctors investigated had administered morphine in twice the lethal dose, without the patient requesting it. Twenty-six percent had been asked to participate in physician-assisted suicide (PAS), and 7 percent of these had complied with this request. Finally, 30 percent of the physicians had been asked to administer a lethal injection (containing a drug other than morphine), and 13 percent of these doctors had done as their patients asked.

In Norway, in 1996, Förde et al. sent a questionnaire to a sample of 1,476 physicians, and the response rate was 66 percent (Förde, 1997). Six percent of the doctors had performed actions intended to hasten a patient's death. However, whether this involved active euthanasia, passive euthanasia or physician-assisted suicide was not clearly defined. Controlling for gender and the number of years since graduation from medical school, regression analysis showed that the doctors exercising most restraint were those with the specialities of internal medicine, surgery and psychiatry. Physicians who had been educated outside Norway or who were opposed to the idea of the patient's autonomy proved to have more liberal views on euthanasia.

In Sweden in 1998, Valverius et al. sent a questionnaire to a random sample of 952 physicians and also to 122 doctors in palliative care and 130 physicians in the Swedish Association of Algologists (Valverius et al., 1998). The aim of the study was to determine the extent to which Swedish physicians talk to their adult patients about euthanasia, the preferences expressed by the patients and the ways in which the doctors act.

The response rate was 79 percent. Half of the physicians studied had experienced their patients expressing a wish to die or received a request to withhold potentially life-sustaining or life-prolonging treatment, and 9.5 percent had been asked about PAS. Some 1 percent of the doctors asserted that they might have directly or indirectly participated in a patient's suicide. No cases of active euthanasia were reported. However, some euthanasia cases in Sweden have been publicised, since the physicians involved have been prosecuted. In three of these cases (in 1986, 1987 and 1995), the prosecution has been withdrawn. In recent years, four cases of euthanasia have come to light in Sweden. The Swedish National Board of Health and Welfare is investigating these cases at present.

Conclusions

In Sweden, ever since the 18th century, the majority of suicides have taken place among the older age groups. However, suicide-preventive resources are directed largely at the young or middle-aged, reflecting society's low valuation of the elderly. In recent years, public attitudes towards the elderly in Sweden appear to have become less favourable, possibly reflecting straitened economic conditions in the country, as well as the growing proportion of elderly people in the population.

References

Beskow, J. (1979). Suicide and mental disorder in Swedish men. *Acta Psychiatrica Scandinavica, 277* (Suppl.), 1–138.

Conwell, Y., Duberstein, P. R., Cox, C., Herrmann, J., Forbes, N., & Caine, E. D. (1998). Age differences in behaviour leading to completed suicide. *American Journal of General Psychiatry, 6* (2), 122–126.

Folker, A. P., Holtug, N., Jensen, A. B., Kappel, K., Nielsen, J. K., & Norup, M. (1996). Experiences and attitudes towards end-of-life decisions amongst Danish physicians. *Bioethics, 10* (3), 233–249.

Förde, R., Aasland, O. G., & Falkum, E. (1997). The ethics of euthanasia – attitudes and practice among Norwegian physicians. *Social Science & Medicine, 45* (6), 887–892.

Forsell, Y., Jorm, A. F., & Winblad, B. (1997). Suicidal thoughts and associated factors in an elderly population. *Acta Psychiatrica Scandinavica, 95* (2), 108–111.

Hagberg, B. (1993, July). *Attitudes towards ageing in Sweden*. Paper presented at the XVth Congress of the International Association of Gerontology, Budapest, Hungary.
Isacsson, G., Holmgren, P., Druid, H., & Bergman, U. (1999). Psychotropics and suicide prevention: Implications from toxicological screening of 5281 suicides in Sweden 1992–1994. *British Journal of Psychiatry, 174,* 259–265.
Katona, C. (1997). The symptomatology of depression in the elderly. *International Clinical Psychopharmacology, 12* (Suppl. 7), 19–23.
Katona, C.L.E. (1994). The epidemiology of depression in old age. In C. L. E. Katona (Ed.), *Depression in Old Age* (pp. 29–41). Chichester: John Wiley & Sons.
Kiemo, K. (2000). *Elderly suicide and social change*. Paper presented at the IVth International Congress of Thanatology, Stockholm, Sweden.
Nordentoft, M., Breum, L., Munck, L. K., Nordestgaard, A. G., Hunding, A., & Bjaeldager, P. A. (1993). High mortality from natural and unnatural causes: a 10-year follow-up study of patients admitted to a poisoning treatment centre after suicide attempts. *British Medical Journal, 306,* 1637–1641.
Odén, B. (2000, August). *Unsuccessful ageing*. Paper presented at the IVth International Congress of Thanatology, Stockholm, Sweden.
Paykel, E.S., Myers, J. K., Lindenthal, J. J., & Tanner, J. (1974). Suicidal feelings in the general population: A prevalence study. *British Journal of Psychiatry, 124,* 460–469.
Schmidtke A., Bille-Brahe, U., Kerkhof, A., & De Leo, D. (1993). The WHO/Euro Multicentre project on parasuicide — state of the art. *Italian Journal of Suicidology, 3* (2), 83–95.
Skoog, I., Aevarsson, O., Beskow, J., & Larsson, L. (1996). Suicidal Feelings in a Population Sample of Nondemented 85-Year-Olds. *American Journal of Psychiatry, 153,* 1015–1020.
Valverius, E., Nilstun, T., Fuerst, C. J., Strang, P., & Westrin, C. G. (1998). Läkares erfarenhet av patienter vid livets slut [Physicians' experience of patients in the final phase of life]. *Hygiea Göteborg, 107* (1), 291–292.
Waern, M., Beskow, J., Runeson, B., & Skoog, I. (1996). High rate of antidepressant treatment in elderly people who commit suicide. *British Medical Journal, 313,* 1118.
Wasserman, D. (1999-2000). *Depression, en vanlig sjukdom* [Depression, A Common Illness. Symptoms, Causes and Treatment Options]. *Hans Reitzels Förlag*, Copenhagen (in Danish) and atur och Kultur, Stockholm, Sweden (in Swedish).
Wasserman, D. (2001). *Suicide – An Unnecessary Death.* London: Martin Dunitz Ltd.

Acknowledgment

Thanks to Ludvig Olsson, who produced and processed all the figures and Table 1.

Suicide Among the Danish Elderly

Unni Bille-Brahe and Karin Andersen

Centre for Suicidological Research, Odense, Denmark

Introduction

In most western countries, the age distribution of the population has changed markedly during this century. Since World War II the relative number of elderly has been increasing, and, as people are now living longer, there is also an increasing number of older elderly. On the basis of the demographer Easterlin's theories on the importance of the relative size of the individual birth cohort (RSC), questions have been raised concerning the effect of this development on the frequency of suicidal behaviour among elderly people. The main point of the theories on RSC is that huge birth cohorts need more 'space' than small cohorts do, and the bigger cohorts are therefore subjected to pressure, their members meeting with fewer opportunities and less favourable conditions than do the members of small cohorts. According to Easterlin, a relatively huge cohort leads to increased psychological stress, partly caused by deterioration of the opportunities and squeezed economical conditions (Easterlin, 1978, 1980).

The aim of this paper is to discuss the changes in the age distribution of the Danish population, the changes in the characteristics of the elderly population and any effect these changes may have on the frequencies of suicide among elderly people.

Materials and Method

Data on suicide for the period 1922–1996 is collected partly from 'Causes of Death in Denmark', issued by the National Board of Health, and partly from the 'Register for Suicide', compiled by the Centre for Suicidological Research. Data on the Danish population is obtained from the Danish Statistical Bureau. Due to small absolute numbers, a five-year average is used. As treating all elderly above the age of 65 years as one homogeneous group would present a very incomplete and in fact rather incorrect picture, analysis are carried out on 5 year age groups. However, data distributed on five-year age groups above the age of 65 is available only from 1943, and analysis on differences between the various groups of elderly are therefore based on data from 1945 onwards.

Results

As a point of departure, Figure 1 shows the age distribution of the Danish population in selected years and an estimated distribution in the year 2015.

Figure 1. Changes in the age distribution of the Danish population in the period 1922–1995, and an estimation for 2015.

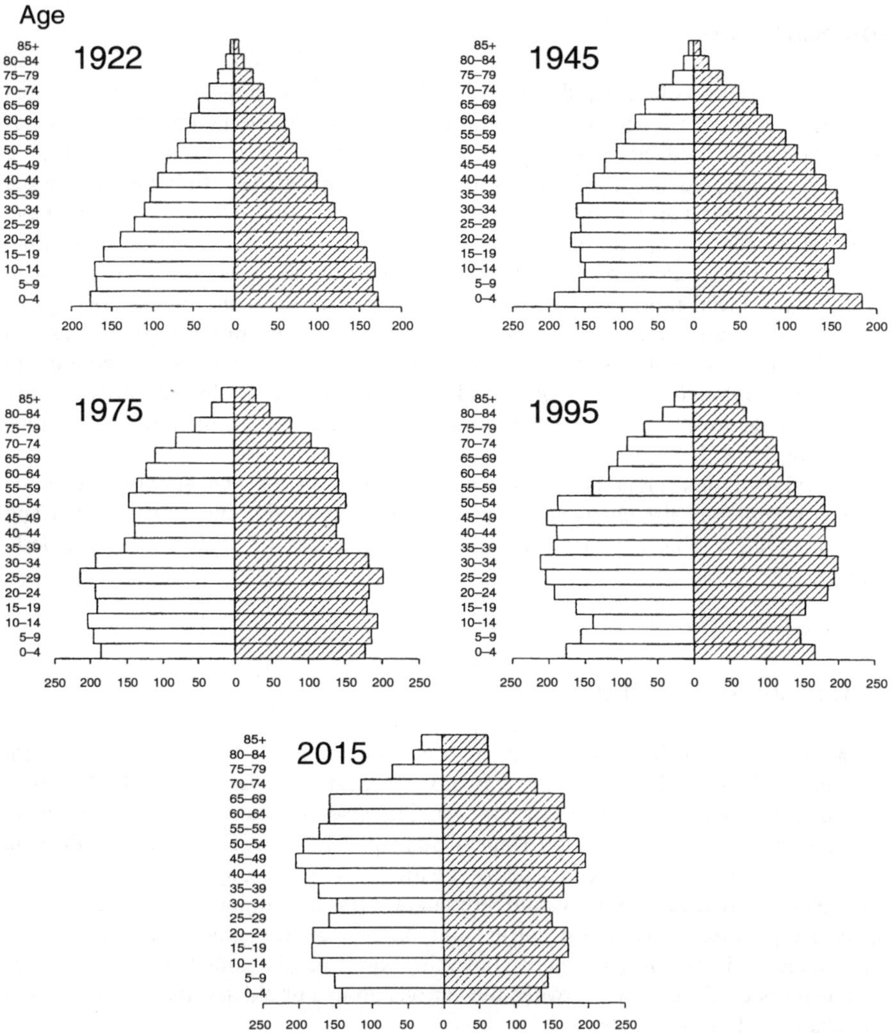

The figure illustrates the change from the neat pyramid-shaped distribution for both sexes at the beginning of the 1920's to the more oval-shaped distribution in mid–1995 with a profusion of men below the age of 50 years and a profusion of women above the age of 65 years.

Figure 2 shows the age and sex-specific rates of suicide among the elderly above the age of 65 compared with the younger age groups. In general, the male age-specific rates followed the same pattern and, with the exception of a period during the mid–1950's, male rates have been peaking among those aged 65 years or older. For women, rates reach their peak among the middle-aged (45–64 years), and the gap between the rate for this age group and rates for other female age groups increased from the early 1960's to the early 1980's, whereafter rates of suicide began to peak among the aged above the age of 65 years too.

Although the rates of suicide among the elderly seem to be following a general pattern over the years, the percentage of all suicides committed by the elderly changes markedly during the period. At the beginning of the 1920's, when the elderly above the age of 65 years comprised about 10 percent of the total population, they completed about 25 percent of all suicides, while at the beginning of the 1990's, when they accounted for about 20 percent of the total population, the proportion of all suicides committed remained the same, namely about one quarter. Figure 3 shows the ratio between the percentage of the population being above the age of 65 years, and the percentage of all suicides committed by the elderly of that age. The appearance of the baby-boomers during the mid–1940's is reflected in the sharp drop in the ratio during this period.

Figure 2. Age and sex-specific rates of suicide 1922–1996.

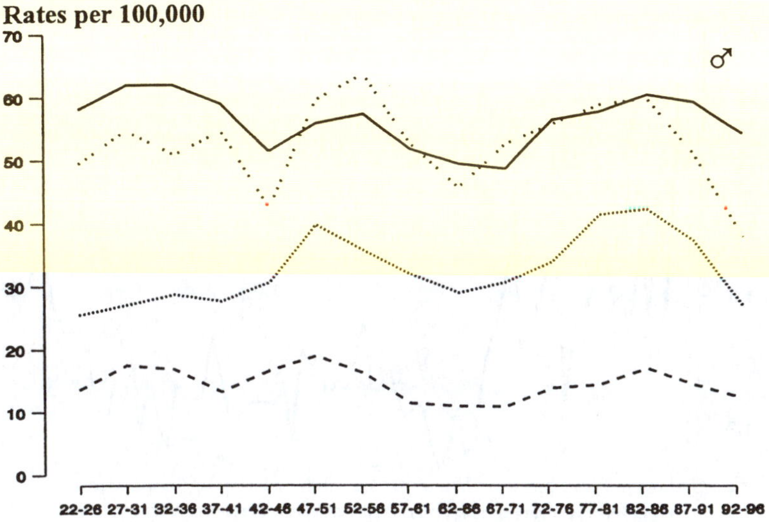

Figure 2. Age and sex-specific rates of suicide 1922–1996 *Continued.*

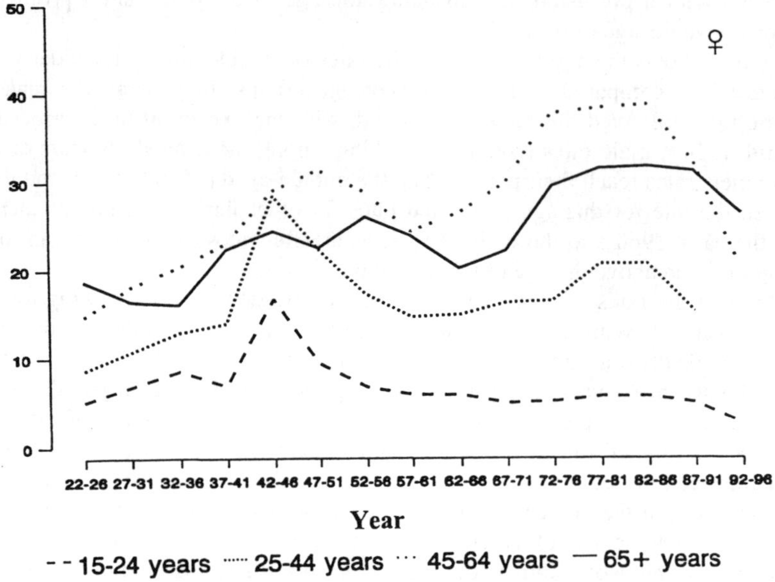

Figure 3. The number of suicides among elderly (65+) as a percentage of all suicides in relation to the number of elderly as a percentage of the total population.

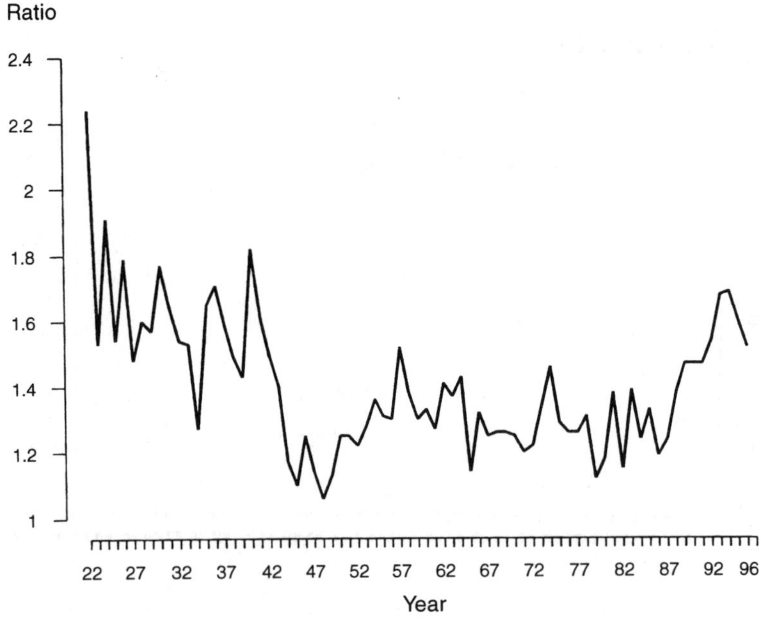

This figure illustrates the fact that even if the risk of suicide continues to increase with age, the relative proportion of suicides committed by the elderly has in general been decreasing. As we can see from Figure 4, the relative increase during the beginning of the 1990's is mainly due to the increasing frequencies among the older elderly.

Figure 4 underlines the fact that as far as the risk of suicide is concerned, people being 65 years or older cannot be seen as one homogeneous group either. This is especially the case for elderly men. The increase in the rate of suicide among older elderly men (80+) around 1980 was steeper than for those younger, and the frequency remained on a high level while rates among the younger elderly decreased.

During the 1970's and 80's, rates increased in all female age groups, especially for those above the age of 30 years, the increase being followed by a general decrease from the early 1990's. However, while female rates of suicide used to reach their peak among the middle-aged (see Figure 2), the rates of suicide (see Figure 4) have now been increasing for the older elderly women (80+): in 1996 reaching 19.6 per 100,000 – compared with 15.0 per 100,000 among the middle-aged.

Figure 4. Age and sex-specific rates for various groups of the elderly.

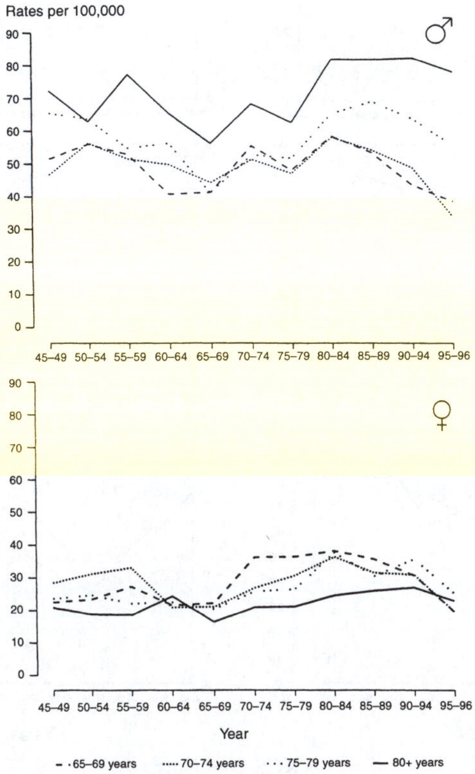

Returning to the question of any relation between RSC and the frequency of suicide, tests for correlations between the two curves shown in Figure 5 were carried out.

Figure 5. The relative size of the cohorts (RSC) and the rates of suicide.

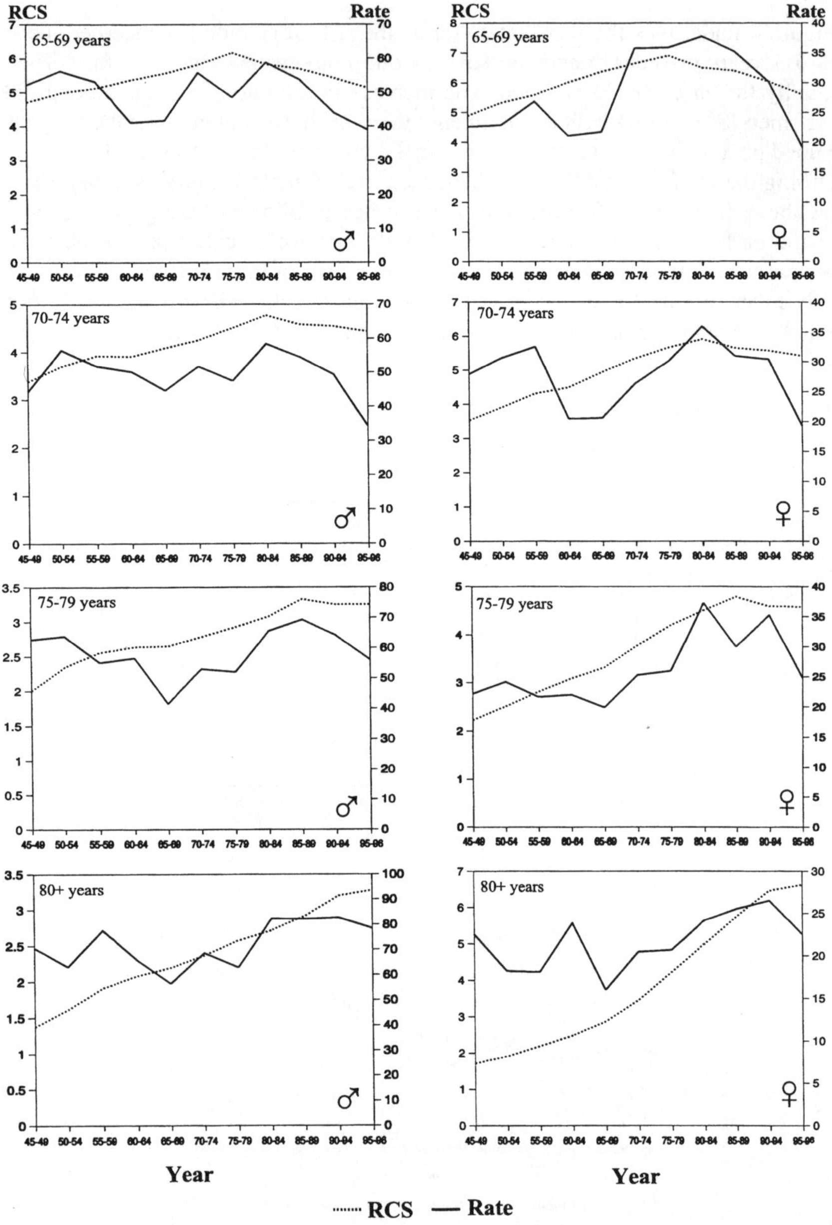

From Figure 5 it seems that through the last 50 years there has been a very close relationship between the rate of suicide and the relative size of the cohort. The figures in Table 1 confirm this, as the correlation coefficients are very high for all male and female age groups, all of them significant on the 99% level. However, two-way analysis of variance with suicide rates as the dependent variable and RSC as the independent one showed no significant interaction effect, that is, RSC explains only a small and insignificant part of the variations in the rates of suicide.

Table 1. Tests on correlations between rates of suicide and RSC

	Corr.coeff.		Sign.		ANOVA		Sign.	
	M	F	M	F	M	F	M	F
65–69 yrs	0.989	0.970	0.000	0.000	0.520	2.111	0.613	1.084
70–74 yrs	0.977	0.952	0.000	0.000	0.238	0.673	0.637	0.537
75–79 yrs	0.971	0.973	0.000	0.000	4.405	5.157	0.075	0.036
80+ yrs	0.962	0.895	0.000	0.000	1.118	0.938	0.373	0.527

Discussion

Most studies on suicidal behaviour among the elderly reported in the literature define elderly as all persons being 65 years or older, that is, all persons above the age of 65 years are seen – and treated in research – as one homogeneous group. This group is usually typified as being poor, lonely, in poor health, miserable, etc. In real life, however, not only are elderly people as different as other people, there are also huge differences between the various age groups of elderly. A so-called young elderly of 65 has very little in common with an older elderly person celebrating his/her 80th or 90th birthday.

Furthermore, a new type of person is now entering the elderly stage, and this type of person is again very different from the elderly people of yesterday: being 70 years old today is quite different from being 70 years old 25 or 50 years ago.

In the mid–1980's, a comprehensive study on three cohorts of the Danish approaching old age (40–44, 50–54, and 60–64 years old) was carried out (Bille-Brahe, 1989; Schroll, 1989). The results indicated that there would be increasing changes to come in the lifestyles and life standards of elderly people, in their attitudes, and as far as various health aspects were concerned. Time has shown that this prediction has come true. Longitudinal studies on the health of 70-year-olds have shown an increasing improvement in health: the 70-year-olds of today are in far better physical and mental health than those at the same age 20 years ago, and they also live longer. Today, people no longer think it is the end of life when one reaches the age of retirement (which in Denmark is 67 years, but with the possibility of withdrawing from the labour market from the age of 60). Instead, people are now looking forward to an active life for still some 15–20 years to come. And the new elderly are in general very active; they are studying, travelling, taking up all kinds of hobbies and engaging in creative or sports activities. This development is going to be even more apparent for those approaching old age, that is, the baby-boomers from the mid–1940's, who will reach the age of retirement around the year 2010.

The new elderly themselves are, of course, fully aware of the problems arising from the change in the age distribution. They are also aware of the fact that because they will probably live longer, they will at some point also be more fragile and in need of more care, and, as they are more accustomed to a higher standard of living, they will be increasingly demanding. Consequently, there will be increasing claims for more and better services and at the same time, a decreasing number of people to carry the burden of support, that is, to procure the resources needed to meet these needs. This problem is exacerbated by the growing number of elderly who chose to retire early from the age of 60.

Already today in Denmark, there are cutbacks on the services provided for the elderly, and steps have been taken to restrict access to early retirement and to revise the system of old-age pensions. Politically, this is creating an interesting situation. In contrast to the elderly of former times, the elderly of today are much more self-conscious, they are fully aware of their position as an interesting target group of voters, and they are prepared to use this power to veto any cut-backs (as, for example, the Grey Panthers in the USA). This situation will come to a head when the politicians who are in power today and arguing for the cut-backs, and who typically belong to the baby-boom generation, themselves reach the age of retirement in another 10 to 15 years. By this time the relative number of breadwinners will have become even smaller.

The effect of this development may have an influence on the rate of suicide, that is, the theories on RSC may have some relevance so that in spite of increasing good health and vigour, the increasing size of the elderly population may relate to the risk of suicide among the elderly. The two-way variance analysis indicates, however, that only a small part of the variance in the rates of suicide can be explained by the relative size of the cohorts.

This brings us to quite another – but very pertinent – aspect which is relevant when discussing the risk of suicide among elderly people. Both Clark (1992) and Kerkhof (1994) in their studies on suicide among the elderly questioned whether it could be that suicide among the elderly is less motivated by, for example, loneliness or general misery than by a fear of becoming dependent on others.

Clark and Kerkhof both argue that the elderly who commit suicide are no more miserable than most other elderly people – but that they do have a specific personality type of personality that may have always had a high regard for independence.

It may be argued that the development of modern society and its individual oriented views on humankind have promoted this personality type. In addition, the new elderly are used to being self-reliant even when getting older, and consequently an increasing number seems to abhor the idea of being dependent on the mercy of a chance care person. The discussion in Holland, for example prior to the introduction of access to assisted suicide, bears witness to this development and to the development of attitudes prevailing among the Stoics and the Epicurean, praising *mors voluntaris* as the (only) decent way to end one's life.

In Denmark, assisting somebody to commit suicide (active euthanasia) is forbidden by law. The act is seen as premeditated homicide and the "assistant" becomes liable for punishment (minimum of 5 years in prison). It is unlikely that this law will be changed in the near future. In the public debate therefore, the focus has been on passive euthanasia, that is, abstaining from or putting an end to futile treatments. In the mid-1970s, a private association was established with the aim of gaining juridical recognition of the individual's right to "a dignified death" (for example, by acknowledging a person's "Life Will") and various forms of passive euthanasia. In 1992, some rules regarding passive euthanasia were included in the Danish Medical Law, and in 1998, a comprehensive Law on Patients' Rights was introduced which included patient autonomy both in general and in relation to abstaining from treatment. The law is followed by a detailed set of supplementing administrative directions.

This means that today, seriously ill patients in Denmark have rather far-reaching access to "a dignified death." The patients and the doctors have been given the legal authority to opt out of futile treatment and especially to use palliatives even if the patient's life is thereby shortened (the double-effect). Furthermore, the wishes of the patient are to be of decisive importance.

In everyday life, there seems to be some variation in the administration of the law. In some places there are over-anxious attitudes towards the opting out of treatment, in some there seem to be tendencies in the opposite direction, and in others there are indications that palliatives are used to deliberately shorten the life of the patient, which is not in line with the intention of the law. Albeit, the Danish Ethical Committee, acknowledging that some kind of grey area will always exist, has recommended that the existing rules be maintained, rather than legalizing more forms of euthanasia.

The changes that have taken place in the Danish legal regulations of passive euthanasia have presumably had little, if any effect on the frequency of suicide. Favourable attitudes, however, among the elderly towards "stepping down with dignity" may have, and this may be behind some of the registered increase during the late 1980's in the frequency of suicide among the elderly over 80 years of age – especially among men.

Conclusion

In most countries, the elderly population has been growing and at the same time, marked changes have taken place both in the society in general and in the conditions and circumstances for elderly people in particular. Analyses carried out on Danish data indicate that in spite of the new elderly staying active and being in good mental and physical health even at a great age, the risk of suicide is increasing among the older elderly. This development may, to a limited extent, be explained by referring to the theories on the importance of the relative size of the cohorts (RSC), while the theories launched by Clark and Kerkhof, speculating on the independent personality type of the suicidal elderly and its possible relationship to increased suicide risk, seem to be of relevance.

References

Bille-Brahe, U. (1989). *Nye tider – nye 'ldre: Holdninger og forventninger* [New times – new elderly: Attitudes and Expectations]. Copenhagen: EGV Foundation.

Clark, D. C. (1992). *Narcissistic crisis of aging and suicidal despair*. Presidential address given at the Conference of the American Association of Suicidology, Chicago.

Easterlin, R. What will 1984 be like? Socioeconomic implications of the recent twist in age structure. *Demography, 15,* 397–432.

Easterlin, R. (1980). *Birth and Fortune: The impact of numbers on personal welfare*. New York: Basic Books.

Kerkhof A. J. F. M., Ormskerk, S. C. R., & Oomes, M. (1994) Assessing rationality in elderly suicidal patients: common sense versus dynamic assessment. In U. Bille-Brahe & E. Schiodt (Eds.), *Intervention and Prevention*. Odense: Odense University Press.

Schroll, M. (1989). *Nye tider – nye 'ldre: Helbred* [New times – new elderly: The health]. Copenhagen: EGV Foundation.

Suicide in Old Age: Swiss Perspectives

Carlos Augusto De Mendonca Lima, José Manoel Bertolote, Italo Simeone and Vincent Camus

Psychogeriatric Service, Department of Psychiatry
University of Lousanne, Switzerland

Introduction

Suicide is a human phenomenon found in all cultures, in both sexes, and throughout history. It has different meanings depending on the context in which it takes place, but as a common feature in all cases of suicide, there is a suffering behind the decision to choose death over the uncertainty of a future perceived as unbearable.

The magnitude of the phenomenon is impressive indeed: it is estimated that world-wide approximately one million people commited suicide in the year 2000, a figure which is bigger than the number of deaths due to wars or to traffic accidents in the same year (WHO, 1999).

Until recently, suicide was a phenomenon typical of the elderly and mainly among men. However, this is quickly changing at a global level, with suicide now predominating among the youth (WHO, 1999). This chapter will analyse the problem of suicide among the elderly in Switzerland, taking into account the peculiarities of this country, and comparing it to other European countries. To better understand the particular context of suicide among the elderly in Switzerland, a brief description of some demographic and mortality-related indicators in this country will be provided.

Epidemiological Data

Structure of Swiss Population

The Swiss population is complex. It is mainly composed of two linguistic groups, the Latin (33% speaking French, Italian and Romansh), and the German (64% speaking Swizerdeutsch). In 1998, the most recent demographic data revealed that Switzerland is composed of 7,123,537 inhabitants, of which 19,4% are foreigners. The Roman Catholic faith is the predominant religion (46%) closely followed by the Protestant faiths (40%) (Office Fédéral De La Statistique, 1995; Swiss Federal Statistical Office, 2000a).

The Swiss population, particularly its elderly population, has suffered important changes during the 20th century. If the group older than 59 years represented 10% of the total population in 1910, it has regularly increased to 13% in 1941, 16% in 1970 and 20% in 1995. Between 1910 and 1940 as well as between 1970 and 1990 there was a relative decrease in the young population. This resulted in a significant increase in the mean age of the Swiss population during these periods (Swiss Federal Statistical Office, 2000b).

In 1998, the population over the age of 65 years represents 15.1% of the total population, with 3.9% aged 80 years or more. Seven percent of the total foreigners are over the age of 64 years. The proportion of people over 64 compared to those aged 20–64 year was 23% in 1990 and is estimated to be 42% in 2040, meaning a huge increase in the proportion of the elderly.

All these data explain why there are now many more elderly persons than in the recent past years. The number of people over the age of 64 is twice more than it was fifty years ago and the number of people over the age of 80 has quadrupled during this period. Increased life expectancy and a low birth rate are the main reasons for this ageing phenomena in Switzerland (Swiss Federal Statistical Office, 2000a).

Images of Ageing in Switzerland

Recent research in gerontology in Switzerland (Stuckelberger & Höpflinger, 2000) has brought to light interesting new data concerning the processes of ageing in the country. The prevalence of extreme old age is increasing very quickly whch possibly explains the absence of a positive culture of ageing among the elderly. Negative and/or false images of ageing can contribute to ageism attitudes that are reflected in society and contribute to a low level of self esteem in the elderly. Some false stereotypes and images of ageing frequently found in the Swiss population include:

- Old age is synonymous of loneliness, isolation and dependence;
- The elderly are not interested on current trends and they have too much cognitive impairments: they are often disorientated and conservative;
- Frequently the elderly are active and benefit from retirement as they are able to develop new activities;
- On the other hand the image of restful old age remains strong and contributes to a misconcpetion about the real level of activity in the elderly;
- To be old often means to be sick but it can also be a time of life that reflects great wisdom.

These contradictory perceptions of ageing are strikingly prevalent in the minds of the majority of the Swiss population. But this combination of positive and negative images points to a gradual change in the image of old age in Swiss society. This is perhaps enhanced by the important volunteers work frequently performed by the older population and the increasing significance of senior citizen associations. The older generations are increasingly participating in political life of Switzerland and, even at the research level on gerontology, they are contributing to towards shared goals together with younger researchers.

The contact between the generation groups may often be difficult as consequence of the specific dimensions of each group. This is particularly relevant in the case of the labour market. Switzerland very recently adopted the trend towards early retirement in order to facilitate the access to the labour market of younger generations. But it seems more and more probable that a rapid shift in the direction of a noticeable demographic ageing of the population will have profound effects on the labour force over the next few years. There may be 3 major consequences:

1. The future economy will no longer afford the prejudicial treatment and discrimI-nation of older workers;
2. Education and professional training over forty will be promoted;
3. The current move toward early retirement will change.

Although the level of well-being in the individual shortly before retirement is generally high, some factors can act to deteriorate well-being after retirement. Low social status, a weak social network, rigid personality characteristics, and being female can all act to diminish the quality of well-being in retired people.

Most particularly, the quality of the well-being of the elderly foreign resident population is problematic. This population is not only over-represented in lower socio-economic groups but their quality of life and social integration also falls clearly below the level of the native population after retirement.

The quality – and not the quantity – of social contacts contribute positively on individual well-being and health. The majority of pensioners can count on at least one surviving child. An increasing lifespan also increases the potential for contact among several generations inside the same family. The older person's network of friends has clearly extended in the last 20 years while the proportion of old people without close friends has fallen. Besides these good indicators, the number of smaller households is increasing and the neighbourhood relationships among older persons are not pronounced.

The level of general well-being of the elderly can be considered quite high but symptoms arousing worry in the older population are fairly frequent (exhaustion, sleeping disorders, headaches, worries about health and anxiety). These symptoms seem strongly affected by subjectivity, thus it is not the person who is actually "sicker" who consumes more health care but rather that one who *feels* "sicker." Healthy ageing is embodied in each personal biography and that heath attitudes over the whole of the lifespan actively contribute to the health level in old age. Finally, sickness in old age is not fate: good physical well-being in old age is linked to self-responsibility and to the conviction that access to care is assured.

Economic analysis of the health care system shows that the link between ageing and an increase in health care expenditure is lower than expected. In fact, the image of "ageing equals illness" is also false, as although the frequency of morbidity increases with age, diseases, health complaints and handicaps only concern a minority of the elderly population. The subjective estimation of the health level is positive in the majority of the elderly population with some differences varying with the social level and the gender of the individual. Only 10–14% of persons over 65 have severe functional disabilities. Despite the efforts of health care policies to help the elderly in their homes, there still are around 30 000 old persons throughout Switzerland whose health needs are not satisfied.

For the elderly whose dependency level is very high, nursing homes offer good quality of living and care. At least 4% of all people aged 65–79 live in residential and nursing homes. For here the proportion of nursing home residents over the age of 80 increases to 25% and the proportion of residents over the age of 85 can reach 38%. The decision to move to a home is determined by several factors, such as the state of health, marital status, income, and the presence of family caregivers. Regional factors also play an important role, as the rural and Catholic regions of the German-speaking part of Switzerland have the highest proportion of old people living in institutions.

Swiss Mortality: Suicide and Accidents

In Switzerland there is a great variation of mortality rates across time and among the different cantons. Between 1881 and 1940 the Catholic cantons (Tessin included) had mortality rates significantly higher than the rest of the country. This has been explained by the differences in the development of the medico-sanitary sector among the different cantons. After World War II, the differences remained unchanged, but the explanation now is to be found foremostly in the variations in the level of industrial development, which in turn reflects the socio-sanitary conditions (Swiss Federal Statistical Office, 2000c).

Since 1970, the high mortality rates observed in the city of Basel, have been explained by the increased ageing rate observed in this city, in comparison with the rest of the country. The accelerated ageing of an urban population explains why, during the last 100 years, there has been an inversion of mortality rates related to place of residence, so that in the beginning of the century mortality rates were higher in rural areas, whereas presently they predominate in urban areas (Swiss Federal Statistics, 2000c).

The progress of medicine during the 19th century resulted in the disappearance of several mortal diseases as well as an extraordinary increase in life expectancy. Concomitantly, extensive access to medical care for all population groups was a contributing factor in the health improvement of the Swiss population. Every Swiss inhabitant is now covered by a mandatory health insurance allowing for good quality hospital and outpatient care. The global density of medical doctors increased threefold during the 20th century. In some regions the ratio is still 1 doctor for 800 persons while in Basel and Geneva it is 1 doctor for 300–400 persons. In general, the Catholic population has better access to care than the rest of the population.

During the last 120 years, there has been a slight reduction in the rates of death due to external (violent) causes, as the number of deaths due to traffic accidents has increased while the number of suicides has remained relatively stable. Suicide rates have oscillated between 17 and 29 per 100,000 in this period. The reduction of suicide rates observed in the 1890s and between 1950 and 1960 has been attributed to an improvement of the overall socio-economic situation of the country, whereas the increases observed in 1878–1887, 1930–1935 and 1975–1980 correspond to periods of socio-economic crises (see Figure 1).

Figure 1. Number of suicides/100,000 habitants and number of deaths by road accidents/100,000 habitants:1875-1995

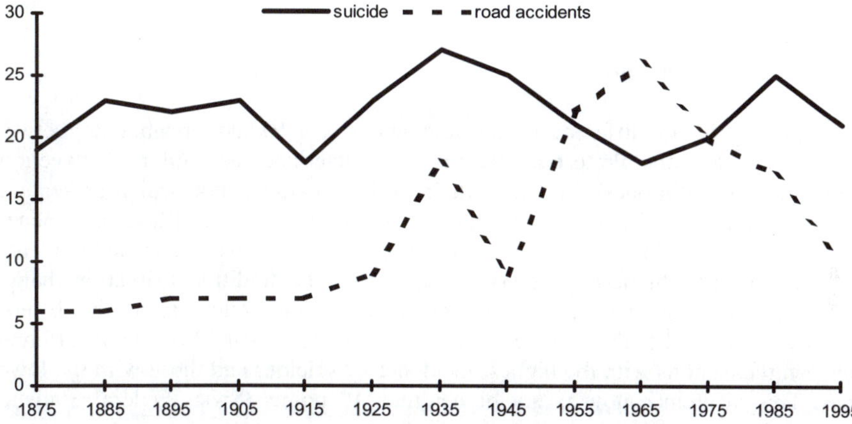

Source:Swiss Federal Statistical Office. (2000c)

In 1996 there were 62,637 deaths in Switzerland, which represents 8.9 per 100,000. Of the total deceased, 50,940 (81.3%) were over the age of 64 years. In this age group, the number of deaths due to external (violent) causes was 1,666 (3.3% of all deaths), and the number of suicides was 381 (0.7% of all deaths; 26.6% of all suicides) (Swiss Federal Statistical Office, 2000a). In the same year, 1,231 elderly people died from accidents, that is, 57% of the total of deaths from accidents and 2.4% of all deaths among the elderly (see Table 1). In brief, approximately 15% of the population (over the age of 64 years) were responsible for almost 27% of all suicides in Switzerland in 1996.

It is not always easy to determine whether the death of a person (particularly if they are elderly) was accidental or a suicide. The taboo that surrounds suicide, religious reasons, issues relating to insurance, police inquiries and the suffering of the family may all, in many instances, make it difficult to ascertain the real cause of a case of death. In these cases the doctor may well sign the death certificate without resorting to a full medico-legal investigation. The high death due to suicide rate among the elderly could, therefore, be at least partially explained by behaviours that are truly a suicide that fail to be recognised as such. Finger (1996) estimates that according to these reasons, suicide among the elderly can be underestimated by up to 20%.

Table 1. Number of suicides, number of deaths, ratio between number of suicides and number of deaths, number of mortal accidents in 1996, by three groups of age

Groups of age	Suicides	Total of deaths	Suicides / total of deaths (%)	Accidents
0–14	4	613	0.7	71
15–64	1046	11084	9.4	762
65+	381	50940	0.7	1231

Source: Swiss Federal Statistical Office. (2000c)

Suicide in the Cantons

There is a significant difference in the suicide rate (per 100,000 inhabitants) between the Catholic and the Protestant regions of Switzerland, as well as between the Germanic and Latin ones. Ticino, of Italian origin, is the canton which presents the lowest suicide rates. The Germanic cantons of Appenzell Ausser Rhoden, Appenzell Inner Rhoden and Basel as well the French speaking cantons of Neuchâtel, Geneva and Vaud have the highest suicide rates. Since 1970 this traditional situation changed to a significant reduction in the difference of the suicide rates among the different cantons. At the end of the 19th century there were more than 20 points of difference between the cantons with the highest incidence of suicides and those with the lowest ones. This difference now is not higher than 10 points (Swiss Federal Statistical Office, 2000c).

Suicide in the Cities

At the end of the 19th century the highest suicide rate was found in some of the most important cities of the French-speaking region (Lausanne, Geneva, La Chaux-de-Fonds) as well as some of the German-speaking onse (Zurich, Bern and Winterthur). Basel and St-Gall had a higher suicide rate than the global country mean after World War I and Luzern had got the same level 20 years ago. Since 1970 the difference in the suicide rate of the cities with the highest rates and those with the lowest rates significantly diminished (Swiss Federal Statistics, 2000b).

Three factors seem to influence the difference in the suicide rates among the different regions:

1. Cultural differences between the cities and the rural regions.
2. Factors linked to Catholic and Protestant religions.
3. Factors linked to the Latin and German communities.

The inhabitants from the rural regions now have lower suicide incidence than those from the cities, possibly because of stronger social links. As the economic differences between the different linguistic regions were not significant until recently, we can suppose that other factors should explain the highest suicide rates in

French-speaking regions of the country. The higher divorce rates and the professional structure of this region may play an important role (Swiss Federal Statistical Office, 2000b).

Data concerning the number and rates of suicides throughout the different age groups in the different cantons and cities are not available, making it impossible look at these variables in relation to suicide in the elderly population. The data identified above simply help us to understand the general context of suicide in Switzerland.

Number of Suicides and Number of Suicides per 100,000 Inhabitants by Age Groups: 1970–1995

In Switzerland, suicide is responsible for around 1,500 deaths every year. In 1995, people older than 64 years (representing 15.1% of the population) contributed to more than 28.2% of the total suicides. We can also observe that the number of suicides per 100,000 habitants in this same year was particularly high in the group aged over 75 years (see Table 2).

Table 2. Number of suicides and rates of suicides per 100,000 inhabitants by age groups: 1970–1995

AGE	**1970**		**1975**		**1980**		**1985**		**1990**		**1995**	
	N	**R**	**N**	**R**	**N**	**R**	**N**	**R**	**N**	**R**	**N**	**R**
5–14	4	0.4	6	0.6	10	1.1	6	0.8	4	0.7	2	0.5
15–24	135	14.1	196	21	231	23.8	189	19.2	147	15.6	132	15.5
25–34	173	18.4	224	22.1	252	26	270	27.5	240	22.1	191	16.3
35–44	145	18.1	235	28.3	259	29.3	291	29.7	229	22.6	219	20.5
45–54	225	32.9	265	35.6	251	33.5	260	33.2	253	29.3	269	27.8
55–64	215	33.4	221	36.3	254	40.5	236	34.9	200	28.8	206	28.8
65–74	158	34.1	173	33.8	216	40.8	218	43.1	187	35.6	199	35.1
75+	95	39.7	109	38.1	148	42.7	150	36.9	207	45.7	201	42.6

N – Number of suicides, R – Rates of suicides per 100,000 habitants

Source: Office Fédéral de la Statistique. (1995), Swiss Federal Statistical Office. (2000c)

In 1970 and 1995, the highest rate of suicide was observed in the 75+ group followed by the 65–74 years group. Besides an important variation in the number of suicides in these two elderly groups (75+ = 111.6%; 65–74 years = 25.9%) we can not find a such an important evolution between the 2 end points for the number of suicides per 100,000 habitants (75+ = 7.3%; 65–74 years = 2.9%). This suggests that the increase in the absolute number of suicides in the elderly group mainly reflects the increase in this population (see Table 3).

Table 3. Evolution of number of suicides and rates of suicides per 100,000 inhabitants by age groups: 1970–1995

AGE	Number of suicides			Number of suicides per 100,000 inhabitants		
	1970	1995	Evolution %	1970	1995	Evolution %
5–14	4	2	–50	0.4	0.5	25
15–24	135	132	2.2	14.1	15.5	9.9
25–34	173	191	10.4	18.4	16.3	–11.4
35–44	145	219	51	18.1	20.5	13.3
45–54	225	269	19.6	32.9	27.8	–15.5
55–64	215	206	–4.2	33.4	28.8	–13.8
65–74	158	199	25.9	34.1	35.1	2.9
75+	95	201	111.6	39.7	42.6	7.3

Source: Office Fédéral de la Statistique. (1995), Swiss Federal Statistical Office. (2000c)

Number of Suicides per 100,000 Inhabitants in 1995: Men vs Women

Data presenting the number of suicides per 100,000 habitants shows firstly, that the suicide rate increases with ageing populations, and secondly, the important prevalence of suicide in men. In 1995 the suicide rate was 2–5 times more significant in men than in women, depending on the age group (see Table 4 and Figure 2). In this same year 26% of the total suicides in men happened in the age group 64 years and over while the same proportion was 28% for women.

Table 4. Rates of suicides per 100,000 inhabitants in 1995: men versus women

Age	Men	Women	Men / Women
5–14	0.5	0	–
15–24	24.1	6.7	3.6
25–34	24.9	7.6	3.3
35–44	30.1	10.6	2.8
45–54	40.1	15.4	2.6
55–64	40.2	18.2	2.2
65–74	49.6	23.8	2.1
75+	88.2	18	4.9

Source: Office Fédéral de la Statistique. (1995), Swiss Federal Statistical Office. (2000c)

Rates of Suicides per 100,000 Inhabitants in Old Age: Switzerland vs other European Countries

With the recent data published by the WHO (1999) we can compare the suicide rates of elderly persons in Switzerland in the age groups 65 to 74 years and 74+ years, with these age samples in 33 European countries. Figure 3 presents the the data of these countries for the age group 65–74 years and Figure 4 presents the data for the 74+ age group (the year when the data was obtained is indicated after the name of the country). Switzerland is situated at the 8th position for the first group and at the 13th position for the second age group, confirming that this country has very high rates of suicide in the elderly population.

Figure 2. Rates of suicides per 100,000 inhabitants (suicide rate) by sex and by age group in 1995

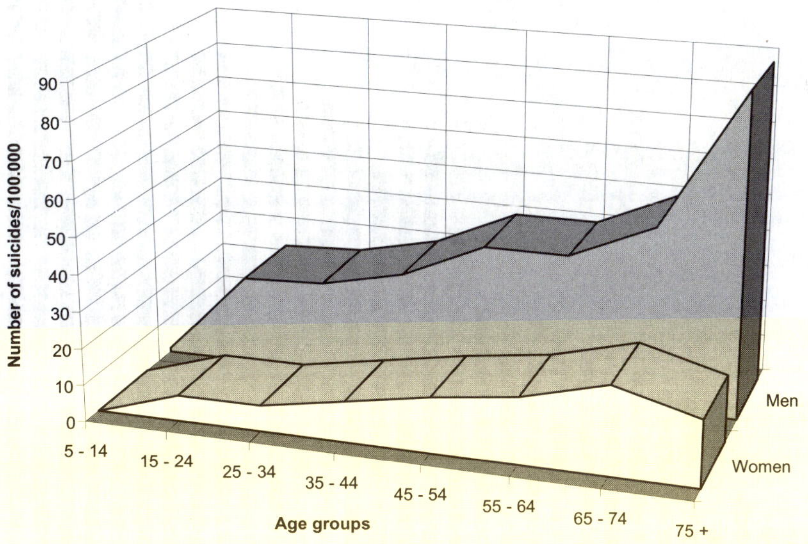

Figure 3. Rates of suicides per 100,000 inhabitants in the group 65–74 years: Switzerland versus other European countries

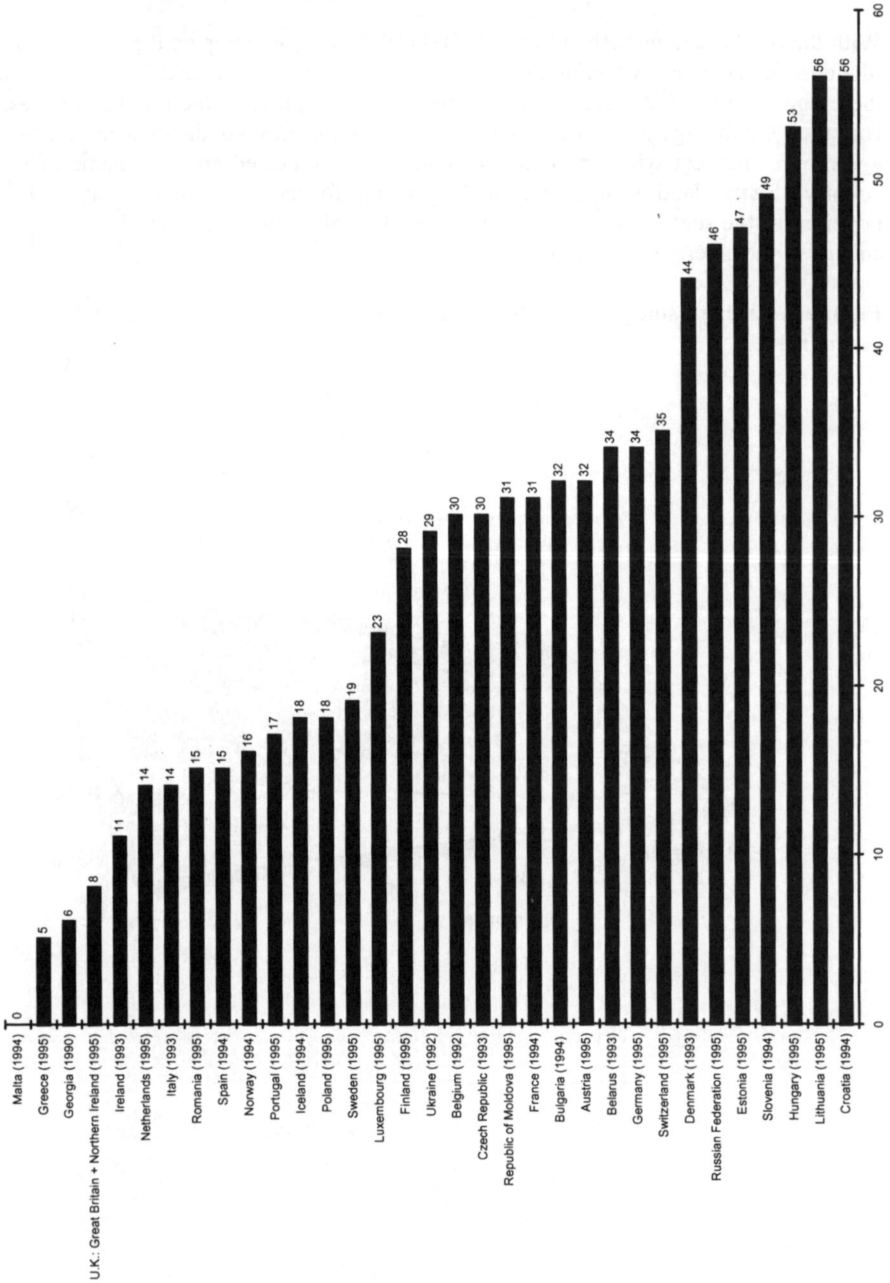

Figure 4. Rates of suicides per 100,000 inhabitants in the group > 74 years: Switzerland versus other European countries

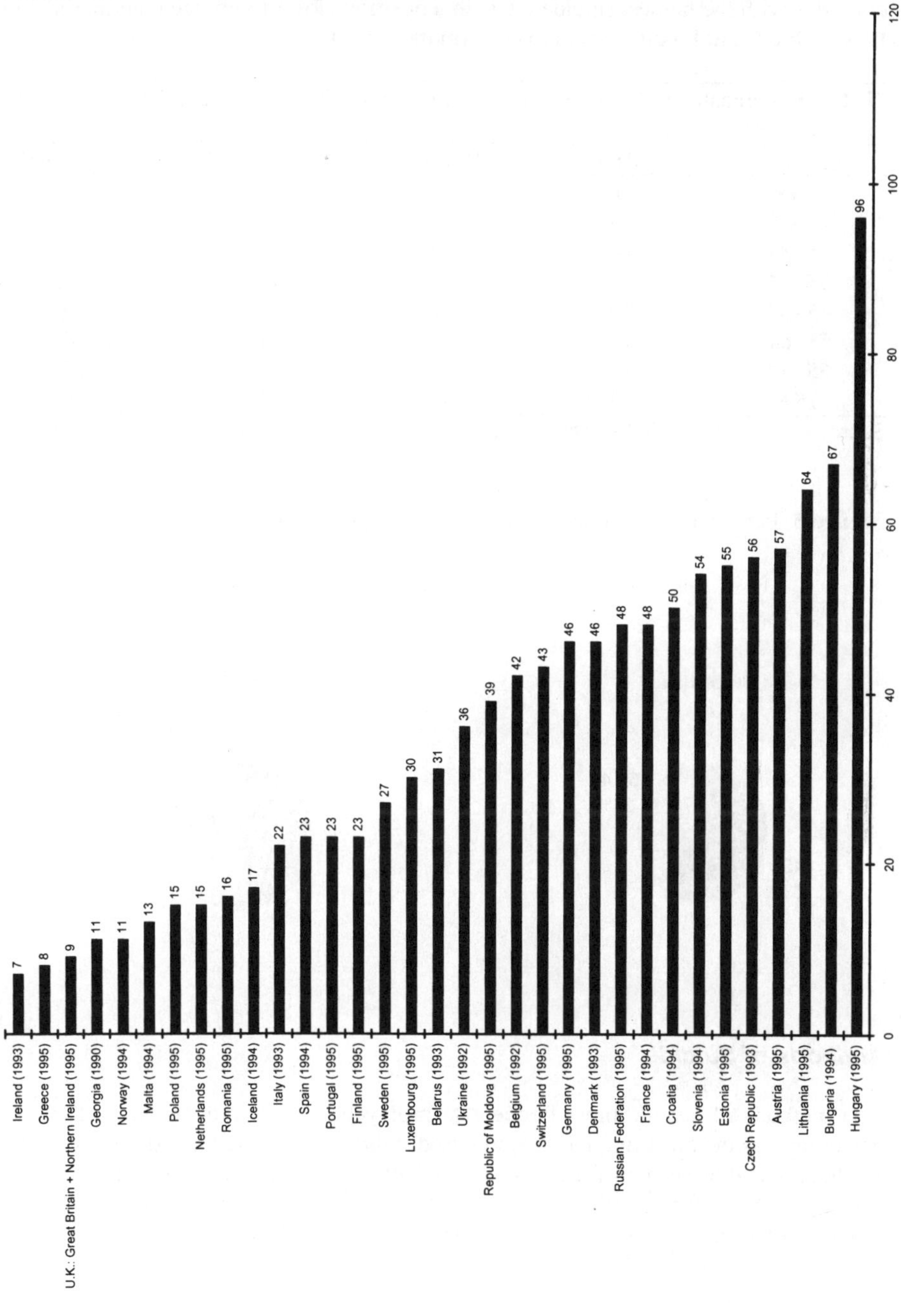

In a study conducted by Gulbinat (Gulbinat, 1996), where the global importance of suicide among the elderly is highlighted, Switzerland ranked 9th among 25 countries with the highest suicide rates, in a position closer to France than to Spain or Italy. Table 5 and Figure 5 seem to confirm these data.

Table 5. Percentage of suicides by age group in 1995 (and by gender): Switzerland and the World

Age (years)	Men	Women	Total CH	Total World
5–14	0	0	0	0.8
15–24	10	7	9	12.5
25–34	14	11	13	17.5
35–44	16	14	15	19.2
45–54	20	18	20	16
55–64	14	17	15	14
65–74	12	19	14	11
75+	14	14	14	9

Source: Office Fédéral de la Statistique. (1995), Swiss Federal Statistical Office. (2000c)

Figure 5. Percentage of suicides by age group in 1995:Switzerland and the World

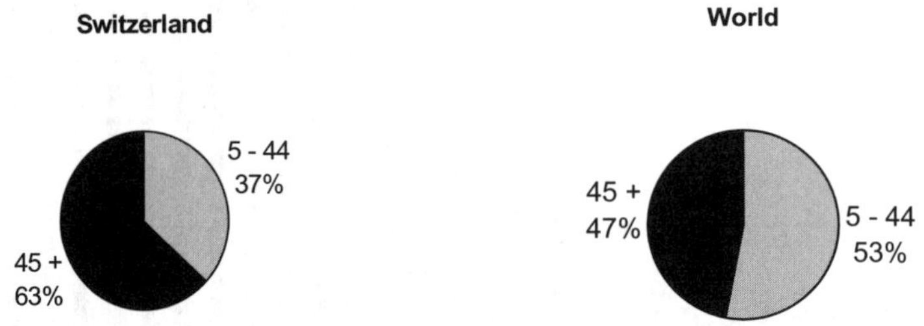

Methods of Suicide

The methods of suicide most frequently employed in 1995 are shown in Table 6. Shooting was the most frequent method used, followed by hanging, indeed, these two methods together account for almost half of all suicides. In addition to the methods identified at the death certificate, the elderly may resort to some methods of suicide that are not easily identified, as such refusing to eat or to drink.

Table 6. Distribution of methods of suicide most often used in Switzerland by persons with more than 64 years of age

Methods of suicide	%
Firearm discharge	25
Hanging, strangulation, suffocation	24
Self poisoning	19
Jumping from a high place	12
Drowning, sumersion	10
Other	10

Source: Office Fédéral de la Statistique. (1995), Swiss Federal Statistical Office. (2000c)

Suicide Attempt and Other Modalities

Several studies suggest that the ratio between suicide attempt and completed suicide decreases in elderly persons (Katona, 1994). Davidson and Philippe (1986) measured in women younger than 25 years one suicide for each 160 suicide attempts, while in women older than 64 years this ratio was one suicide for each 3 suicide attempts. In men older than 64 years this ratio even raises to one suicide for each suicide attempt.

In Switzerland, there are no data about suicide attempts in old age and the number of suicide attempts is difficult to assess. In general only suicide attempts with serious consequences needing medical care are detected. Therefore a significant number of suicide attempts are probably underestimated. Several cases of violent death are considered accidents when they are really suicides or suicide attempts. Detecting these suicide attempts is very important due to the high risk of relapse, as 9% of men and 11% of women who have made a suicide attempt try again to suicide (Picault & Le Gac, 1996).

Tessier (1999) suggested that we should consider other forms of voluntary suppression of one's life. The suicide pact, when a couple decides to die together, is more and more frequent in older people. The debate on active euthanasia is going on in several European countries, but only Holland has authorised this practice. In Switzerland active euthanasia is not authorised and yet the debate is becoming deeper (Baertschi, 1999). Tessier also suggests that further research be performed on some of the more typical suicide behaviours of the elderly, such as refusing treatments, ceasing to eat or drink, intentional self-harm, some kinds of addiction behaviour and focal suicide. No such information is yet available in Switzerland.

Risk Factors for Suicide in Old Age

Age and Sex

In 1995 the suicide risk associated with ageing was almost 5 times greater for those aged 75 years and over when compared to those under 24 years of age. This suggests the existence of different specific risk factors at different age groups.

However, these rates also fluctuate in a complex fashion which difficult to explain. For instance, although the males' rates are consistently higher than the females', the male/female ratio decreases constantly from 3.6 to 2.1, between 15 and 74 years of age, but increases again to 4.1 in the 75 years and over age group. Among females a peak was observed in 1987-1988, whereas for males, two peaks were observed, between 1970 and 1978, and again since 1990 up until now.

The aspects linked to the generations (cohort) are very important when considering suicide in old age. Behaviours observed in a group of elderly persons can be better appreciated by their life experiences (wars, natural catastrophes, economic crises) than by aging problems only. In Switzerland, it is difficult to establish a hypothesis which links risk factors and cohort aspects to explain why a particular generation of the elderly would commit suicide.

Older males seem more vulnerable to suicide than females within the same generation. Gallager et al (1981–1982) suggests that the higher vulnerability of men at the time of retirement and widowhood may explain this difference, especially during the first year after both events.

Social and Economic Factors

The economic situation of the Swiss population is quite comfortable. Annual per capita GNP in Switzerland is approximately US$23,200 and is one of the highest in the world. Current inflation rate is around 3.4% and the unemployment rate covers 4.4% of the active population (Office Fédéral de la Statistique, 1995) .

These favourable economic conditions contributed to a life expectancy of 81.6 years for women and 75.1 years for men in 1994. In this same year, Switzerland spent US$17 billion in retirement pensions, making the income of retired people in Switzerland the highest in Europe (Office Fédéral de la Statistique, 1995). However, in view of the real size of the active population and the growth of the elderly population, it seems difficult to maintain the economic power of the retired people in the near future, which leads to constant debates in search of a solution.

In 1990 the proportion of elderly households was estimated to be 24% of the total Swiss households. The proportion of the elderly living alone increased from 16% in 1960 to 32% in 1990, whereas in the same period the proportion of those living with a family member decreased from 27% to 12%. This explains, in part, why in 1990,

8.4% of the population over 65 years were institutionalised (Lalive D'epinay et al. 1998).

Current policies which enable the elderly to continue to live at home, thus avoiding institutionalisation, contribute to the development of smaller sized households. Hence, in 1990, 48% of the households of elderly people were made up of couples only, and an additional 34% of persons living alone (Lalive D'epinay et al. 1998).

All these data substanciate the importance of social isolation to the elderly in Switzerland. Among several factors, family structure changes seem to be the main cause of isolation. The increase in the number of divorces, migration of offspring who live far from their parents, and the decrease in family size are all facts contributing to that isolation. Isolation particularly contributes to suicide when it is associated with feelings of abandonment (Conwell et al. 1991). The link between suicide and isolation becomes even stronger in certain individuals such as those who are unmarried or widowed, or those with serious handicaps, or those who have moved homes (Katona, 1994). As suggested by Tessier (1999), apart from the fact of being alone and feeling alone, the fear of dying alone can particularly contribute to the decision of suicide.

Physical Factors

Theories which stress physical factors try to establish correlations between severe somatic diseases, chronic pain and suicide. These physical factors could act alone or in combination with other social and psychological factors (Shah & Tamal, 1998).

Difficulties in adaptive mechanisms may lead elderly people to refuse normal physical and mental changes linked to ageing, particularly for those with vulnerable personalities. These adaptive difficulties can be reinforced by the occidental way of life which frequently over evaluates youth values.

For Cattel (1988) and Tressier (1999) the suicide, which can be considered as a response to avoid physical suffering, can follow several steps:

- the suicide as a way to escape unbearable physical pain;
- the physical suffering acting together with other pathogenic independent factors (depression, loneliness, conflicts, etc);
- the physical suffering as a cause of a depressive episode;
- the physical suffering as a symptom of a depressive episode.

Psychiatric Factors

Psychiatric theories have highlighted the importance of mental disorders – such as depressive disorders, alcohol and other substances abuse – in those who commit suicide. These two types of disorders represent an elevated risk of suicide and, alone or in combination have been found in up to 80% of all cases of suicide (Katona,

1994; Baldwin, 1997; Baldwin, 1998; Ernst, 1999; Conwell, 1994; Simeone & Goda, 1994; Goda, 1994; Camus, 1999).

In the younger age groups, depressive psychopathology is heterogeneous but in the elderly its most frequent clinical feature is a mild late onset depressive episode (Conwell, 1994). An old person with depression has a risk of suicide estimated as 4 times higher than a younger person (Katona, 1994). The impact of depressive sub-syndromes on suicide is very high, especially when it is the first episode (Ernst, 1999).

Depression alone is not enough to explain the high rate of suicide in old persons. Very often it is associated with a difficult family context, a recent widowhood, an objective and subjective experience of loneliness, the presence of a serious medical problem, the fear of dependence, problematic social relationships and to alcohol abuse (Katona, 1994). Indeed, the loss of a man's partner can increase his risk of suicide threefold (De Leo & Ormskerck, 1991).

Other psychiatric disorders that can be found in suicidal people include personality and anxiety disorders, although in approximately 13% of elderly people who had committed suicide no psychiatric diagnosis could be established (Tessier, 1999; Camus, 1999). These theories are the basis for the development of neuropsychiatric theories trying to establish a link between suicide and changes in brain neurotransmitters, such as serotonin (WHO, 1998).

Prevention Measures

It seems illusory to want to extinguish suicide behaviour but some appropriated prevention measures can significantly reduce its prevalence. These possible measures are limited only to some forms of intervention.

The characteristics of depression in late life suggests a role for prevention of suicide in this particular age group. Elderly persons who suicide rarely consult health care professionals regularly (Conwell, 1994; Camus, 1999; Ernst, 1995). But, in three quarters of cases they do during the month before their suicide (Ernst, 1999). Some authors point to the absence of adequate antidepressant treatment to the elderly in several and different care contexts (Duckworth & McBride, 1996; Koenig et al. 1997). That is why some authors propose the above measures to prevent suicide in old persons (United Nations, 1996; WHO, 1993, *Groupe latin*, 1998):

- to combat the traditional therapeutic pessimism of caregivers face to an old person with depression;
- to get the confidence of the patient: to speak to him about death and suicide;
- to make the diagnostic of depression as soon as possible and to treat it;
- to increase the competencies of caregivers to assess the risk of suicide;
- to be particularly alert:
  - to any change on the religious interests and in the legal will;
  - to the anniversary of losses;

  - to any suicide threat;
  - to control somatic treatments and to give palliative treatments when necessary;
  - to the presence in the environment of any kind of objects with which the person can suicide (arms, cords, drugs, etc.);
- to create adapted programs, strategies and facilities to give support (De Leo & Ormsteck, 1991);
- to give adapted information to general public.

Swiss authorities are well aware of the importance of mortality from suicide. Many efforts have been made to include suicide prevention as a public health priority, particularly through its integration into some local health-related legislation (*Nouvelles orientations*, 1997). In addition, the Swiss Medical Federation has developed a major information and training program concerning suicide prevention through a series of publications and organisation of seminars and workshops (Ernst, 1995; Federation des Medecins Suisses, 1995). As since 1986 we observe a progressive increase in the ratio between the suicide rate in the elderly and that in youngest people, we can suppose that the impact of prevention measures adopted was lower in the first group. Adapted preventive measures to the group of old persons are necessary.

Conclusion

In 1995 the group of old persons in Switzerland contributed to almost one third of the total number of suicides in this country. The high prevalence of suicide in this age group is found in the majority of European countries (Pritchard, 1992; Haenel, 1996; Michel & Spuhler, 1988; Andrian, 1991) wheras the world tendency is towards an increase in the suicide rate of young people (WHO, 1999).

We don't believe that the situation in Switzerland will change in the next few years. Haas & Hendin (1983) estimated that the number of suicides in the elderly will double until 2030, in light of the increase of the old people represented in the total population. Demographic data on Swiss ageing seems confirm this hypothesis because the proportion of elderly in 2025 is expected to be 23% of the total population instead of the 15.1% observed in 1998 (Swiss Federal Statistical Office, 1996; WHO, 1998).

Suicide rates in Switzerland show dynamic and complex fluctuations and should be analysed not only in terms of sex distribution, but also on regional characteristics. Between 1970 and 1995 the proportion of suicides of the elderly in relation to the total of suicides increased from 22% to 28.2%. Within this same period the proportion of suicides in the under 25 years age group was reduced from 12% in 1970 to 9.4% in 1995 and in the age group aged between 25 to 64 years the proportion diminished from 66% to 62.4%. This progression of suicides among the elderly, particularly noticeable after 1985, indicates that the preventive measures adopted so far have been less effective among this group (de Mendonca Lima, et al. 2000).

There is a great concern about the further increase of suicide in the elderly, making it a serious public health problem, considering the ageing of the Swiss population that is forecasted for the coming years.

In conclusion, although the living conditions of the elderly in Switzerland seem to be on the favorable side, they nevertheless do not prevent these people from having a high rate of suicide. This problem has been increasing in recent years and although it is not as big as in other age groups, its rate of increase is far higher. Within the elderly population the problem is unevenly distributed being highest among the men aged 75 years and older.

Methodological difficulties prevent us from knowing more precisely the number of suicide attempts. It seems that this knowledge is highly relevant for effective preventive programs. In fact, the positive experience of the reduction of suicide rates among the young and adults, indicates that we could perhaps be as effective in the reduction of suicide among the elderly as well. Additional research proposed by the literature (Conwell et al., 1991) are necessary to determine:

- the role of somatic disorders as precipitant factor of suicide in old age;
- the role on suicide of the pre-morbid personality, cognitive functioning, social support and recent and old stressing events;
- the participation of normal and pathological ageing on the expression of the suicide behaviour;
- the biological markers of suicide in old age;
- the potential impact on suicide rates of educational interventions for the general public and for caregivers.

References

Andrian, J. (1991). Le suicide des personnes âgée. Comparaisons nationales et internationales. *Gérontologie et Société, 56*, 101–113.

Baertschi, B. (1999). *Respect de l'autonomie et bienfaisance: la médecine face au suicide* (Folia Bioethica No. 25). Geneva: Société Suisse d'Ethique Biomédicale.

Baldwin, R. (1997). Depressive illness. In R. Jacoby & C. Oppenheimer, *Psychiatry in the Elderly* (pp. 536–573). Oxford: Oxford University Press.

Baldwin, R. (1998). Dépression. In R. Butler & E. Pitt (Eds.), *Seminars in Old Age Psychiatry* (pp. 102–124). Glasgow: Royal College of Psychiatrists.

Camus, V. (1999). Dépression du sujet âgé: Obstacles au diagnostic et au traitement en médecine générale. *Gériatrie Pratique, 3,* 14–19.

Cattell, H. (1988). Elderly suicide in London: an analysis of coroners' inquests. *International Journal of Geriatric Psychiatry, 3,* 251–261.

Conwell, Y. (1994). Suicide in elderly patients. In L. S. Schneider., C. H. Reynolds III., B. D. Lebowitz, & A. J. Friedhoff (Eds.), *Diagnosis and treatment of depression in late life.*

Results of the NIH consensus development conference (pp. 397–418). Washington: American Psychiatry Press.

Conwell, Y., Olsen, K., Caine, E., & Flannery, C. (1991). Suicide in late life: psychological autopsy findings. *International Psychogeriatrics, 3,* 59–66.

Davidson, F., & Philippe, A. (1986). *Suicide et tentatives de suicide aujourd'hui: étude épidémiologique*. Paris: Inserm-Doin.

De Leo, D., & Ormskerk, S. (1991) Suicide in the elderly: general characteristics. *Crisis, 12,* 3–17.

de Mendonca Lima, C., Bertolote, J., & Simeone, I. (2000). Le suicide chez la personne âgée en Suisse: à propos de quelques chiffres. *Médicine & Hygiène, 58,* 313–317.

Duckworth, G., & McBride, H. (1996). Suicide in old age, a tragedy of neglect. *Canadian Journal of Psychiatry, 41,* 217–222.

Ernst, C. (1999). Suicide in old age. In M. Maj & N. Sartorius (Eds.), *Depressive disorders. Volume 1 WPA series: evidence and experience in psychiatry* (pp. 398–400). New York: John Wiley & Sons.

Ernst, K. (1995). Médecin practicien et approche du risque suicidaire. *Bulletin des médecins suisses, 11,* 454–458.

Fédération des médecins Suisses & Office Federal de la Santé Publique. (1995). Crise et suicide. Berne: Fédération des médecins suisses.

Finger, S. (1996). L'Europe du suicide. *Abstract Neuro et Psy, 144,* 16–20.

Gallagher, D., Thomson, L., & Peterson, J. (1981–1982). Psychological factors affecting adaptation to bereavement in the elderly. *International Journal of Ageing and Human Development, 1412,* 79–83.

Goda, G. (1994). Le suicide à l'âge avancé. *Cahiers Psychiatriques Genevois, 16,* 127–135.

Groupe Latin pour la Prévention du Suicide. (1998). *Le Suicide en Questions 4: le Suicide de la Personne Âgée.* Paris: DepRelief, Lundbeck.

Gulbinat, W. (1996). The epidemiology of suicide in old age. *Archives of Suicide Research, 2,* 31–42.

Haas, A., & Hendin, H. (1983). Suicide among older people: projections for the future. *Suicide & Life Threatening Behavior, 13,* 147–154.

Haenel, T. (1996). Epidemiologie und Bedeutung der Suizidalität im Alter. *Geriatrie Praxis, 3,* 21–23.

Katona, C. (1994). *Depression in Old Age*. Chichester: John Wiley & Sons.

Koenig, H., George, L., & Meador, K. (1997). Use of antidepressants by nonpsychiatrists in the treatment of medically ill hospitalized depressed elderly patients. *American Journal of Psychiatry, 154,* 1369–1375.

Lalive D'Epinay, C., Brunner, M., & Albano, G. (1998). *Atlas suisse de la population âgée.* Geneva: Réalités sociales – âge et société.

Michel, K., & Spuhler, T. (1988). Suizid in der Schweiz 1970–1986. *Scweizerische Ärztezeitung, 69* (41), 1732–1737.

Nouvelles Orientations de la Politique Sanitaire. (1997). Suisse: Canton de Vaud.

Office Fédéral de la Statistique. (1995). *Memento statisique de la Suisse.* Berne: Author.

Picault, L., & Le Gac, J. (1996). Tentatives de suicide chez les personnes âgées. *Gérontologie Pratique, 77,* 4–5.

Pritchard, C. (1992). Changes in elderly suicides in the USA and the developed world 1974–1987: comparison with current homicide. *International Journal of Geriatric Psychiatry, 7,* 125–134.

Shah, A., & Tamal, D. (1998). Suicide and the elderly. *International Journal of Psychology and Clinical Practice, 2,* 3–17.

Simeone, I., & Goda, G. (1994). L'hypersuicidalité du sujet âgé. Pourquoi le sujet âgé se suicide-t-il? *Gazette Médicale, 15,* 915–917.

Stuckelberger, A., & Höpflinger, F. (2000). *Ageing in Switzerland at the dawn of the XXIst century. Main results of the national research program on ageing* (National Research

Program on Ageing Report NRP32). Berne: Swiss National Science Foundation and Gerontological Economic Research Organization.
Swiss Federal Statistical Office. (2000a). *Population: age structure and an ageing society* [On-line]. Available: http://www.statistik.admin.ch/stat_ch/ber01/eu0101-107.htm.
Swiss Federal Statistical Office. (2000b). *L'histoire de l'Etat fédéral* [On-line]. Available: http://www.statistik.admin.ch/ch150/ffrach.htm
Swiss Federal Statistical Office. (2000c). *Health: causes of mortality 1996* [On-line]. Available: http://www.statistik.admin.ch/stat_ch/ber14/eu1401.htm.
Tessier, J. (1999). Suicide du sujet âgé et autres conduites autodestructrices. In J. M. Léger, J. P. Clément, & J.Wertheimer, *Psychiatrie du sujet âgé* (pp. 133–146). Paris: Flammarion.
United Nations. (1996). *Prevention of suicide. Guidelines for the formulation and implementation of national strategies* (ST/ESA/245). New York: Author.
WHO. (1993). *Guidelines for the primary prevention of mental, neurological and psychosocial disorders*. Volume 4: Suicide (WHO/MNH/MND/93.24). Geneva: Author.
WHO. (1998). *Demographic data for health situation assessment and projections – 1998* (WHO/HST/HSP/98.4). Geneva: Author.
WHO. (1998). *Suicidal behaviour in Europe. The situation in the 1990s.* Copenhagen: WHO regional office for Europe.
WHO. (1999). *Figures and Facts about suicide* (WHO/MNH/MBD/99.1). Geneva:Author.

Elderly Suicide in Slovenia

Onja T. Grad, Aleš Kogoj and Jože Trontelj

Department of Psychiatry, University of Ljubljana, Slovenia and the National Medical Ethics Committee of Slovenia

A man can age and die like a Gothic cathedral,
or like an old shoe.

(The words of a depressed patient, who eventually committed suicide)

Introduction

Slovenia is one of those middle European countries that suffer from a long-lasting problem of high suicide rates. Currently, Slovenia ranks the sixth in Europe with a suicide rate of around 30 per 100,000 inhabitants, which has remained the same for the past twenty years (see Table 1). The average profile of the Slovenian that dies from suicide is a male (the M:F ratio is 3.5:1), in his late forties (49.8 years), who hangs himself (62.5%), had problems in his relationship (22%), was poorly educated, had a long history of alcoholism and had some additional health problems (Milčinski et al., 1998).

Table 1. Suicide rates in Slovenia from 1873–1998 (Data apply to the present territory)

Year	Suicide Rate per 100,000
1873	3.0
1881–1890	6.8
1931–1935	19.4
1950–1957	20.4
1960–1969	26.9
1970–1979	28.6
1980–1989	31.6
1990–1998	30.1

We surely have to agree with Shneidman's statement that suicidal phenomena are enormously complex, and if we look at the suicide trajectory model (Stillion et al., 1996), we can see that it applies more to the individual risk factors than to the sociological or cross-cultural ones. This model includes several commonalities that exist in suicidal behaviour: biological, psychological, cognitive and environmental risk factors, warning signs, triggering events and different suicidal behaviour. If we hypothesize that most of them are more or less common worldwide, we have to look at the environmental ones closely to see the differences of one particular country compared with another.

Slovenia is bordering four countries, three of which share the problem of very high suicide rates in comparison with the EU average of 19,4 (see Figure 1). While Italy on the one hand has a relatively low suicide rate (7.2, from the latest data for 1993), Austria (19,9), Hungary (31,4), Croatia (21,9) and Slovenia (29,2 – all data for the year 1996) have always had a serious problem with suicidality (World Health Organisation, 1999).

All four of these countries with high suicide rates were parts of the same Austro-Hungarian Empire and thus used to share many important facets of living. There are many socio-cultural and historical determinants that influence and are connected to the phenomenon of suicide and contribute to an atmosphere of high suicide risk in the society. Even though the four countries have had different histories in the last century, some basic commonalities prevail. These include similar general attitudes towards suicidal acts, the style and norms of living, the main values and beliefs, education systems and the upbringing of children, problems with alcohol (specially in Slovenia, Croatia and Hungary), and attitudes which contribute to the perception of the elderly as a high risk population for suicide.

Slovenia's development in connection with the so-called withdrawn and individualistic character of their inhabitants is currently directed towards a society of high material standards of living, which is expanding and growing too rapidly. Accompanying this trend is a loss of traditional patterns of support and the security of close social networks. These attributes of a society in transition add to the long-standing problem of alcoholism with its connection with the introjected aggressive impulses of the average Slovenian. Aggression has traditionally been suppressed at the national level because of the centuries of foreign rule, and at the individual level because of an authoritarian, paternalistic pattern of child rearing.

The general attitude towards suicide in Slovenia could be described as ambivalent. On the one hand it is a taboo subject and talking about it is discouraged, but on the other hand, it is accepted and understood as a solution for those who have "failed" in their lives, or have nothing to expect from life any longer (such as the elderly). In addition, suicide has frequently been present in Slovenian literature. One of the most popular Slovenian poets brings this feeling up in one of his sonnets:

Dear Death, do not delay to break the spell!
O happy road, O key to our endeavour,
You lead us where mortality shall sever
Life's chains and free us from these pains of hell;

(F. Prešeren [translation by K. Bray])

When we talk about the elderly we have to mention that Slovenia is one of those European countries which have a very low birth rate (1.7 child per fertile woman, natality decreasing to 10 per 100,000 between 1995–1997), while the number of people over 65 years of age increases rapidly and constantly (in 1999 this age group represented 13.6% of the whole population), bringing the problems associated with old age into focus.

Figure 1. Suicide standardised death rate (SDR) in Austria, Croatia, Hungary, Italy, Slovenia and Europe

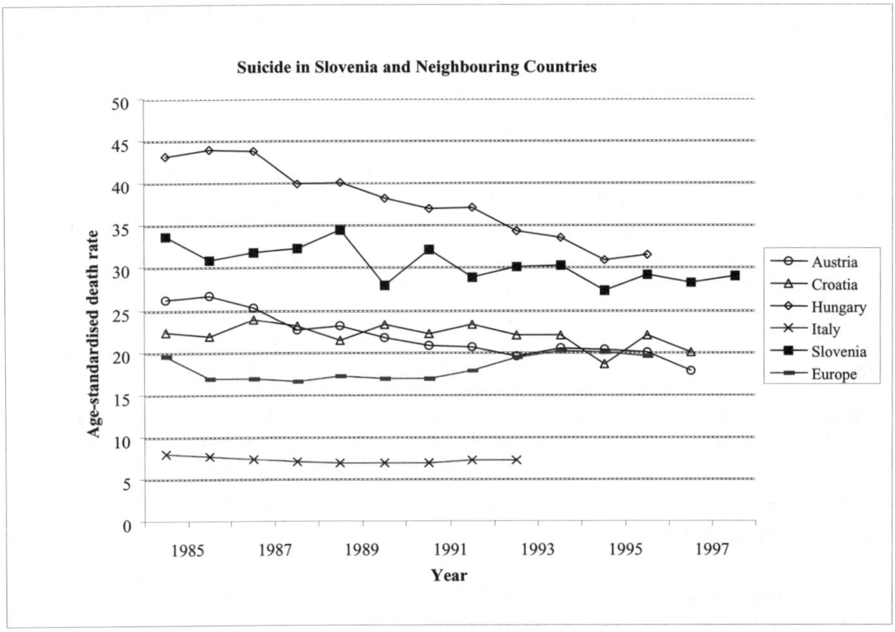

By the year 2009 it is estimated that in Slovenia the number of people over the age of 65 will exceed 15%, while 3.5% will be older than 80 years of age. Life expectancy at birth is now 71.0 years for males and 78.6 years for females. Approximately every four years life expectancy at birth increases by one year. Thus, Slovenia is rapidly becoming an ageing nation.

Epidemiology of Elderly Suicide

When a nation becomes older, all the problems associated with the ageing process become more prominent. This certainly includes elderly suicide in a country with high general suicide. Table 2 reveals a higher suicide rate in the elderly group in comparison with the general rate, matching the years of the highest and the lowest annual rates in both groups in the years 1989 and 1995, respectively.

Table 2. Suicide rate for persons over 65 per 100,000 in Slovenia – standardised death rate (SDR)

Year	Total	Male 0–64	Female 0–64	Total 0–64	Male 65+	Female 65+	Total 65+
1985	33.6	49.1	13.1	30.7	113.4	24.2	57.4
1986	30.8	44.3	11.4	27.5	112.5	26.9	57.5
1987	31.8	44.1	13.6	28.5	95.5	39.2	58.8
1988	32.3	42.5	15.2	28.8	126.5	27.3	60.9
1989	34.5	48.4	13.5	30.7	124.5	33.7	65.4
1990	27.9	40.6	9.9	25.1	92.3	29.3	50.6
1991	32.1	45.9	12.8	29.3	120.9	21.9	55.0
1992	28.8	40.1	10.0	25.0	99.2	38.3	59.6
1993	30.1	44.7	9.4	27.0	106.7	29.6	55.0
1994	30.2	44.3	11.3	27.7	99.5	24.5	50.3
1995	27.2	40.5	10.1	25.3	84.1	21.4	43.0
1996	29.2	41.3	11.8	26.5	99.4	24.1	50.7
1997	28.2	42.1	9.4	25.7	97.8	20.6	47.9
1998	29.0	42.1	10.8	26.5	95.6	22.9	48.6

It is interesting to note a small but significant drop in suicide rates after Slovenia gained independence. The first remarkable drop was noticed in 1990, when Slovenia was preparing several political and social acts to become independent, while it was still annexed by the former Yugoslavia. Grad (1995) proposed the following possible explanations for this phenomenon:

- There was a clear "political spring" and an awakening of new perspectives with many democratic changes on the horizon;
- The "enemy" was openly named (Serbia) and there was a fight against it by and through political means and the media. This allowed formerly suppressed aggression to vent freely (even) with the approval of local authorities;
- Most of Europe and Slovenia's neighbouring countries supported the democratic changes in Slovenia, which was perceived as a small but justified rebel (the David versus Goliath syndrome);
- In the time leading up to the gaining of independence, the last Yugoslav government tried to bribe the citizens for political peace with artificially inflated local currency and a relatively comfortable standard of living.

In spite of the general drop in the suicide rate that year, the drop was not so dramatic and quickly increased again in men over the age of 65. The new developments and uncertainty probably scared and burdened the elderly, who are usually more rigid and experience difficulties in adapting to rapid social changes.

Cultural Aspects of the Ageing Process in Slovenia

If we look again at the trajectory model for the elderly (Stillion et al., 1996), we can see that the predominant risk factors for suicide in the elderly include all sorts of physical decline and illnesses in connection with neurotransmitter decline, loneliness associated with different losses (retirement, poverty, widowhood) and increasing feelings of despair and depression.

When an old person becomes debilitated or loses the capacity to take care of him or herself, it is either up to the children to take charge or arrange care, or else they are forced to seek admission to one of the old people's homes. This is not a popular solution for most as it is considered the last stop before the cemetery. Unfortunately there are not enough non-government, social programs for those elderly who, despite their need for care, prefer to stay in their home environment. The first two-day care centres were opened last year. In the next few years there should be at least seven more such centres. Care centres come as a great relief to children who live together with their parents. In Slovenia it is the women who usually take care of the parents (and spouses) when they become disabled through old age. A lot of women in Slovenia are employed, especially those in urban areas. Indeed, in the 25–49 age group, 88.4% women are employed. Although they possess the physical capacities to take care of the elderly, they do not have sufficient time to attend to their work and take care of their elderly relatives. In the over 50 age group, only 18.3% women are employed, but being older and more often ill, they themselves need care from others.

There are very few flats for elderly available in the community or in the connection with old people's homes. The long-term goal of our government is to provide sufficient enough services to assist 20 % of the elderly, while presently this percentage is much lower.

Much too often proper care and connections with the environment depend on the financial possibilities of the aged or their family. The financial constraints represent a major difficulty and lead to the isolation of the elderly and produce many additional problems. The average pension reaches 68 % of the average salary, while the lowest pension (for farmers) amount to no more than 26% of the average salary. A radical change in post-communist Slovenia was the dropping of the "high security-low risk" principle, which included the numerous benefits of unlimited social, economical and medical care. Slovenia is now in a "high risk-low security" period of extreme, liberal capitalism with very little solidarity for the under-privileged (such as retired, old, chronically ill), which has resulted in an increase in social pathologies, such as suicide, alcoholism, and poverty.

Retirement is not only a financial problem for the elderly as it is also associated with psychological and social difficulties. Once retired, people lose their status, their position in the society, their power, a source of gratification, and even their vocation, as officially they are no longer a physician, a teacher, a salesman, but "just" a retired person. In Slovenia there are currently no systematic courses to prepare people for their retirement. Nor are there any peer support groups organized by employers to prepare employees for this new stage in their life cycle. However, since 1987 more and more peer self-support groups for the elderly have been organized in different parts of Slovenia. Approximately 1.6 % of the elderly are included in these groups (Kladnik, 1998).

In Slovenia, loneliness is an extremely important risk factor for the elderly. Unfortunately there are insufficiently developed networks of different activities for the aged. Although in rural areas families are larger than in urban settlements (the rural/urban ratio for the number of children in the family is 1.37:1.24), the elderly living on farms are often alone due to the daily migration of predominantly younger people to the urban areas. In one third of the Slovenian communities, the village population has dropped by about 20% over the last ten years. In the period between 1981–1991 the number of single-member households in urban settlements has increased by 8.5%, and in rural settlements by 22.1%. In Ljubljana, the capital of Slovenia, 33% of all people who are living alone are older then than 65 years of age (13.6 % of the population). Thus, living alone and being lonely is one of the major risk factors for suicide in Slovenia (Kostnapfel, 1986). This problem is compounded in rural areas where there are few organized activities for the elderly.

The data in Table 3 confirm the findings by Stroebe & Stroebe (1993) where they report on a remarkably consistent pattern cross-culturally, whereby suicide rates are lowest for those who are married. The excess of widowed men (compared with married men) is greater than that of widowed women (compared with married women). Obviously the marital status carrying the highest suicide risk is that of divorced men (in both age groups) or widowed men (in the older age group).

Table 3. Suicide rates by gender and marital status for those aged over 55 years of age, 1992–1998

	Mean suicide rate			**Mean suicide rate**	
	Age 55–64	**Age 65+**		**Age 55–64**	**Age 65+**
Women	**21.5**	**26.4**	**Men**	**93.1**	**96.7**
Married	21.5	44.8	Married	95.2	94.5
Widowed	26.3	23.4	Widowed	68.1	108.6
Divorced	16.2	23.5	Divorced	121.8	119.7
Single	13.6	22.2	Single	87.2	56.8

The next two major factors that are very influential in increasing the suicide rate among the elderly are depression and the general attitude towards the old age in the society. Physicians and family members are not sufficiently aware of the depressed elderly and their depression remains unrecognized and untreated, and often leads to suicide.

General practitioners are most appropriately situated to recognise and treat depression in the elderly and yet their numbers are very low with one family doctor per 1503 inhabitants. Psychiatric and psychotherapeutic help, on the other hand, is easily accessible and available to all, either in public or private institutions. However, the elderly in particular, frequently have prejudices against these services and avoid seeking psychiatric help. All old people's homes in Slovenia have a part time psychiatrist.

The social status of the elderly population in Slovenian society is generally low and is not respected. The elderly are an effectively marginalized social group. They are frequently perceived to be "worth less" than those working and producing and are seen as non-contributors to the general welfare of the country. The perception of the elderly as a burden for younger generations begins at a young age and is accepted by nearly everybody, striking as a boomerang upon those who are growing old but had low respect for the old age when younger. Two typical elderly suicide scenarios follow.

Case Vignettes

Case One

A 66-year old farmer was the second child in a peasant family with nine children. He began working on the farm when he was 6 years old and had been a farmer all of his life. He married but the couple could not have any children. He had been paying social insurance only for 12 years and so was unable to receive the farmers' pension in his old age. The only source of income was his wife's modest pension. In his old age he was not able to work as he had done before. He was worried about the future of his farm. He often had headaches and he was melancholic. One day he went to the barn where he hanged himself. His wife found him hanging. In the hospital he had extension posture and he breathed spontaneously. He was successfully resuscitated but he remained amnestic about his suicidal attempt.

Case Two

A 72-year old retired engineer and professor had a history of mild manic-depressive spells throughout his adult life, and was treated regularly by his psychiatrist and had to be hospitalized from time to time when depressed. All of his depressions obviously stemmed from the troublesome relationship with his wife. When this was better, he was coping all right. When he had problems with his wife, he became severely depressed and suicidal. He didn't see his worth as a man and as an intellectual any more. His wife was not supportive and often tortured him with her jealous outbursts. As long as he continued working part time in previous job, he could fight his feelings of worthlessness, but when this stopped he just felt useless. He took an overdose of his medications and died while his wife was sleeping at his side. He was a nice and gentle old man and everybody who used to know him believed that he was ageing as a Gothic cathedral, while he perceived himself during his last years as an old shoe – forgotten and discarded, without any place to be.

Recent Developments in Human Rights and the Dignity of the Terminally Ill and the Dying

These days it is harder to die than it used to be a hundred or more years ago. In previous times, dying was a life event whose meaning was clear and well understood. Our ancestors lived in much closer contact with the rhythms of nature and most often died of natural causes. Death usually occurred at home, and had a humane, moral, and social purpose. The community felt each individual's death; it became part of its emotional experience, moral conscience, and culture (Echeverri & Acosta, 1996).

Since those times, death and dying have changed dramatically. There are so many more people around, and old people have become more numerous than ever, often as a burden to their family and to the society. The traditional family bonds have loosened. Many people die away from their homes, often after a long illness and suffering, among strangers, and in an emotionally cold environment. Throughout the developed world, death has lost a lot of its original meaning, values and impact. In this regard, Slovenia is no exception.

At the same time, values associated with human life have changed. Independence and autonomy have become highly valued. Many of those incapacitated by disease feel humiliated and embarrassed because of their increased helplessness and dependence upon other people's assistance. Many feel bad when noticing the increasing fatigue and exhaustion of their caregivers. Others would like to leave before they lose control of both themselves and the things they used to control. Still others would like to depart before becoming disfigured by illness and suffering; they would like to be remembered by their loved ones the way they were when at their best (Compassion in dying v. State of Washington, 1996).

The concept of *"lebensunwertes Leben", life which is not worth living*, was introduced in Germany by the professors of law and medicine, Binding and Hoche, in 1920. They went on to propose a state controlled, enforced euthanasia program in order to solve medical and social problems and get rid of "useless" human lives (Binding & Hoche, 1920). The ideas of Binding and Hoche were immediately and vigorously opposed by two Slovene professors of law and medicine, who predicted what less than two decades later actually happened – mass killing as part of the Nazi euthanasia program (Dolenc & Šerko, 1921). Indeed, the notion of "*lebensunwertes Leben*" contributed to a gradual change in social attitudes towards human life whereby life's intrinsic and transcendental values were degraded, with the holocaust as a final consequence.

In the recent years, the idea of euthanasia upon request and the right to physician-assisted suicide have become a subject of heated public debate, triggered by the well known movements in several countries towards making *"mercy killings"* socially and legally acceptable. The public media have also taken up the debate in Slovenia, and requests started to appear in the media to legalise euthanasia or physician-assisted suicide as one of the human rights.

These developments prompted the National Medical Ethics Committee of Slovenia (NMEC) to express its opinion on both euthanasia and the ethical aspects of care for the terminally ill. Indeed, the NMEC was one of the first of the Central and

Eastern European countries to produce a position paper on these highly controversial issues.

The NMEC recognised that it was impossible to deny the validity of certain arguments claimed by the proponents of the legalization of euthanasia and physician-assisted suicide. However, it believed that legalization of euthanasia would produce significant and long-lasting damage to the medical profession, as well as to the society. Effects of this kind may not yet be fully evident even in countries where euthanasia in one form or another has been practised for some time. Therefore the NMEC considered it timely to express its views in detail, taking into account the principles of medical ethics as well as the national legislation.

In preparing its opinion, the NMEC relied on ethics codes and other ethical documents, and on certain published guidelines, in particular on those of the Swiss Academy of Medical Sciences (SAMS, 1996). The main purpose was to help medical doctors in their clinical decisions; however the text was also intended for those interested in the problems of end-of-life decisions. The following summarises some of the main points of the document (Trontelj, 1997a, 1997b).

The NMEC emphasised the physician's duty to assist the patient with all reasonably accessible measures so that their suffering is alleviated and their life may be saved. It added however, that the physician's duty to save life is exhausted when the disease process has taken an irreversible course towards patient's death, or when injuries are so severe that survival is no longer possible. In such cases, the physician's duty remains to alleviate symptoms and relieve the patient's physical and mental suffering. Then is the physician in charge is justified in abandoning or discontinuing life prolonging therapeutic measures. The method of reaching such a decision depends on whether the patient is able to understand their condition and declare their own will and wishes. Before taking the final decision, the physician should consult with the nursing personnel, the patient's family, and, if appropriate, with a colleague. In the case of a patient in chronic vegetative state that is diagnosed as irreversible, the physician may, after consulting with patient's closest relatives, discontinue not only active treatment but also nursing care, such as nutrition and hydration.

If a conscious and mentally competent patient refuses treatment or life sustaining measures, or requests that such (existing) treatment be stopped, this wish must be respected. In this case, the doctor in charge must explain to the patient the medical facts that will be the likely consequence of his or her decision. When the physician believes that the patient's refusal of treatment is not in his or her best interest, it may be appropriate for physician to suggest consultation with another physician. The wishes of older children or the mentally handicapped should be taken into account within the context of their ability to understand and act on their own behalf.

Physician-assisted suicide, however, is ethically unacceptable and is prohibited by law. The patient who wishes to die because of severe physical and mental suffering must be helped as much as is possible so that his or her suffering is relieved. In case of an unconscious or mentally incapacitated patient, the doctor in charge has to carefully consider the most likely prognosis of his or her medical condition. When an advance directive exists forbidding active treatment, made while the patient was conscious and competent, such a wish has to be respected, except when the requests are contrary to the law or to ethical and deontological principles. In the view of the NMEC, the physician may not comply with the patient's advance directive to abandon life saving measures, if there is reason to believe that patient's consciousness, ability to communicate and will to live can be restored.

In cases where the prognosis is not established beyond reasonable doubt and a variety of decisions about the treatment are possible, the physician is obliged to respect the known or presumed patient's wishes. Furthermore, if the patient shows signs suggesting that he or she is still fighting to survive, such signs oblige the physician to do his/her best to preserve the patient's life. In the absence of such signs, the physician should consider the previously expressed patient's wishes, in particular any written advance directive, and the family's testimony regarding the patient's views in this regard.

If it seems that the patient may survive and regain consciousness and the ability to communicate, his desire to live may as a rule be expected to return. Such likelihood obliges the physician to undertake active treatment. This also applies to a person who is unconscious after an attempted suicide. In the majority of cases, the wish to terminate one's own life is temporary, as suggested by the fact that only about 10–14% of those (physically healthy) persons who survive a suicidal attempt will successfully repeat it within the next 10 years.

The NMEC recommended that in planning national health care strategies, the concept of hospice and palliative care, preferably offered at patients' homes, should become a priority (Rowe, 1996). Such care should, as far as is possible, ensure that the human rights of the terminally ill and dying patient are respected. In particular, patients should have the right to autonomy, dignity, truth regarding their medical condition, psychological support and spiritual comfort, and above all, the right to relief of unnecessary suffering. In this, the doctor in charge may use sufficient doses of opiates and sedatives to provide adequate relief, even if this shortens life, as long as he/she acts in accordance with responsible medical practice, with the objective of relieving pain or distress, and with no intention to kill (that is, the "double effect", House of Lords, 1995). This position is in accord with the Slovene law and the principles of medical ethics and deontology.

The NMEC reiterated the exceptional significance and value of human life. Prohibition of killing is one of the cornerstones of our civilisation. It is possible to predict that the legalization of "mercy killings" would profoundly affect the status of human life, and thus attitudes towards any individual. This would jeopardise our right to life, as well as our right to dignity – the basic human rights that are now acknowledged after many centuries of abuse and denial, although even today they are far too little respected. The obvious alternative is better care for the terminally ill, and particularly effective pain control and the alleviation of their physical and mental suffering, by means of effective palliative care. Indeed, assuring such care is technologically possible, relatively inexpensive, and is a moral duty of any civilised society (Trontelj, 1998).

The NMEC position paper was well received among the medical community, and various aspects of it were debated at a number of professional meetings within the framework of the Slovene Medical Association. Although no reliable information is available, it is estimated that the Slovene physicians very rarely resort to acts of euthanasia and assisted suicide. On the contrary, physicians, particularly those in large hospitals, often feel themselves under pressure to prolong the life of terminally ill patients, not just because of misunderstandings about their duty to preserve patients' lives, but also in order to avoid suspicions of malpractice or professional misconduct. The position paper has provided doctors not only with ethical advice but also with some kind of legal support. A further advantage to the legitimacy of this paper is its extensive agreement with the recent Recommendation by the Parliamentary Assembly of the Council of Europe (1999).

References

Binding, K., & Hoche, A. (1920). *Die Freigabe der Vernichtung lebensunwerten Lebens. Ihr Mass und ihre Form* [Allowing the extermination of life not worth living]. Leipzig: Verlag Felix Meiner.

Compassion in dying v. State of Washington. 79 F.3d 790 (9th Cir. 1996).

Dolenc, M., & Šerko, A. (1921). Ali se naj da na prosto, da se sme uničiti življenje, ki je postalo življenja nevredno? [Should it be made free to take the life which is no longer worth living?]. *Slovenski pravnik, 35,* 23–30.

Echeverri, T. A., Acosta, O. V. (1996). Palliative care: The hospice concept. *Pain – Clinical Updates, 4,* 1–4.

Grad, O. T. (1995). Why is the incidence of suicide in Slovenia one of the highest in Europe? In O. T. Grad (Ed.), *How to reduce suicide in Slovenia?* Geneva: WHO.

House of Lords. (1995). *Report of the Select Committee on Medical Ethics* (HL Paper 21-I). London: HMSO.

Kladnik, T. (1998). Skupine starih za samopomoč v Sloveniji. [Peer groups for elderly in Slovenia] (pp. 27–34). In I. Hojnik-Zupanc (Ed.), Dodajmo življenje letom. Ljubljana: Gerontološko društvo Slovenije.

Kostnapfel, J. (1986). Suicide among the aged. *Zdrav Vestn, 55,* 237–8.

Milčinski, L., Virant-Jaklič, M., & Jeraj, T. (1998). Samomor in samomorilni poskus v Sloveniji v letu 1996 [Suicide and suicide attempt in Slovenia in the year 1996]. Ljubljana: Psihiatrična klinika.

Parliamentary Assembly of the Council of Europe. (1999). Protection of the human rights and dignity of the terminally ill and the dying (Recommendation 1418). *Official Gazette of the Council of Europe.*

Prešeren, F. (1983). Sonnets of unhappiness. Translated by K. Bray. Ljubljana: Cankarjeva založba.

Rowe, J. W. (1996). Health care myths at the end of life. *Bulletin of American College of Surgeons, 81,* 11–18.

Stillion, J. M., & McDowell, E. E. (1996). Suicide across the life span. Washington: Taylor & Francis.

Stroebe, M. S. & Stroebe, W. (1993). A mortality of bereavement: A review. In M. S. Stroebe., W. Stroebe & R. O. Hansson (Eds.), Handbook of bereavement: Theory, research and intervention. Cambridge: Cambridge University Press.

Swiss Academy of Medical Sciences (SAMS). (1996). Medical-ethical guidelines for the medical care of dying persons and severely brain-damaged patients. *Schweizerische Medizinische Wochenschrift, 126,* 136–139.

Trontelj, J. (1997a). Position paper of the National Medical Ethics Committee on the care for the dying and on euthanasia [In Slovene]. *Zdravniški vestnik, 66* 269–270.

Trontelj, J. (1997b). Explanatory notes to the Position paper of the National Medical Ethics Committee on the care for the dying and on euthanasia [In Slovene]. *Zdravniški Vestnik, 66,* 270–271.

Trontelj, J. (1998). On euthanasia and other end of life decisions [In Slovene] (pp. 310–347). In A. Polajnar-Pavčnik, D. Wedam-Lukić (Eds.), *Pravo in medicina.* Ljubljana: Cankarjeva založba.

WHO. (1999). *Health for All Data Base*. Geneva: Author.

Elderly People and Suicide in Turkey

Isik Sayil[1] and Cigdem Aydemir[2]

[1]Department of Psychiatry, Faculty of Medicine, University of Ankara
[2]Psychiatric Department, Ankara Numune Hospital, Turkey

Introduction

Turkey is a rapidly developing country extending from Asia to Europe where quality of life and primary health care standards are improving. The mean age of the Turkish population is currently increasing and the elderly are occupying a larger proportion of the overall population. According to the most recently collected statistics (1995), the population of Turkey is approximately 62.8 million, 47% of whom are over the age of 65 (Development of Turkish Population, 1995). This percentage was expected to increase to 5.2% by 1999, with the a population explosion and general increase in life expectancy. While life expectancy for the period 1980-1985 rested at 59.0 years, it increased to 66.7 years in 1990 and was expected to reach 69 years in 1999 (Development of Turkish Population, 1995).

In accordance with these demographic changes in Turkey there is a mounting interest in geriatric medicine. Both in Istanbul and Ankara there are geriatric departments in medical schools and the first psychogeriatric service was established in Istanbul University Cerrahpasa a Medical School in 1993. In addition, the medical school at Ankara University also has a psychogeriatric unit which operates on an outpatient basis and a third unit has recently been established in the Medical School of the Army (GATA).

In Turkey, as in many countries of the world, the family is the basic social unit and may be conceptualised in the form of extended families or a confederation of nuclear families with linear and collateral ties. Regardless of where people live (whether rural or urban areas), whether the family structure is traditional or modern, extended or nuclear, the elderly have an impact on family life and are respected as individual members. This is true despite a gradual alteration in the Turkish family structure from an extended model to a nuclear model, whereby elderly people generally continue to function within this new structure. Within these families, they may take care of grandchildren and participate in housework to some degree. Elderly family members have important roles in the decision making and future planning processes of the family and younger people usually respect their advice and expect their support.

In addition, the senile elderly are rarely institutionalised and attempts are generally made to care for them until the time of their death. Whenever elderly people are placed in institutions, family members are made to feel guilty about neglecting their responsibilities (Öztürk & Volkan, 1971) which may account for the limited number of nursing homes or elderly residences in Turkey. However, a small number of elderly people do prefer to live in nursing homes or homes for senior citizens where they are able to keep their privacy. Table 1 reveals that there are a total of 116 homes for the elderly in Turkey, 62% of which are owned and managed by the public and local authorities, whilst the remainder are non-government organisations. It is relevant to note that six of the total of 116 organisations were opened prior to 1950 and the remainder after 1970, with most of these opening after 1985 (Nursing Homes in Turkey, 1998).

Table 1. Nursing homes and elderly houses in Turkey

Type of Nursing Home	Number	Capacity
Nursing homes belonging to social services and children's protection association	44	5182
Nursing homes belonging to ministries	4	763
Nursing homes belonging to municipalities	19	1868
Nursing homes belonging to associations	21	1356
Nursing homes belonging to minorities	6	900
Private nursing homes	22	770
Total	116	10870

Source: Nursing homes in Turkey, 1998.

Table 2. Distribution of the psychiatric problems in the elderly in Turkey

Psychiatric Condition	Percentage Affected
Alzheimers disease	17%
Vascular dementia	7%
Other dementia	11%
Major depressive disorder	35%
Dysthymic disorder	0.8%
Bipolar 1 disorder	5.3%
Mood disorder due to general medical condition	2.2%
Psychotic disorder	9%
Generalized Anxiety disorder	1.7%
Anxiety disorder due to general medical condition	0.8%
Obsessive compulsive disorder	4%
Adjustment disorder	1.2%
Medication induced disorder	0.8%
Personality disorder	0.8%
Somatoform pain disorder	0.4%
Delirium	2.2%
Mental retardation	0.4%
Substance related disorder	0.4%

Source: Güngen et al, 1998.

Biological changes, illness, retirement, financial concerns, the loss of loved ones, and residency issues are the main difficulties of the aging process. In addition, depression is the most common psychiatric condition in elderly populations (Table 2) (Güngen et al, 1998).

Indeed, many studies have highlighted the importance of the above factors in the frequent prevalence of depression (Aydemir, 1994; Palabıyıkoglu et al, 1992; Sayil & Aydemir, 1998).

Suicide is a feared outcome of depression. The problem of suicide in the elderly population of Turkey can be discussed within the framework of DIE (State Institute of Statistics) data which dates back to 1962 and identify age-differentiated statistics after 1974 and sex differentiated data after 1987 (Table 3 & 4) (Suicide Statistics, 1996). These data reveal that suicide amongst the elderly is an escalating problem with an increase from 47 suicides in 1974 to 139 in 1996. This roughly amounts to a tripling of elderly suicides over the 22-year period. Sex distribution data show that Turkish men are a higher risk group than Turkish women, which is consistent with international data. In addition, the western part of Turkey and the greater metropolitan areas exhibit higher suicide rates than the eastern and less urban regions of the country.

Table 3. Elderly suicides between 1974 and 1996 in Turkey

Year	Number of suicides in age group 65-74	Number of suicides in age group 75+	Total number of elderly suicides
1974	39	8	47
1975	39	32	71
1976	52	24	76
1977	49	28	77
1978	39	26	65
1979	42	26	68
1980	52	29	81
1981	52	25	77
1982	62	33	95
1983	75	47	122
1984	72	65	137
1985	80	53	133
1986	47	64	111
1987	55	44	99
1988	59	26	85
1989	58	64	123
1990	57	64	121
1991	64	50	114
1992	54	33	87
1993	62	59	121
1994	77	57	134
1995	90	45	135
1996	85	54	139

Source: Suicide Statistics, 1996.

Like many other countries, the authorities are inclined to report suicides as accidents or intoxications, to protect the families from the convicting attitude of the society. In reality, distinguishing suicides from accidents may sometimes prove to be difficult. For these reasons, epidemiological data on suicide have to be considered reliable only to a degree.

Table 4. Sex distribution in the elderly suicides in Turkey

Years	65-74		75+		Total	
	Male	Female	Male	Female	Male	Female
1987	41	14	25	19	66	33
1988	48	14	18	21	66	35
1989	40	18	50	14	90	32
1990	37	20	43	21	80	41
1991	47	17	33	17	80	34
1992	32	22	23	10	55	32
1993	43	19	46	13	89	32
1994	59	18	34	23	93	41
1995	64	26	34	11	98	37
1996	66	19	34	20	100	39

Source: Suicide Statistics, 1996.

Table 5. Suicide by age and method

Year	Age group	Hanging	Jumping	Chemicals	Firearms	Others	Total
1987	65–74	32	9	3	3	8	55
	75+	24	13	2	1	4	44
1988	65–74	26	15	7	4	7	59
	75+	24	9	1	-	5	39
1989	65–74	30	14	4	6	4	58
	75+	35	13	4	3	9	64
1990	65–74	39	6	6	2	6	57
	75+	35	14	3	7	5	64
1991	65–74	40	6	5	5	8	64
	75+	28	9	3	4	6	50
1992	65–74	35	12	2	2	3	54
	75+	19	6	6	4	1	33
1993	65–74	36	11	5	7	3	62
	75+	23	22	1	5	8	59
1994	65–74	39	17	5	6	10	77
	75+	34	11	5	5	2	57
1995	65–74	59	19	4	3	5	90
	75+	27	14	1	2	1	45
1996	65–74	51	13	7	8	6	85
	75+	25	13	3	6	7	54
Totals		661	246	72	83	108	1170

Source: Suicide Statistics, 1996.

The most common method of suicide in the elderly is hanging, while jumping from heights and firearms are the second and third most common methods respectively (Table 5) (Suicide Statistics, 1996). This would indicate that the elderly are inclined to use more lethal methods and form more serious intent to die. The stated reasons for elderly suicide have been analysed in Table 6. These data suggest that the substantial causal factor in elderly suicide in Turkey is illness, followed by family and economic problems (Suicide Statistics, 1996).

Table 6. Suicide by age and cause

Years	Age group	Illness	Family problems	Economic problems	Total
1987	65-74	28	8	3	55
	75+	26	2	1	44
1988	65-74	31	5	10	59
	75+	31	1	–	39
1989	65-74	35	9	2	58
	75+	40	4	5	64
1990	65-74	35	8	4	57
	75+	40	10	4	64
1991	65-74	50	10	2	64
	75+	48	4	-	50
1992	65-74	34	1	5	54
	75+	27	1	1	33
1993	65-74	50	9	1	62
	75+	53	6	–	59
1994	65-74	63	9	3	77
	75+	34	10	3	57
1995	65-74	69	7	7	90
	75+	35	8	4	45
1996	65-74	62	8	10	85
	75+	44	2	8	54
Totals		835	122	73	1170

Source: Suicide Statistics, 1996.

In spite of social support systems and religious affiliations which prohibit suicide, these data reveal a dramatic increase in suicide rates within these age groups. The westernisation of traditional Turkish society, industrialisation, and the trend towards nuclear family structures, are all factors which may have contributed to social alienation and the loosening of family ties, resulting in the isolation of the elderly. An increase in depression and suicide are likely consequences of the 'loss of place' endured by this age group.

As mentioned above, demographic changes in the constitution of Turkish society mean that the elderly population will continue to be a prominent group. The ramifications of these phenomena are that Turkish society need to develop the organisations and institutions to deal with the elderly as soon as possible. In particular, the establishment of small urban residences which enable the elderly to live independently with some support, would seem to be the most logical solution. Furthermore, structures need to be developed whereby elderly people could reside more or less independently in their own homes, with the supplementary support of telephone checks, home visits, housekeeping services, in conjunction with preventative strategies addressing isolation such as social clubs, day hospitals, etc (Aydemir, 1994).

Assisted Suicide and Euthanasia

Suicide and self-mutilation are the manifestation of aggression directed towards the self, whereas alcohol and drug dependence and risk taking behaviour may be considered gradual or indirect consequences of such aggression. Within this definition, assisted suicide or euthanasia could also be regarded as a form of indirect aggression.

In Turkey, death in hospital is seen to be an unnatural occurrence, especially by the elderly. Instead, elderly people prefer to pass away in their homes surrounded by their loved ones and may deliberately avoid attending hospital for treatment. This avoidance behaviour can be considered a type of passive euthanasia.

The concept of euthanasia has been prevalent in Turkey for the last twenty-five years as a result of technological and medical developments around the world (Sayil & Oguz, 2000). Physicians, patients, communities members and insurance companies have colluded together to discuss the concept of euthanasia and its social and ethical repercussions. In particular, the media have been primarily responsible for attracting attention to the issue of euthanasia, through their extensive reporting of cases such as that of Cees Van Mendel de Joe from Holland (1994), Romam Sampero from Spain (1998), and various incidents occurring in Turkey. The mass media representation of euthanasia provides the opportunity for social comment on the legal, religious, ethical and medical aspects within the euthanasia debate.

Medical doctors and academics in Turkey have also expressed an increasing interest in the subject in recent years (Sayil et al, 1990; Oguz 1996). In 1990 Sayil et al performed a study on the attitudes of psychiatrists toward euthanasia, the results of which indicated that younger psychiatrists (those with less than ten years of professional experience) seemed more flexible towards euthanasia than their older counterparts (Sayil & Oguz, 2000; Sayil et al, 1990).

In a study by Gündüz in 1996, 510 medical students and doctors were interviewed about their attitudes and knowledge about euthanasia. One third of the subjects claimed that they did not have enough knowledge of euthanasia while 63.72% supported the application of euthanasia (Gündüz , 1996). On the other hand, 68.82% of the subjects refused to take responsibility for the application of euthanasia even if the process became legal. All of the subjects were of the opinion that although passive euthanasia is not legal, it is currently being applied in the field when necessary.

Another study by Oguz et al (1996) explored the attitudes of clinicians towards euthanasia by distributing questionnaires to 1343 clinicians (Oguz et al, 1996). The results suggested that 75.3% of clinicians were willing to take active steps to hasten death, while 26% believed euthanasia to be unethical and never justified. 63.9% reported that they would feel comfortable about assisting euthanasia if the decision was made and administered by a committee. These results are consistent with several other studies examining the attitudes of medical staff to euthanasia.

It remains to be said that the euthanasia debate in Turkey will stay within the limits of academic discussion for a few more years. However, the transformation of Turkish society is rapid. Economical, social and technological developments put a considerable pressure on the state for a legislative arrangement whereby euthanasia may be accepted legally. This escalating process of demanding government attention has been evident in a range of bioethical considerations including abortion, organ transplantation, genetic technology and in vitro fertilisation. As a secular structure, the Turkish legal system is both rational and open to change after careful consideration of contemporary opinion and further study.

References

Aydemir, Ç. (1994). *Deisik ortamlarda yasayan yaslılar üzerine bir çalısma.* (A study on elderly people living in different environments) Uzmanlık tezi.

Gündüz, T. (1996). Hekim Ötenaziye karsı mı? (Do the Physicians Defend Euthanasia?) *Adli Tıp Bülteni, 1,* 170–171.

Güngen, C., Ertan, T., Eker, E. (1998). Admission to the first psychiatric unit in Turkey. Presented in Joint Meeting of International Psychogeriatrics Association and Turkish Society of Psychogeriatrics. Istanbul.

Intihar Istatistikleri Devlet Istatistik Enstitüsü 1974–1996 (Suicide Statistics, State Institute of Statistics, 1974–1996 data) (1996). DIE Yaynlar, Ankara.

Oguz, Y., Senol, S., Devrimci Ozgüven, H., Arıkazan, M., Özen, A. R., Unal, S. (1996). *Ankara da hekimlerin ötenazi ile ilgili görüslerini belirlemeye yönelik bir anket calısması* (A survey on clinicians attitudes toward euthanasia) 3P dergisi 4 (ek 3).

Oguz, Y. (1996). Euthanasia in Türkiye. *Eubios, Journal of Asian and International Bioethics, 6,* 170–171.

Öztürk, O., Volkan, V. (1971). Theory and Practice of Psychiatry in Turkey. *American Journal of Psychotherapy, 25,* 240–271.

Palabyıkoglu, R., Yücat, T., Haran, S. (1992). Yaslılarda depresyon ve yasam doyumu (Depression and life satisfaction in elderly people) *Kriz Dergisi Cilt 1,* Say Güz, 26–33.

Sayil, I., Oguz, Y. (2000). Attitudes towards assisted suicide (euthanasia) in Türkiye. *J Ankara Medical School, 22,* 45–49.

Sayil, I., Aydemir, Ç. (1998). Elderly people and suicide in Türkiye. Presented in *Therapeutische Ansätze bei Suizidalität im Alter,* Würzburg, 20–22 November.

Sayil, I., Gogus, A. K., Sözer, Y., Ceyhun, B. (1990). Attitudes of clinicians toward suicide in Türkiye. In G. Ferrari, M. Bellini, & P. Crepet (Eds), *Suicidal Behavior and Risk Factors.* Bologna: Monduzzi Editore, pp. 803–808.

Türkiye 'de Nüfusun demografik yapısı ve gelisimi (1923–1995) (1995). (Development of Turkish Population) DIE yayınları Ankara.

Türkiye'de huzur evleri (Nursing Homes in Turkey) (1998). Sosyal Hizmetler ve Çocuk Esirgeme Kurumu Kaytlar (Social Services and Childrens' Protection Association data) Ankara.

Suicidal Behavior in the Hong Kong Elderly

Paul S.F. Yip[1,2] and Iris Chi[2,3]

[1]Department of Statistics and Actuarial Science,
[2]Medical and Health Research Network,
[3]Department of Social Work and Social Administration,
The University of Hong Kong, China

Introduction

Suicide is a very complex problem. It is caused by a variety of factors, including social, psychological, emotional and situational factors. Prolonged illnesses, death of loved ones, family troubles, frustrations, despair and hopelessness are just some of the reasons often cited in cases of suicide attempts in the elderly (Health and Welfare Branch, 1994; Chi et al. 1998). Research studies of suicide notes have indicated that elderly people are much more likely than other age groups to see suicide as a way of escaping from life, or a means of alleviating pain. Their motive is simply to end their life (Mcintosh, 1992; Ho et al. 1998). Suicide in the elderly is an important issue, especially in view of a growing aging population. However, very few studies have been conducted on this topic; this is partly because the subject is not easy to study, and partly because of social bias against elderly persons. Yip et al. (1998) and Chi et al. (1997) provided useful information about suicides in the elderly in Hong Kong. They made use of the data collected in 1992 from police files, which investigated the cause of death. Here, we make use of updated information obtained from the Census and Statistics Department as well as the Coroner's Office, to examine suicidal behaviour in the elderly in Hong Kong.

Table 1 gives the suicide rates for a selection of countries, including Hong Kong and represents a cross section of the world community. Care should be exercised in interpreting these data because they refer to different years, and there is the possibility of age and gender differences in the populations of those countries. For Western countries, the suicide rate in the elderly was not much higher than the average; whereas elderly suicide rates in Asian countries (e.g., Singapore, China and Hong Kong) were shown to be 2 to 3 times higher than average. The suicide rate in the elderly in Hong Kong was much higher than the rates reported in Australia and the United States (Yip, 1998a,b; Yip et al. 1998).

For the purposes of this discussion the chosen definition of suicide was "a fatal act in which an individual deliberately causes self-injury or ingests a substance in excess of the generally recognised therapeutic dosage" (Kreitman, 1977).

Table 1. An international comparison of elderly suicide

Country	Elderly suicide rate	General population	Year
Australia	16	13	1994
China (Beijing, Urban)	13	4	1994
China (Beijing, Rural)	38	14	1994
Hong Kong	30	12	1997
New Zealand	12	12	1993
Singapore	50	14	1994
U.S.A.	20	12	1991

The objectives of this discussion were, firstly to examine the trend of elderly suicides in Hong Kong over the past 17 years (1981–1997), and secondly to describe the socio-economic characteristics of suicides in the elderly. A third aim of this chapter is to identify the high risk factors for suicides among the elderly.

Data and Methods

Two sources of data were utilised. The first being data from the Census and Statistics Department of the Government of Hong Kong Special Administrative Region and the second from the Hong Kong Coroner's Office. The statistics include all deaths where the underlying cause is determined as being suicide or self-inflicted injury (E950–E959), as classified under the tenth (1992) revision of the International Classification of Diseases (ICD) (World Health Organisation, 1992). These statistics are related to the number of deaths in the years shown. The yearly data included is related to cases where judicial inquiries established that the deaths were due to suicide within the calendar year. There are two different data files on deaths available from the Census and Statistics Department; known deaths and registered deaths. It is important to make use of the registered death files to reconstruct the number of deaths in each calendar year, as a significant proportion of the suicide deaths are not recorded if the known death files alone are used. It has been found in previous studies on suicides, that using the known death files resulted in underreporting of up to 20% when compared with data obtained from the registered death files. This is mainly due to the delay in reporting deaths from the Coroner's Office to the Registry of Births and Deaths. The Census and Statistics Department imposed a cut-off date in May the following year to collect the death data from the Registry of Births and Deaths. All other deaths reported after May were therefore not recorded in the known death file, under the relevant ICD classification. Although the percentage of deaths in comparison with the overall total number of deaths is low (about 1–2%), the proportion of suicides among these deaths is significant (20–30%). All the unclassified deaths in the present year would not be updated in the known death file until the following year.

The definition of elderly in this paper is 60 years of age or over, since the normal retirement age in Hong Kong is 60 for most occupations. It is shown later that retirement is an important factor which affects suicidal behaviour. All rates are expressed as the number of deaths per 100,000 persons. The Census data on territory-wide suicide is analysed to determine the profile of elderly suicides in Hong Kong. Both the number and rate of suicide in the elderly over the past 17 years have included a detailed breakdown of socio-economic characteristics such as: sex, age, occupation, month of occurrence, and the method of suicide. Also, with the assistance of the Coroner (Mr. Andrew Chan), the death records from the Hong Kong Coroner's Office on suicides in the elderly in 1997, were scrutinised to find out the major reason(s) for self-inflicted death. Usually, the Coroner's death files consist of reports from police investigations and any medical and autopsy reports. In Hong Kong, the police are required by law to investigate any unnatural deaths. The information collected by the police for the Coroner's Office, may however be incomplete, or may even be biased, since the principal concern of the police investigation is the possibility of homicide. Based on the findings and recommendations of the police, the Coroner(s) will then decide whether a death inquest is necessary. Coroner(s) would return a verdict of suicide if a death results from self-inflicted injuries or is proved beyond reasonable doubt (Coroner's Offices, 1999). Death inquests for suicides in the elderly are very uncommon. Of the 283 suicides in the elderly that occurred in 1997, none were subject to an inquest.

The extraction of information from the Coroner's files was performed according to a schedule that has been developed for a similar study in Chi et al. (1997). Only relevant information and relatively complete data are included, that is: age, sex, marital status, occupation, type of accommodation, district of household, living arrangements, family relationship, date, time and place of the incident and any previous attempts undertaken, method used, precipitating factors, chronic illnesses and their type, smoking and/or drinking habit, previous medical and/or psychiatric treatment, severity of illnesses, self care ability, and perceived burden to the family. The incidence rates are calculated and based on the estimated Hong Kong mid-year aged population in persons aged over 60 in 1997.

Limitations of Data

The Census data is limited by the nature of its scope. Only a few socio-economic data are available. The Coroner's files are also limited by the nature of the data collection method. The major purpose of the police investigation is the possibility of a homicide. As a result, some of the information may be incomplete or biased.

Results

This section consists of two parts, firstly the suicide rates and trends based on Census data analyses, and secondly, the characteristics of suicides in the elderly based on information from Coroner's files.

Epidemiological Profile of Elderly Suicide Based on Census Data

Trends

In the 17 years between 1981–1997, the total number of deaths in Hong Kong increased from 24,911 in 1981 to 31,711 in 1997, and the number of suicide deaths increased from 501 in 1981 to 777 in 1997. As a proportion of total deaths, suicides increased by 2.0% in 1981 and by 2.5% in 1997. Table 2 shows that during the reference period, the crude suicide rate increased by 24% from 9.6 to 11.9 deaths per 100,000. However, on an age standardised basis the increase over the 17 years between 1981–1997 was only 6% from 10.3 to 10.9, reflecting the trend towards a larger elderly population in Hong Kong. The highest standardised suicide rate in the reference period was 12.9 in 1985, placing suicide among the top ten causes of death. It ranked 10th in 1982 and has ranked 7th since 1985. Furthermore, suicide was the leading cause of death in females aged 15–24 in 1997. The proportion of elderly suicides among suicide deaths of that year was about 36% and accounted for 1.1% of all deaths aged 60 or above. In the same year, the elderly contributed only 14% to the total population. A breakdown of suicide rates by age for the period 1981–1997 is given in Figure 1. The suicide rate in the elderly remained more or less the same in 1981–1997, of which 35% of all suicide deaths were those that included elderly persons. On average, the number of suicide deaths is 32 per 100,000 for those aged 60 or above, while males aged 75 years or above recorded suicide deaths at 61 per 100,000, giving this age group the highest suicide rate among all age groups in the population. The suicide rate for the elderly is 7 times higher than that for younger individuals. Suicide rates for the period 1981–1997 were relatively stable.

Table 2 Elderly Suicide Rates (per 100 000) by Gender, 1981-1997

Year	Person	Male	Female	M/F Ratio	All Ages*
1981	27.6 (27.1)	32.0 (31.7)	24.1 (23.5)	1.3	10.3 (9.6)
1982	23.4 (23.4)	21.0 (21.5)	25.4 (25.0)	0.8	8.2 (7.8)
1983	29.5 (29.3)	33.7 (33.7)	26.1 (25.8)	1.3	9.2 (8.8)
1984	29.4 (29.2)	35.1 (34.7)	24.8 (24.7)	1.4	10.7 (10.4)
1985	34.3 (34.2)	39.4 (39.3)	30.2 (30.0)	1.3	12.9 (12.8)
1986	37.0 (37.0)	42.5 (42.5)	32.6 (32.6)	1.3	12.0 (12.0)
1987	33.8 (34.0)	39.5 (39.8)	29.1 (29.2)	1.4	10.9 (11.1)
1988	32.3 (32.6)	35.7 (36.2)	29.5 (29.6)	1.2	10.3 (10.6)
1989	31.5 (31.9)	37.7 (38.1)	26.5 (26.6)	1.4	10.9 (11.3)
1990	37.0 (37.8)	44.6 (45.7)	30.8 (31.1)	1.4	12.1 (12.8)
1991	34.1 (35.2)	40.7 (42.3)	28.7 (29.0)	1.4	12.0 (12.8)
1992	35.3 (36.5)	40.2 (41.5)	31.3 (32.1)	1.3	12.1 (12.9)
1993	31.6 (32.8)	35.6 (36.8)	28.4 (29.3)	1.3	10.6 (11.6)
1994	34.9 (36.4)	42.4 (44.1)	28.8 (29.6)	1.5	11.9 (12.9)
1995	30.2 (32.4)	35.4 (38.3)	25.9 (27.0)	1.4	11.7 (12.9)
1996	26.0 (27.2)	28.7 (30.0)	23.7 (24.6)	1.2	10.3 (11.4)
1997	27.6 (29.6)	32.6 (35.4)	23.6 (24.3)	1.4	10.9 (11.9)
Average	31.6 (32.3)	36.6 (37.5)	27.5 (27.9)	1.3	11.0 (11.4)

Remarks: a) *Rates are standardised per 100 000 for mid-year 1986 population
b) The values given in parentheses represent the crude suicide rate.

Age Group and Gender

In 1997, suicide rates for the age groups 5–14, 15–24, 25–59, 60–74 and ≥ 75 were .7, 8.9, 11.8, 24.0, 45.4 respectively. (see Figure 2). The average number of suicides was 12. Male suicide rates were usually higher than those of females. The gender ratio for the elderly was 1.4 in 1997. The suicide rate increased sharply for the group aged 75 or over. For people aged 75 or over, the rate is 3.8 times higher than the average and 5.1 times higher than for young people aged 15-24. Indeed, the elderly aged 75 years or over, had the highest suicide rate in the population during the reference period. The gender ratio of all suicides was about 1.3. A relatively higher male to female suicide ratio 1.5 was observed in the 25-64 years age group. There was not much variation between the years in these ratios during the reference period.

Figure 1. Age-specific suicide rates (per 100,000), 1981-1997

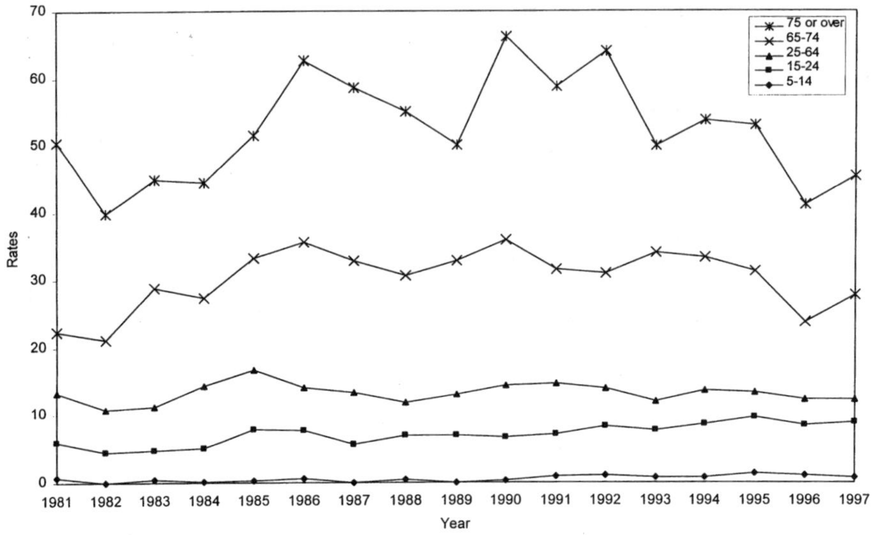

Figure 2. Age-specific suicide rates (per 100,000) by gender, 1997

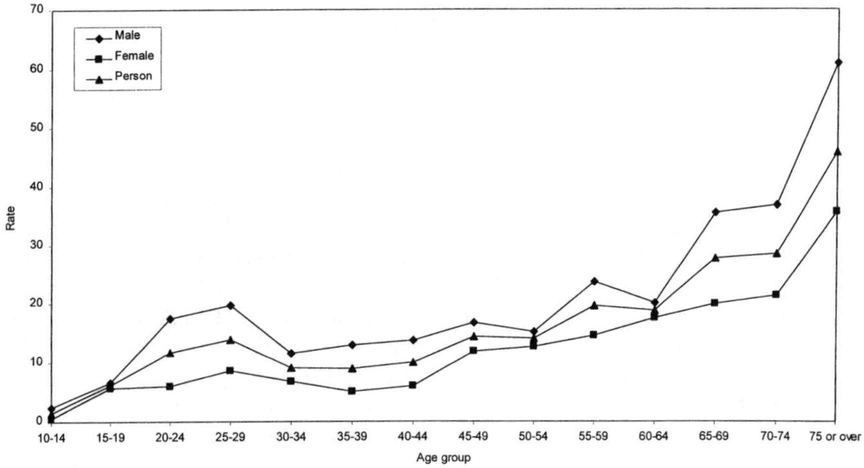

Method of Suicide

Figure 3a portrays the different methods used by elderly persons as a proportion of the different methods used by the total population between the years 1981 to 1997, while Figure 3b compares the percentages of the different suicide methods of the same population during the same period. Jumping and hanging were the most frequently used methods and accounted for more than 80% of the cases. However, the proportion of jumping gradually increased from 29% to 52% whereas, hanging decreased from 59% to 37% for the reference period. The small number of suicidal deaths from firearms and explosives in Hong Kong is mainly due to the strict control and heavy penalties imposed upon individuals for the possession of firearms and explosives.

Occupation

Table 3 shows the suicide deaths and rates of the elderly by economic activity from 1981 to 1995. The Census and Statistics Department introduced new job classification systems in 1996, which makes it very difficult to compare data with previous years. Hence, we only provide information from 1981–1995. The population can be divided into two groups, economically active and inactive. The inactive group consists of housewives, students, retired and jobless persons. The active ones are professional, technical and related workers; administrative and managerial workers; clerical and related workers; sales workers; service workers; agricultural, animal husbandry, forestry workers and fishermen; production and related workers, transport equipment, operators and labourers. The average crude suicide rates for economically active and inactive persons aged 60 or above were 6 and 38 per 100,000 in 1981–1995 respectively. The ratio was higher than that of the general population, which was 4 and 20 per 100,000 respectively. In 1995 alone, 4 economically active and 213 economically inactive persons aged 60 or over committed suicide, the rates being 3 and 30 per 100,000 respectively. In this same year for the group aged 60–64, 1 economically active and 28 economically inactive persons committed suicide, the rates being 1 and 17 per 100,000 respectively. Overall, males had a higher suicide rate than females with the ratio being about 1.5 to 2. Retired individuals also showed the highest suicide rate followed by housewives aged 65 and over with average rates of 44 and 35 per 100,000 respectively.

Month of Occurrence

During the summer months there were more suicide deaths than average, compared with February, November and December which had fewer reported suicides. The cumulative number of suicide deaths by month in 1981–1997 is given in Figure 4.

A more detailed profile of suicides in the elderly based on 1997 Coroners' death files is given in the next section. A similar study was performed on 1992 data and a comparison with 1997 data is given, where possible. Such detailed information concerning suicide deaths was not available in the Census data.

Figure 3a. Elderly suicide rates by method, 1981-1997

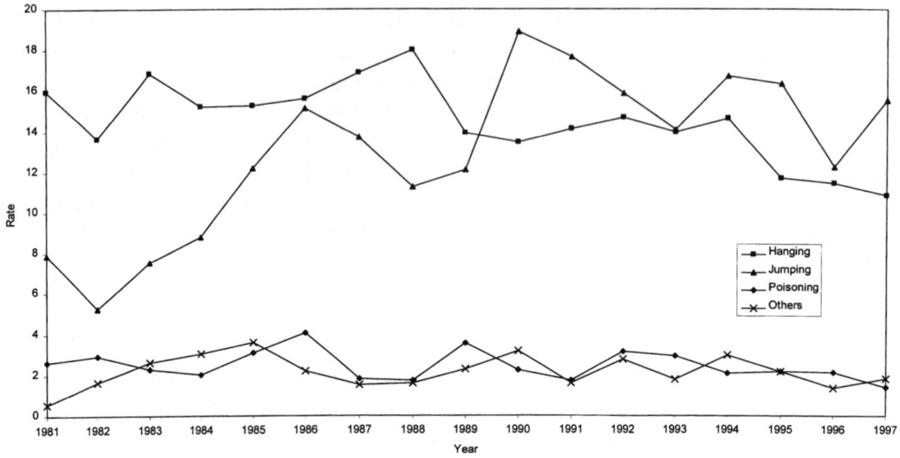

Figure 3b. Methods of suicide among the elderly, 1981 and 1997

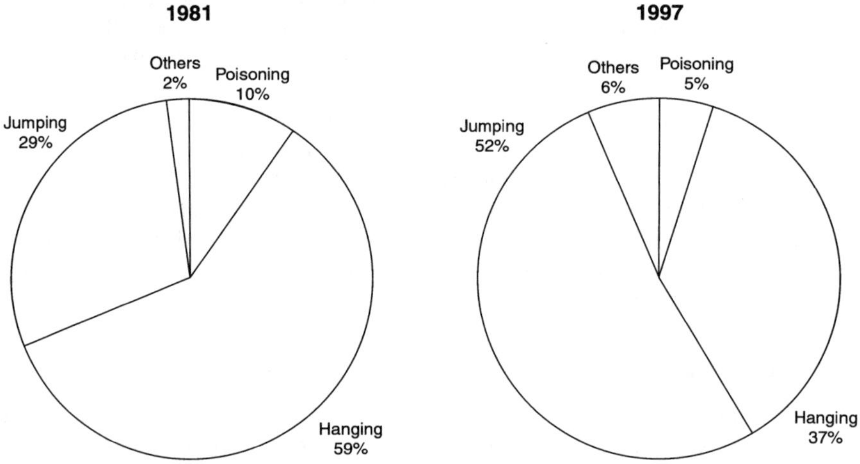

Table 3. Elderly suicide rates (per 100,000) by economic activity, 1981-1995

		1981	1982	1983	1984	1985	1986	1987	1988	1989	1990	1991	1992	1993	1994	1995	Average
Economic Active	60-64	5	10	10	7	8	2	6	3	2	6	3	6	0	3	1	**5**
	65 or over	9	9	6	7	0	4	9	7	6	5	5	9	13	6	6	**7**
Economic Inactive	60-64	30	22	26	33	35	37	29	30	27	28	33	34	23	33	17	**29**
	65 or over	36	31	39	38	47	50	46	43	43	48	42	44	39	41	34	**41**
60 or over	Economic Active	7	10	8	7	4	3	7	5	4	5	4	7	5	4	3	**6**
	Economic Inactive	35	28	36	37	44	46	41	40	39	43	39	42	35	39	30	**38**

Remarks:

(a) The population of economic active people is calculated by multiplying the age-specific participation rate to the respective population.

(b) The population of economic inactive people for each age group is calculated by subtracting the population of economic active people from the respective population.

(c) The number of econmic active and inactive do not add up to the total number of suicides since information about occupation of some suicide deaths was missing.

(d) Source: Census and Statistics Department, Yip (1997) and Chi et al. (1997)

Figure 4. Cumulative number of elderly suicide deaths by month, 1981-1997

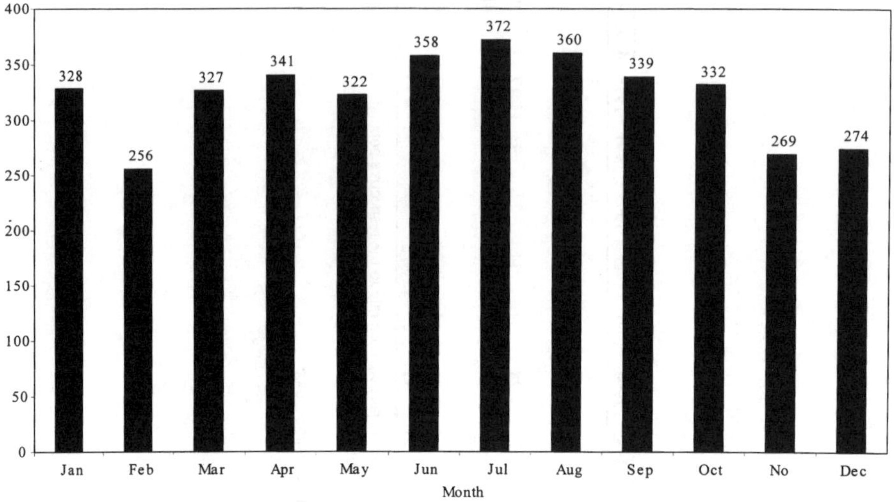

Socio-economic Profile of Suicides in the Elderly, Based on Coroner's Files

The following findings are related to the profile of elderly suicide persons based on the 1997 Coroner's suicide death files. None of the 283 suicides in the elderly that occurred in 1997 were subject to a death inquest by the Coroner's Court. Most of the cases were straightforward and no evidence of foul play was detected.

Marital Status

Table 4 suggests that marriage provides protection against suicide for males and females. Males who have never married and widowed males had the highest suicide rate (101.6 and 104.1 per 100, 000 respectively), whereas, the never married females were about the same as married females, 17.9 and 15.7 per 100,000 respectively.

Table 4. Elderly suicide rates (per 100,000) by gender and marital status, 1997

	Male	Female	Person
Marital status			
Single	101.6	17.9	65.1
Married	23.9	15.7	20.4
Divorced	24.4	24.1	24.2
Widowed	104.1	35.2	48.2

Accommodation

About 55% of the elderly population lived in public housing, whilst 38% lived in private housing and 5% lived in homes for the aged. The proportion of elderly persons that lived in public housing was more than that in the 1992 sample. Generally speaking, those at the lower end of the economic class lived in public housing provided by the Government. The proportion of suicide deaths for those persons that lived in public housing is over-represented in that only 44.5% of the elderly population live in public housing in the community.

Health Status

Table 5a shows that 87% of suicide cases under the age of 24, 61% of suicide cases aged 25–59 and 10% of suicide cases aged 60 or over were free from any illness prior to the suicide event. About 10% of the total cases were free from any disease, while illness was observed in 3% of the 1992 samples. About 82% and 72 % of the cases were found to have severe or terminal illness in 1992 and 1997. Compared with suicides in other age groups, our finding show that the elderly were more likely to suffer physical illness prior to the suicide event, but that this effect was reduced in the 1992 samples. For mental illness, only 17% of elderly suicides exhibited a history of receiving psychiatric treatment and 7% had the diagnosis of schizophrenia compared with 17% found among teenagers. The proportion of elderly persons who had financial problems was 4%, a history of drug abuse 3%, and drinking problems was 7%. It is also important to note that very few cases had totally lost their self-care abilities. Table 5b, shows that only 8.2% of the elderly suicides who suffered from terminal illness were totally dependent whilst 44.9% were totally independent. About 58% of the elderly suicides were independent and were able to look after themselves in their daily lives.

Table 5a Proportion of Elderly Suicide Deaths by Age Group, Physical Illness and Gender, 1997

Age group	Illness Level	Male	Female	Person
Under 24	Terminal	0%	0%	0%
	Severe	2%	8%	3%
	Not Severe	11%	4%	9%
	No illness	87%	88%	87%
	Total	*100%*	*100%*	*100%*
25-59	Terminal	2%	4%	3%
	Severe	19%	21%	19%
	Not Severe	13%	26%	17%
	No illness	66%	50%	61%
	Total	*100%*	*100%*	*100%*
>=60	Terminal	22%	12%	17%
	Severe	55%	56%	55%
	Not Severe	14%	23%	17%
	No illness	10%	10%	10%
	Total	*100%*	*100%*	*100%*

Table 5b. Proportion of Elderly Suicide Deaths by Physical Illness and Self-care, 1997

Illness Level	Totally Dependent	Partially Dependent	Independent	Total
Terminal	8%	47%	45%	100%
Severe	5%	42%	53%	100%
Not Severe	2%	24%	73%	100%
No illness	0%	18%	82%	100%
Total	4%	37%	58%	100%

Family Relationship

About 22.6% of elderly persons who committed suicide lived alone which was higher than that of the general population of which only around 11% lived alone. The majority had the support of the family and only 16% reported to have family problems. About 9% had indicated the existence of interpersonal conflict. Nevertheless, 95% claimed to have been under a lot of stress. Financially speaking, in 1997 data 14% received government assistance whilst only 7% were found among the elderly suicides in 1992 sample.

Clues to Suicide and Help-Seeking Behaviours

There are often actual signs to suggest that an elderly person is about to commit suicide. Nearly 36% indicated suicidal ideas to their family members or significant others before their fatal act. About 22% and 11% of elderly suicides had performed a previous suicidal act in the 1992 and 1997 samples, respectively.

Motivation to Suicide

About 17% of the cases of elderly suicide had written a suicide note whilst 86% of the total written suicide notes were from males. This is similar to the 1992 sample. This might be related to the literacy factor, as many female elderly persons in this age cohort are illiterate. The majority of suicide notes expressed the unbearable pain from prolonged illnesses, regardless of whether the illness was terminal. In addition, some of the notes indicated explicitly that their suicide was to relieve the burden of their dependency on the family.

Some of the elderly with terminal illnesses committed suicide because they had an incontestable intention to ease the burden they were inflicting upon the family and to alleviate the suffering from their illness. Even so, it is important to recognise that most of the elderly could still look after themselves without relying on family or significant others for help (Table 5b), although family members were usually supportive. Sometimes, it was their own sense of guilt of being a burden to the family that led them to end their lives.

Euthanasia

According to the Medical Council of Hong Kong, euthanasia is defined as direct intentional killing of a person as part of the medical care being offered. The Medical Council does not support this practice because it is illegal and unethical (Medical Council of Hong Kong, 2000). However, the withholding or withdrawing of artificial life support procedures for a terminally ill patient is not euthanasia. Withholding or withdrawing life-sustaining treatment (when taking into account the benefits to the patient and the wishes of the family, and when based upon the principal of the futility of treatment for a terminal patient), is therefore legally acceptable and appropriate.

According to the instructions given by the Council to its members, it is important that the rights of the terminally ill patient or their relatives be respected and that their views be solicited. The decision to withhold or withdraw life support should be made on the basis of the consent of the patient themself, and if possible their immediate family, who should be provided with full information relating to the circumstances and the doctor's recommendation. Doctors should also exercise careful clinical judgement and whenever there is disagreement between doctor and patient, or between doctor and relatives, the matter should be referred to the Ethics Committee of the hospital concerned or relevant authority for advice. In case of further doubt, direction from the court may be sought as necessary. The Government has been very careful in dealing with such a sensitive issue, as they recognise that the elderly might be at particular risk if physician-assisted suicide and euthanasia were to become legal and available in Hong Kong. In Hong Kong at this stage, it is premature to set up any legislation regarding this matter. The issue of euthanasia or assisted suicide has not been fully debated in the society. However, the community tends to be more receptive to this idea especially for the elderly with terminal and painful illness. Hong Kong has an ageing population where people tend to live longer but not healthier in terms of the hospitalization rate among the elderly. We do need to examine the matter seriously in the future.

Discussions

The number of suicides in the elderly reported by known death files in 1997 was 243, although the actual number of elderly suicides that occurred during the calendar year was 283. The extent of underreporting using known death was 14% and the overall underreporting is 18% for the total population (645 and 784 from the known deaths and Coroner's record, respectively). Therefore, it is important that the registered death files be used in compiling the suicide death statistics in Hong Kong. However, much delay in obtaining the official data is expected and from the author's experience, the best available information is obtainable from the Coroner's Office. Furthermore, suicides in the elderly may be even more prevalent than is suggested by the statistics. In some cases, intentional overdoses of prescribed medications may go unrecognised or unreported. Older persons may also commit "chronic" or "passive" suicide: that is, they lose the will to live and simply stop caring for themselves. They may cease taking medication or simply delay treatment for medical conditions, which all increase health risks. In addition, they may also slowly stop eating and drinking until they become ill and die (Devons, 1996).

Suicide rates among the elderly have been declining in many industrialised countries, such as England and Wales, in recent years. In these countries the suicide rates for men in the 55–64, 65–74 and 75–84 age bands have fallen by 30–40% between 1983 and 1995 (Harwood and Jacoby, 2000). However, suicide rates among the elderly in Hong Kong remain very stable for the study period 1981–1997. Though Hong Kong's GDP has risen to a very high standard (up to US25, 000 per annum), there has been no effect on suicides in the elderly. On the other hand, the Gini coefficient index measuring the discrepancies in the distribution of wealth, has increased to .52 which suggests a widening gap between rich and poor. Significantly, most elderly suicide cases were reported to have primary education or less (93%). Poverty among this elderly group is very serious. In addition, the pension support provided by the Hong Kong Government for the elderly is minimal, and medical and health services for the long-term patient are far from adequate. Also, the elderly in Hong Kong are increasingly isolated in the sense that the average household size has decreased to 3.2 in 1999 which indicates that the traditional large family is disappearing rapidly. This is partly explained by the limited living area available per household, as Hong Kong simply does not have enough space to house families for two generations. It may also be that the young of today would prefer not to live with their parents after marriage, which was quite a common practice in the past.

Hong Kong's suicide rate for elderly females is much higher than that of Western countries (Yip, 1996, 1997), and the male to female ratios in this age group also differ. In Western countries, suicides in older males outnumber those of elderly females by 4:1 (Bharucha and Satlin, 1997) whilst in Hong Kong the male to female ratio is only 1.5: 1. In most Western countries, suicide rates are highest among the divorced followed by the widowed and then the single, with lowest rates existing among the married (Smith et al., 1988). However in Hong Kong, single and widowed elderly males have the highest rates, which are over 100 per 100,000. In addition, there is no difference between elderly females who have never married and those who have married. The high suicide rate among males that have never married could be explained by the selection bias. They are usually not very wealthy, have poor health and have no supporting network, therefore, the probability of getting married is slim. Also, depressed persons marry less often and are therefore the most vulnerable group (Chi et al., 1997). On the other hand, most of the never married elderly women are financially better off than their male peers (Yip, 1998). Marriage provides a much stronger protection against suicide for males than females. The coefficient of preservation (rate of never married to married) for elderly males and females in Hong Kong was 4.26 and 1.14 respectively.

Studies conducted in Australia and the UK suggest that the suicide rate in elderly immigrants is largely determined by their country of origin (Raleigh and Bablarajan, 1992; Burvill, 1995). In Hong Kong, about 80% of the elderly suicides studied were immigrants from Mainland China. The proportion of elderly immigrants from Mainland China in the Hong Kong community is about the same. The suicide rates among the elderly in Mainland China are very high (Yip et al., 2000) especially in rural areas. This may help to explain the elevated rates of elderly suicide in Hong Kong.

The methods of suicide used by the Hong Kong elderly are lethal and highly effective with 52% of suicides completed through jumping and 37% by hanging. In addition, there was no difference in the methods used between males and females, which might explain the possible high suicide rate among the female elderly in Hong Kong. The non-lethal and non-violent methods used by females in Western countries lead to more non-fatal outcomes. The methods used by elderly persons in Hong Kong are very much determined by their availability and the individual's determination to die. 85% of the population in Hong Kong live in high-rise flats and the proportion of elderly suicides involving jumping from a high-rise building has increased from 29% to 52% for the period 1981–1997. However, this change of method reflects the change of preference rather than an increase in the overall suicide rate.

Psychiatric illness was found to be present in over 71% of older people who commit suicide in U.S.A. (Conwell, 1997). In Hong Kong, only 17% of elderly suicides have a history of receiving psychiatric treatment, which is more often frequently associated with suicide among the group of age 25–59 (37%). Certainly, it can be argued that the prevalence of mental illness among the elderly is underreported due to the inadequate provision of a geriatric psychiatric service and the prejudice associated with consulting psychiatrists in Hong Kong. However, from the author's point of view, the large difference between West and East in the prevalence of psychiatric illness reflects genuine regional difference rather than underdiagnosis. Among the suicides deaths in the elderly that had history of psychiatric illness 33% (15 persons) had a consultation with a psychiatrist within a week before committing the act. Can these suicides be prevented?

Less than 10% of the suicide deaths in Hong Kong involved alcohol and/or substance abuse, which is low in comparison with the figure of 20% reported from U.S.A. (Carney et al., 1994; Conwell et al., 1996). The proportion of suicide cases that had a criminal record is also low at 1.8% and 0.0% for males and females respectively. According to other studies, physical illnesses are the most frequent life events preceding suicide in older people (Heikkinen and Lönnqvist, 1995). About 72% of suicide deaths in the elderly involved a severe or terminal illness, for example, cancer. In addition, the most prevalent illness amongst elderly suicides was arthritis, which can be very painful especially in the humid weather in Hong Kong. About 58% of the elderly suicides were independent and could look after themselves and among those with terminal illness, 45% were independent. Nevertheless, fear of becoming a burden on family members is likely to be an important factor (Chi et al., 1997). About 75% of the elderly had consulted a General Practitioner in the three months leading up to the suicide event. Therefore, it can be argued that the opportunity to make a referral or provide proper treatment for the suicidal elderly has been missed.

Living alone is shown to be a risk factor for suicide among the elderly. The suicidal risk of those living alone is twice that of the elderly who live with others. Furthermore, employment for the elderly might be very important for those who prefer to work, not only as a means to support their own living, but also to facilitate an active lifestyle. Retirement, especially without sound financial support can lead to a loss of self-esteem. The proportion of elderly persons receiving Government assistance has increased from 7% to 14% for 1992 and 1997 respectively. The impact of poverty among the elderly is serious, especially in the recent financial turmoil.

Summer months had an excessive number of suicides when compared with the winter months (November, December). The Chinese New Year usually falls in the month of February which reports fewer suicides than any other month. This phenomenon might be due to the fact that there are more holidays in these months. The family members and significant others might be able to spend more time with their elderly relatives. More frequent family gatherings in the major festivals would reduce the feeling of isolation. It might also defer or reduce suicidal feelings in the elderly.

Conclusion

Late life is often a time of profound losses – employment, social status, health, independence, spouse and family members. Those losses may result in stress and eventually depression, at a time when the individual is least able to cope with it. Many elderly persons are left with feelings of emptiness and loneliness. Most of the elderly in Hong Kong are not prepared to live in a world very different from the one in which they grew up, and a mismatch of expectations exists between the old and younger generations. In such an urbanised city as Hong Kong, the elderly are left behind. The support from the Government is very minimal and medical and health supports leave much to be desired. It is important to raise public awareness about suicides in the elderly, and to educate family members to be more alert in detecting any early warning signals, so that they can reassure their elderly relatives about their demands for love and care. In addition, family members should be prepared to seek external help as it is often difficult for family members to seek help to prevent suicides in the elderly. This is because traditional Chinese culture stipulates that the family should take care of its elderly members and the family may feel like they are not fulfilling their filial obligations by going to outsiders for help.

The majority of those elderly suicide victims studied, suffered from chronic diseases. However, very few of them were totally dependent. Older persons may decide to kill themselves out of fear of being a burden to their family. This raises a very interesting question about our high technological development in medical care. Advances in medicine keep us alive longer, and yet new medical technology does not promise good quality of life in later years. We add age to life but not life to age. The elderly who committed suicide due to prolonged suffering from a chronic disease, perhaps testify that an extended life is not necessarily worth living. Euthanasia is a highly sensitive and controversial issue among both the medical profession and the community at large, and as yet little consensus has been reached. Even though some might feel that suicide and assisted suicide among the terminally ill should be ethically and legally acceptable, most elderly suicides are not related to terminal illnesses, but the result of social bias and professional neglect.

Suicides in the elderly is an issue loaded with value judgments. Goodman (1990) raised a series of questions about suicides in the elderly. Why are suicides among the young, the healthy, and the depressed considered a waste, whereas those among the elderly are understandable if the people are old enough and sick enough? Are there any good reasons for suicide? Can suicide be a rational decision that we can accept as tragic and wasteful?

There are no easy answers to any of these questions. However, this paper tries to point out that we cannot dissociate the prevention of elderly suicide from negative societal stereotypes and myths about the elderly, social isolation, inactive lifestyle, health-related stresses, and other factors that are correlated with elderly suicide. Education and public awareness are central ingredients in the prevention of suicide in the elderly. Awareness efforts must be broadly targeted to include mental health professionals, health care providers, volunteers, caregivers of the elderly, family members, the media, and the community (Osgood, 1985). With a solid understanding of suicides in the elderly and a proper attitude towards elderly persons, we can then start to plan programs and allocate resources to help this high-risk group. The phenomenon of suicides in the elderly will not stop. It is a social problem that is not going to cure itself. This problem is a human challenge to raise collective consciousness and to develop innovative interventions, creative public actions, professional cognisance, and comprehensive programs to address suicide among the elderly (Mercer, 1992). Therefore, we should all work together to overcome this challenge which will provide us with an ideal opportunity to address the needs of our senior citizens.

References

Bharucha, A.J., Satlin, A. (1997). Late-life suicide: a review. *Harvard Review of Psychiatry, 5,* 55–65.

Burvill, P.W. (1995). Suicide in the multiethnic elderly population of Australia, 1979–1990. *International Psychogeriatrics, 7,* 319–333.

Carney, S.S., Rich, C.L., Burke, P.A., & Fowler, R.C. (1994). Suicide over 60: the San Diego study. *Journal of the American Geriatrics Society, 42,* 174–180.

Chi, I., Yip, P.S.F., Yu, G.K.K. (1997). *Elderly Suicides in Hong Kong.* Hong Kong: Befrienders International.

Chi, I., Yip, P.S.F., Yu, K.K. (1998). A study of elderly suicides in Hong Kong. *Crisis, 19,* 35–46.

Conwell, Y. (1997). Management of suicidal behavior in the elderly. *Psychiatric Clinics of North America, 20,* 667–683.

Conwell, Y., Duberstein, P.R., Cox, C., Herrmann, J., Forbes, N.T., Caine, E.D. (1996). Relationships of age and axis I diagnoses in victims of completed suicide: a psychological autopsy study. *American Journal of Psychiatry, 153,* 1001–1008.

Devons, C.A.J. (1996). Suicide in the elderly: How to identify and treat patients at risk. *Geriatrics, 51(3),* .67–72.

Goodman, E. (1990) Bettelheim leaves us looking for meaning. *Arkansas Gazette,* 11.

Harwood, D., Jacoby, R. (2000). Suicidal behaviour among the elderly. In K. Hawton & K. Van Heeringen (Eds.), *The International Handbook of Suicide and Attempted Suicide.* Chichester: John Wiley & Sons.

Health and Welfare Branch. (1994). *Working group report on the care for the elderly.* Hong Kong: Hong Kong Government Printer.

Heikkinen, M.E., Lönnqvist, J.K. (1995). Recent life events in elderly suicide: a nationwide study in Finland. *International Psychogeriatrics, 7,* 287–300.

Ho, T.P., Yip, P.S.F., Chiu, C.W.F., Halliday, P. (1998). Suicide notes: What do they tell us? *Acta Psychiatrica Scandinavica, 98,* 467–473.

Kreitman, N. (Ed.). (1977). *Parasuicide.* London: John Wiley & Sons.

Mcintosh, J.L. (1992). Suicide of the elderly. In B. Bonger (Ed.), *Suicide: Guidelines for assessment, management and treatment.* New York: The Free Press.
Medical Council of Hong Kong. (2000) *Professional Code and Conduct.* Hong Kong: Author.
Mercer, S.O. (1992). Suicide and the elderly. In F. J. Turner (Ed.), *Mental health and the elderly: A social work perspective.* New York: The Free Press.
Osgood, N.J. (1985). *Suicide in the elderly: A practitioner's guide to diagnosis and mental health intervention.* Rockville, MD: Aspen.
Raleigh, V.S. and Balarajan, R. (1992). Suicide levels and trends among immigrants in England and Wales. *Health Trends, 24,* 91–94.
Smith, J.C., Mercy, J.A., & Conn, J.M. (1988). Marital status and the risk of suicide. *American Journal of Public Health, 78,* 78–80.
World Health Organisation. (1992). *The tenth revision of the international classification diseases and related health problems.* Geneva: Author.
Yip, P.S.F. (1996). Suicides in Hong Kong, Taiwan and Beijing 1981-1994. *British Journal of Psychiatry, 169,* 495–500.
Yip, P.S.F. (1997). Suicide in Hong Kong 1981-1994. *Social Psychiatry and Psychiatric Epidemiology. 32,* 243–250.
Yip, P.S.F. (1998a). Age, gender, marital status and suicides – An empirical study from East and West. *Psychological Reports, 82,* 311–322.
Yip, P.S.F. (1998b) Suicides in Australia and Hong Kong: An East and West Experience. *Crisis, 19,* 24–34.
Yip, P.S.F., Chi, I. and Yu, K.K. (1998) An epidemiological profile of elderly suicides in Hong Kong. *International Journal of Geriatric Psychiatry, 13,* 631–637.
Yip, P.S.F., Callaran, C. and Yuen, H.K. (2000) Urban/rural and gender differentials in suicide rates: East and West. *Journal of Affective Disorder, 57,* 99–106.

Acknowledgment

The author would like to thank the Coroner's Office and the Census and Statistics Department of the Hong Kong Government (Special Administrative Region) who provided data for the study. The research was also assisted by a group of dedicated research assistants, Patsy Chau, Ada Cheung, Wil Lee and Michael Wong.

An Investigation into Resilience and Suicide in Japan's Elderly

Naoki Watanabe

Department of Psychiatry, Saint Marianna University School of Medicine, Kawasaki, Japan

Introduction

Japan is a country with a population of 125,197,000, situated in East Asia. The land is small for its occupants, such as 377,727sq/km when compared with the United States where the area is 9,809,386sq/km and the population 263,034,000 (The Times Atlas of the World, 1999). After World War II, Japan experienced rapid technical and economical growth which lead to abrupt changes in life style, prolongation of life and shifts in life values.

Figure 1 shows the updated annual change of suicide rates by sex and age groups. Across males and females, youth suicide rates have decreased between 1950 and 1997. Just after World War II, there was a general feeling of disappointment with the defeat of the war and disorientation of the young people (who are now elderly) with their life goals. Also, it was a time of the epidemic expansion of tuberculosis and low expectations from treatment. The average life expectancy in 1949 was 56.2 for males and 59.8 for females. The proportion of elderly in 1950 was 4.9%.

In spite of the fact that there are many suicides among young students today with identified problems of bullying and violence in school classes, youth suicide rates are decreasing. The recent increase in suicide rates of middle-aged males could be associated with the recent economic depression since 1989. The total amount of suicides increased to 23,494 and the total suicide rate in the year 1998 was 18.8 per 100,000 population. As for the elderly, suicide rates (see Figure 1) declined between 1950 and 1997. Nevertheless, suicide rates of the elderly are much higher than those of other age groups. Compared with other countries, suicide rates in Japan increase as people age in both males and females.

There is a rapid growth of the elderly population in Japan. In these 50 years since World War II, the average life expectancy has increased by about 30 years from the age of 50 to 80. Such a rapid growth of the average life expectancy has brought about several problems for the elderly such as dementia, the increasing incidence of various diseases, increasing burden for families and medical costs. Until the year 2050 it is estimated that the elderly proportion will increase to over 30 % of the total population (see Table 1). In the year 1998, the average life expectancy for males was 77.16 and 84.01 for females. In addition, Japan is still the country with the highest longevity rate in the world, and life expectancy is still getting higher in females. However, there is a slight decline in males (down from 78).

Figure 1. Annual change of suicide rates by sex and age groups

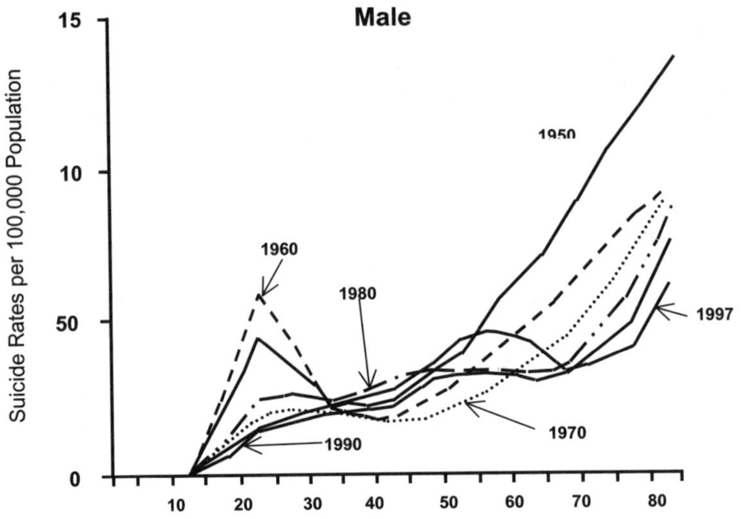

From Ministry of Welfare and Health. Population Census

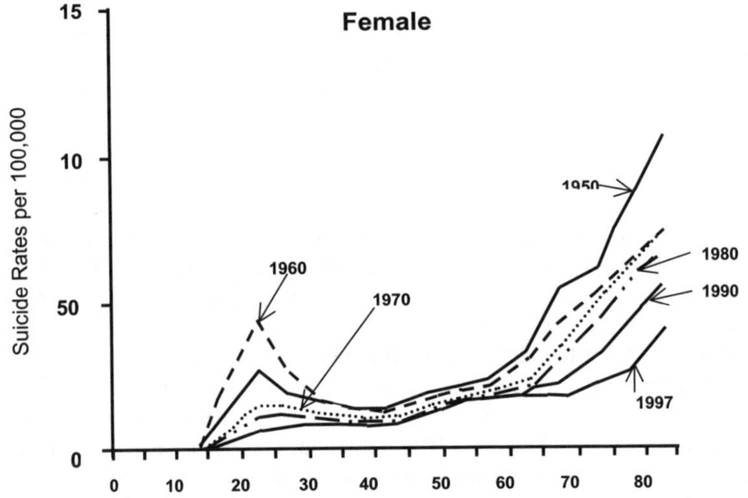

From Ministry of Welfare and Health. Population Census

Table 1. Estimated population and elderly proportion in Japan

Year	Population (1000)	Over 65 (1000)	Proportion (%)
2000	126 892	21 870	17.2
2010	127 623	28 126	22.0
2020	124 133	33 335	26.9
2025	120 913	33 116	27.4
2050	100 496	32 454	32.3

Source: National Institute for Social Security and Population problems (January, 1997).

Suicide Rates of the Elderly

As seen in Figure 2, Japan is a country with high suicide rates. When comparing national suicide rates, Japan falls in the middle spectrum akin to Germany (Takahashi et al., 1995). However as for the elderly, Figure 2 shows that Japan is one of the countries with higher than average elderly suicide rates both for males and females. Japanese males have similar trends to the U.S.A. or Sweden wherein suicide increases with age. In the U.S.A., women across age groups have much lower suicide rates than men. In Japan, in general, males have slightly higher suicide rates than women in all age groups. However, there is little data from which to conclude reasons for these differences.

Regional Differences in the Suicide Rates of the Elderly

In order to gain an understanding of suicide patterns, this chapter focuses on some regional differences in Japan. Two prefectures in Japan, Akita and Niigata, take annual first and second place positions among other prefectures concerning suicide rates of the elderly (65+). The highest national rates of elderly suicide occur in the Akita prefecture. By contrast, the Okinawa prefecture has the lowest elderly suicide rate. The Akita prefecture is situated in the northern part of Japan with the population of 1,204,000 in the year 1997. The area is famous for rice production and as an agricultural area and in winter it is snow-laden.

Figure 2. Annual change of suicide rates by sex and age groups – international comparison (1995)

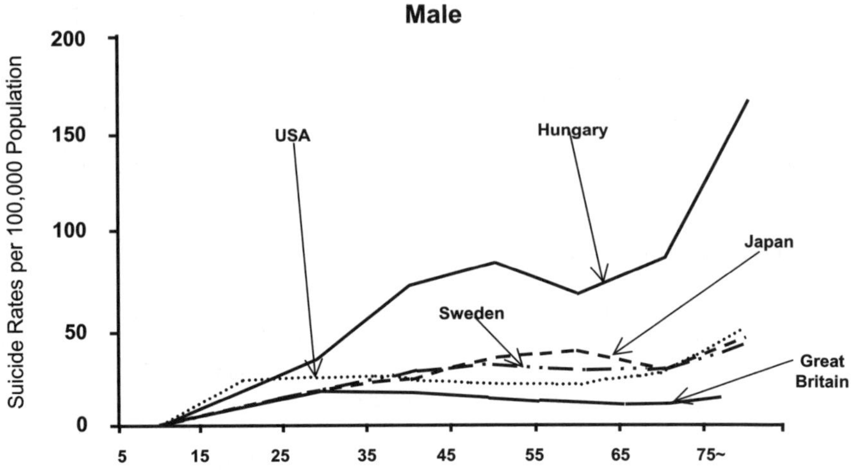

From Ministry of Welfare and Health. Population Census
WHO [World Health Statistics Annual 1996]

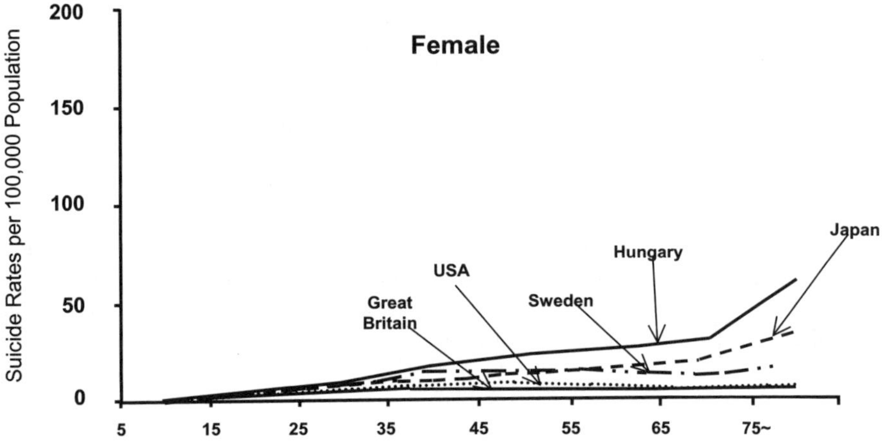

From Ministry of Welfare and Health. Population Census
WHO [World Health Statistics Annual 1996]

The Okinawa prefecture is in the southern island with a population of 128,5000 in the year 1997, and it is well known for the severe battles fought there at the end of World War II. It is warm in all seasons. The Akita Prefecture has an elderly suicide rate four times higher than the Okinawa prefecture. Table 2 shows the suicide rates of the elderly for the year 1995 between the Akita prefecture and Okinawa prefecture. In the Akita prefecture, rates are 66.62 suicides per 100,000 inhabitants whereas Okinawa had 20.72 per 100,000 inhabitants. And an interesting finding is that elderly women in the Okinawa prefecture have much fewer suicides than elderly men. Suicide rates in males are 79.04 per 100,000 inhabitants and 57.86 per 100,000 inhabitants for females in the Akita prefecture. In the Okinawa prefecture, rates for males were 42.42 and 6.84 per 100,000 inhabitants for females.

Table 2. Comparison of elderly suicide rates (65+) per 100,000 inhabitants, 1995

	Akita Prefecture	Okinawa Prefecture	Japan as Total
Male	79.04	42.42	38.2
Female	57.86	6.84	25.9
Total	66.22	20.72	30.9

Suicide methods of the elderly

In the year 1995, a research team visited Y-city in Akita prefecture with ca. 140,000 inhabitants and checked the death records at the Public Health Center. Comparisons were made between Y-city in Akita prefecture and Kawasaki-city with a collective population of million inhabitants. Table 3 shows suicide statistics between 1982 and 1990 across Y-city in Akita prefecture and Kawasaki city.

Table 3. Suicide rates in a rural versus urban area, 1982–1990

	Y-City		Kawasaki City	
Age groups	Male	Female	Male	Female
10–19	3	2	32	8
20–39	14	4	324	145
40–64	31	18	490	199
65+	20	29	156	116
Total	68	53	1002	468

Kawasaki city is an industrial district where the higher proportion of male suicides cluster in the age groups of 20–64. Table 4 shows that in both cities hanging is the most common method of suicide in all age groups, both in Y-city and Kawasaki city. In the United States, suicide by firearms is the most common method. However, suicide by firearms in Japan is rare (Japan has much stricter gun control when compared with the U.S.A.). In addition, the national Japanese data shows that hanging is the common method of suicide across all age groups. In the older age groups, hanging is the most usual method; whereas in the younger age groups jumping from heights is seen relatively often.

Table 4. Methods of elderly suicide (65+), 1979–1990

Methods	K-City	Y-City
Hanging	65.6%	69.4%
Jumping from a height	10.5%	3.3%
Burning or being run over by a moving vehicle	9.4%	3.3%
Drowning	6.6%	7.4%
Poisoning by solid or liquid substances	4.4%	5.0%
Stabbing with knives or swords	1.9%	3.3%
Poisoning by domestic gas, car exhaust, and other gases	1.6%	5.0%
Others	0	3.3%

After the age of 65, most males retire from their life-long occupations. What might be productive ways of living? What facilitates "successful" aging? How does one maintain a secure state of health that is associated with physical, psychological, emotional and psycho-social well-being? The following is a report about a recent study on life styles of the elderly in the district of Akita Prefecture and Okinawa Prefecture.

Research and Methodology

Psychological Autopsy Study

In 1995, the Public Health Center in Yuri-town investigated whole family units in which older persons had completed suicide as a kind of psychological autopsy study. Public health nurses interviewed the family survivors about the victim's psycho-social background. The subjects of this investigation were family members of the victims (mostly spouse, sons or daughters, or sons or daughters-in-law). The victims committed suicide between 1992 and 1994 and included 8 males and 8 females, with a mean age of 71.9 years (range 50–80). Family members were interviewed about possible factors inducing suicide, illness, number of family members, presence of a spouse, personality, suicide of other relatives, activities of daily living (ADL), role in the family, social engagement and suffering of the victims.

Survey Component of Research

In March 1997, a survey was mailed to 10% of inhabitants about their awareness of suicide prevention in the elderly. The questionnaire consisted of questions about life satisfaction, important things in life, health consciousness, thoughts on elderly suicide and prevention methods and on public support and services (see appendix one). The questionnaire was sent to 504 inhabitants of Yuri-town.

Research in Akita in 1997

In the summer of 1997 a research team of four stayed for 4 days in Yuri-town and visited 8 villages Prior to the team's visit, the public health officials called for volunteers (elderly) to attend interviews at the public halls of each village. 111 elderly people participated (30 males and 81 females), with an age range of 57–92 (mean = 76.6).

It should be pointed out that the Youri town is an agricultural district that has a population of ca. 6000 inhabitants. The population showed a gradual decrease through the years because the young productive population wanted to move into big cities where they could find better jobs with higher incomes. The proportion of the elderly was ca. 20%. The district not only has high suicide rates (30.7 per 100,000 inhabitants in 1997) but, in comparison with other districts, also has very high prevalence of cerebro-vascular disease (181.6 per 100,000 inhabitants in 1997) and also of vascular dementia.

Research in Okinawa in 1998

Using the same research protocol (minus the Geriatric Depression Scale and items c, d, e of the Suicide Ideation Questionnaire), a similar investigation was conducted in M-town (150,000 inhabitants) in the Okinawa prefecture. In M-town suicide rates of the elderly were not yet been reported. Hundred-and -five elderly subjects, with a mean age of 74.0 years (26 males, mean age 73.4; 79 females, mean age 76.1) participated in the study. Comparisons were made between answers from the elderly from Yuri-town in Akita prefecture and M-town from the Okinawa prefecture.

Researchers attempted to identify common patterns of response related to choices in life style among the non-suicidal. In addition, researchers reported on the natural religious practices of elderly women who worshiped a god-figure: it was hypothesised that this popular practice may positively impact on the living status of elderly women and in turn prevent their suicide.

It should be noted that during the course of the research, the Public Health Officials impeded the use of the term 'suicide' by researchers, fearing that this might stimulate self-destructive behaviours in citizens.

Through the investigation, we tried to obtain reliable answers to the following questions:

- Were there significant differences in depressed feelings, awareness of quality of life factors, and coping ability between the Akita-Group (high suicide rate area) and the Okinawa-Group (low suicide rate area)?
- Were there significant differences in socio-demographic factors between the Akita-Group and the Okinawa-Group?
- Were there any significant relationships between depressed mood, socio-economic status, quality of life knowledge, and coping behaviours? And finally,

- Were there significant regional differences on depression factors between the Akita-Group and the Okinawa-Group?

Results

Psychological Autopsy Study in 1995

This research project represented the first active engagement with the national Public Health Center on suicide problems. Prior to this study, there was only one other district (in Niigata prefecture) which was investigated for its high suicide rates. As a cultural note, there is a strong taboo in Japan against suicide studies, because people have concerns that they could be excluded from the community if they participate. In general, people attempt to hide their family member's suicide as much as possible.

Results indicate that:

1) Most victims (14/16) had physical illnesses such as hypertension, arthritis, liver diseases, myocardial infarction, cerebral infarction, intestinal cancer, gynaecological diseases and kidney diseases. Some of them were also undergoing treatment for depression;
2) An assessment of pre-morbid personality features of victims, as seen by significant others, was sought. Four out of 16 subjects were regarded as having personality features related to emotional and social sensitivity, 2/16 were identified as socially withdrawn, and 2/16 were regarded as over-sensitive in general;
3) Of significance is that none of the victims lived alone at the time of their suicide and most of them (10/16) lived with more than 3 generations of family members;
4) Over half of the victims had experienced the prior suicide of a relative;
5) Regarding contacts with family members, most of the victims (11/16) were used to meeting with family members several times a day;
6) Most victims (13/16) were regarded by family members as having satisfactory ADL;
7) Most victims (13/16) were identified as having meaningful roles and enjoyment in their families;
8) Among victims, 9/16 had contact with other persons outside the family several times a week, and
9) Only 1 victim was identified as having had an "important personal" factor, 2 victims were identified as having had family problems, and the suicide of 13 victims were associated with "socio-ecological" factors.

From the view of family survivors, 68.7% of the victims seemed to have had some of the following concerns:

- fear and worry that family members might detect a worsening of their disease, indicating that he/she was afraid of being re-admitted to the hospital;
- fear of knowing the progress of their disease;
- fear of dependency, wherein the victim had observed another family member causing trouble to their family carers; there was fear that he/she might fall into the same situation and place a burden on his/her family;
- the constant worry to become a burden for their family members;
- the feeling/belief that they would have no relief from their illnesses;
- depressed feelings caused by the death of spouse, friends and other family members;
- concern for the household economy of their family, and,
- concern about repaying the debt their family had incurred through their incapacity with insurance money arising from their death.

Surviving family members indicated that these victims had anxiety, melancholy, and a rigid way of thinking. Victims were heard saying, "I might be a burden for the family" which may have lead to their hopeless feelings.

Results from the questionnaire

The results of the questionnaire revealed that good communication was considered to be important for quality of life. Even in later life, the most important factor indicated was health care and second, good family relationships. Family knowledge and awareness of beliefs/feelings of elderly members who committed suicide was far higher in Yuri Town than in the other town. This inquiry-survey was firstly performed on the basis of the hypothesis that people in this district would better accept someone's suicide that would be a burden to their family and surrounding community. However, 80 % of people who responded, regarded suicide as serious problem and believed something should be done to prevent suicide and to promote mutual relationships in the family.

There were 328 answers to the 504 mailed questionnaires (65%) in an age range from 20 to 80 years. The most interesting responses were the following:

1. *How do you enjoy your life? What do you find important in your life*?
   42.1 % of respondents answered with "spending time with family members", 38.7% responded with "communicating with friends." Adults over the age of 60, particularly, tended to answer in the same way.
2. *What is important for you in late life?*
   Eighty-six and three percent of respondents focussed on health care, 59.8% of respondents answered with "good family relationships", 40.2% of respondents answered with "contact with the neighbours."
3. *What do you think about when you get ill?*
   32.0% of respondents answered with "doing the best while depending on others", 21.3% of respondents indicated that they would concentrate on the

treatment, while 7 respondents (2.1% between 40 to 80 years of age) answered that it would be of no use to live.

Akita prefecture in the year 1997

As for family composition, 78.4 % of the subjects lived with their spouse and the average members in each family was 5. There were only 2 elderly persons (1.8%) who lived alone; 78 (70.3%) lived with spouse; 63 (56.8%) lived with their sons and their wives; 75 (67.6%) lived with their grandchildren; and 14 (12.6%) lived with their own father or mother. As for educational data only 1 person (0.9%) graduated from university; 36 elderly (32.4%) had completed 8 years of education, and 31 (27.9%) had finished 6 years of education under the old educational system.

As for occupation, 26 (23.6%) claimed they had no occupation, and 84 (76.4%) had some work, including farming. As for hobbies, 32 (29.4%) declared that they had no hobbies, and 77 (70.6%) declared that they did. As for physical illness, 26 (23.4%) declared that they were free from physical illnesses whilst 85 (76.6%) had some kind of somatic problem: 35 (41.2%) of them had a history of hypertension, 24 (28.2%) had neuralgia or joint pain, 28 (25.2%) were taking medications [however, only 3 (3.5%) of them were under treatment]. As for smoking and drinking, 8 subjects (7.3%) had a history of smoking and 32 (29.1%) had a history of drinking.

Correlation Between QOL and GDS

By dividing the scores of the Geriatric Depression Scale (GDS) into three groups, we found that a Low GDS-Group showed significantly high awareness of the Quality of Life (see Figure 3). The Low GDS-Group showed significantly higher scores for "present life satisfaction," "psychological stability," and "energy for living" (*p<.05).

Correlation Between GDS and CISS

As for the CISS, or coping behaviours inventory of the elderly for stressful situations, results showed that the Low GDS-Group was significantly lower for the emotion-oriented coping behaviours (*p < .05). Thus, the higher the depressive tendency, the higher the emotion-oriented coping behaviour scores (see Figure 4).

Figure 3. Correlation between QOL and GDS

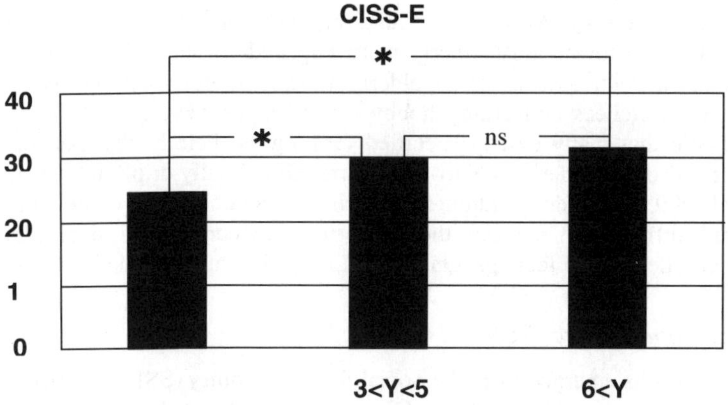

Figure 4. Correlation between GDS and CISS

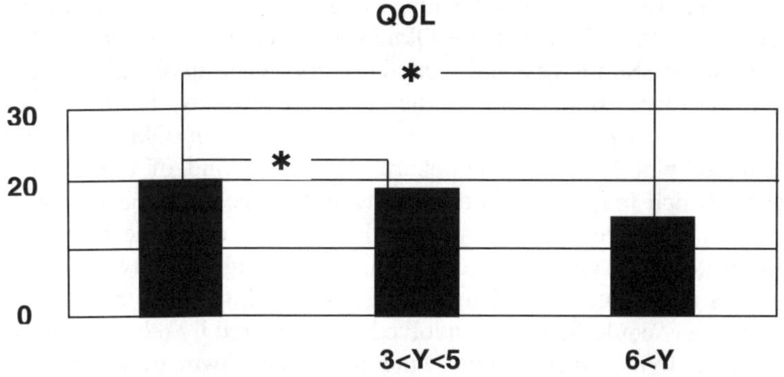

Y=GDS score

Comparison with Okinawa Prefecture

Socio-Demographic Data

As for socio-demographic data, there were no significant differences in most variables except in living and working situations, and in drinking habit. In Yuri-town, only 2 of the elderly (1.8 %) lived alone, whereas in M-town 16 (15.4%) lived alone. In Yuri-town the extended family with family membership comprised more than 3 generations. Whereas in M-town we found that most elderly lived with their spouses (39.4%). In Yuri-town, most elderly were engaged in some farm work (77.1%), whereas in M-town 39.6% of the elderly worked more regularly. We found no significant differences concerning hobby activities. However, in Yuri-town it was characteristic that many elderly specified farming as their hobby. As for drinking habits, 28.4% of the elderly in Yuri-town admitted to "daily drinking" whereas in M-town only 4.9% of elderly admitted to drinking alcohol. We could not find any significant differences between the 2 districts concerning physical illness, loss experiences, depressive feelings, Quality of Life-scores and suicide ideation.

Social Support Inquiry (SSI)

Interesting results emerged from the Social Support Inquiry (SSI). Compared with the Akita prefecture, the older adults in Okinawa showed significantly lower scores of negative support. The elderly in the Akita prefecture were very sensitive concerning negative support by their spouse, other family members, family members living away from the home, friends and neighbours. Figure 5 shows the comparison between social support in the Akita and the Okinawa prefectures, concerning friends and neighbours. In the SSI, the first and second categories (positive and physical support: four items each) were similar in both the Akita and Okinawa prefectures except for the item *"people would be ready to lend money"* (in Okinawa, there is an organization of elderly called "Yuimahru" that is a kind of traditional self-help organization which may have contributed to differences in expectations from outsiders). A major difference was found in the category of the negative support (remaining four items). In Okinawa older adults showed significantly fewer answers for the negative support questions. This contrasts with Akita where most of the elderly admitted that they could be overly involved and bothered by others such as spouses, family members living together, family members living away from the home, friends and neighbours.

Discussion

Results from this study do not support existing research on suicide in the elderly. For instance, Tamura (1979) suggests that the elderly at risk in regions with high suicide rates, have extended family support and have a tendency to drink alcohol every day; their hobby activities are minimal and they set higher value on their work as farmers. In our study, depressed feelings in the elderly in both groups were not correlated with suicidal ideation. Other studies suggested that illness could not be considered as one of leading factors to suicide and no correlation of illnesses with the intensity of depressed feelings has generally been reported (Dorpat et al., 1968; Whitlock, 1986; Conwell et al., 1991). In our study, suicide was inversely related to hobby activities and subsequent intensity of depressed feelings as reported by survivors. For instance, the subgroup with depressed feelings had fewer hobbies, and this subgroup was dominant in Yuri-town. Therefore the encouragement to develop hobbies for the elderly might be one of the ways to reduce suicide.

In this study, the intensity of depressed feelings was correlated with QOL and coping behaviours. The higher the depressed feelings, the lower the "present life satisfaction", "psychological stability" and "energy for living" and also the higher the emotion-oriented coping behaviour. These features were found equally in the Akita and the Okinawa region. The comparison of the data between Akita and Okinawa made it clear that the elderly in Yuri town in Akita prefecture are very sensitive to their surrounding social environment. They are mostly afraid to "lose face" towards others which could be correlated to the "masochism" as described by Nakakuki (1994). They want to be regarded by others as "diligent and self-sacrificing." As long as the elderly devote themselves to their family and work hard, they feel respected and safe in their family and also in the community as a group. However, given the changes in their financial status, social role and identity as farmers, they become at risk due to these loss factors (Tamura, 1979). When comparing communities, the elderly in the Akita prefecture seemed more concerned not to "lose face." As long as they were healthy and hard working they felt safe, secure, and accepted in the community. However, once they were disturbed in their activities due to severe-illnesses, they tend to withdraw from the community and suffer symptoms of depression which increase their suicide thoughts and behaviours. Most of the elderly seemed to be afraid to lose their mental and physical activities due to severe illness as they made frequent visits to their medical centers. This could be a strong indicator of anxiety in this population (perhaps as much as depression).

In the Okinawa prefecture, the female elderly were especially stable and seemed to feel secure and safe in their community even though they lived alone or only with their spouse. The female elderly carry important roles in their community and participate in religious ceremonies by taking on the role of mediator between God and the people. They are respected and are also able to take on leadership duties in various ceremonies throughout the religious cycles of the year. They have strong emotional ties with other community members. As it is warm enough throughout the year their houses are also open to the outside community.

Figure 5. Social Support Inquiry

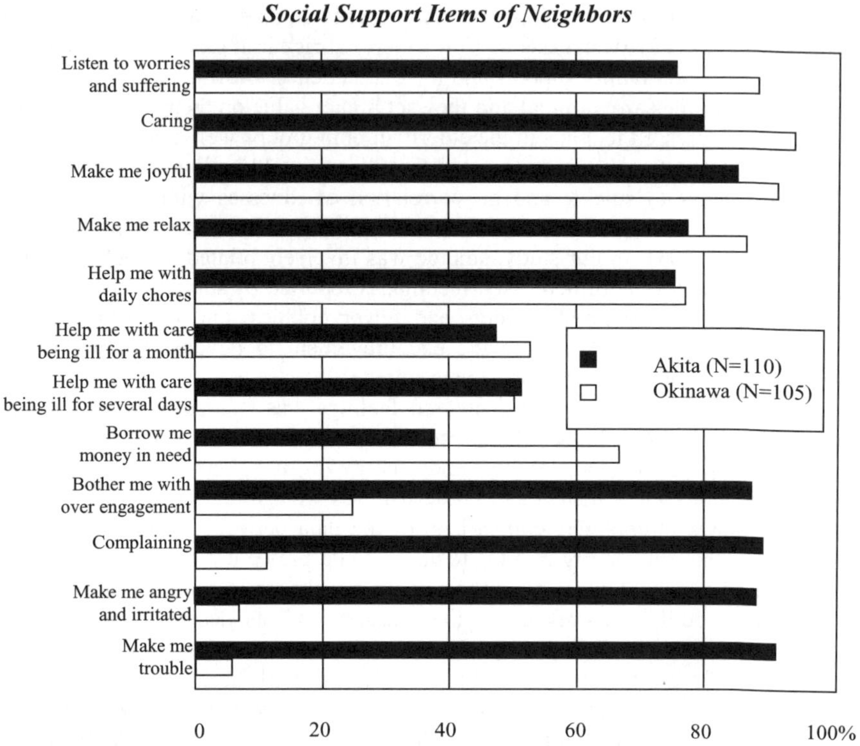

Everybody can take a look at their houses, providing the opportunity to develop social relationships. There is no strict barrier between individuality and community.

Perhaps the so-called "masochistic thinking" by the elderly in the Akita prefecture is rather a traditional way of thinking in Japan. It seems to be found less in Okinawa where they have nourished their own culture as an island. In big cities other values for development and meaningful activities are evident. The elderly tend to live separately from their children. However they have a lot of opportunities to meet them and friends, and enjoy social activities and so on. There is a good transport system which allows the elderly to maintain good communication, even if they live alone.

This research began as an inquiry to better understand resilience against and risk factors for suicide. The study was developed following the observation of differences in suicide rates between rural and urban areas in Japan (Watanabe et al, 1995). In particular, two northern prefectures have significantly higher elderly suicide rates when compared with Southern regions in Japan. This research focussed on factors that contributed to an elderly person's decision to commit suicide despite their older age (the highest suicide age in Niigata-prefecture was reported as 103). There was a curiosity about the suicide of those who seemed to benefit from family support, as many victims had shared their lives with 3 generations of family members, resided in beautiful surroundings, lived together with their spouse, had daily connection with other family members and kept social roles in the community. Results from our interviews and literature review indicated that the elderly people who completed suicide were especially careful about their physical conditions and once they became ill, they interpreted this as a great loss. The older people in this district were regarded by community members as honest and hard working and were highly respected. However, once they experienced some stressful events such as loss experiences and abandonment experiences, their suicide risk increased and they were reported by family to have had a lower quality of life and emotional coping behaviour.

Results from this study may be useful for establishing effective intervention programs for those at risk for suicide. Summing up our main results, these were:

1) we could find significant differences only in age, number of family members, and emotion-oriented coping behaviour;
2) we could find significant differences only in work and drinking habits;
3) intensity of depressed feelings was correlated only with hobby activities. The higher the depressed feeling, the lower the "present life satisfaction", "psychological stability" and "energy for living" in QOL and higher emotion-oriented coping behaviour in CISS;
4) we could not find any significant difference in subgroups of the GDS-scores between the Akita-Group and the Okinawa-Group.

Status of Ethics with Regard to Euthanasia

There is a growing interest in Japan concerning the issue of euthanasia. The following example may clarify how Japanese are thinking on this matter. In May 1991, a physician at the T-University hospital injected an intravenous dose of sodium chloride to a multiple myeloma patient who was in a comatose state. The physician stated that he performed this procedure because the patient's family begged him to let the patient be free from his suffering. Subsequently, the doctor was accused of murder and went on trial. The doctor was found guilty with a stay of execution. After the trial a discussion about euthanasia emerged in the mass media, with particular reference to the boundaries between suicide and euthanasia. In Japan the knowledge of euthanasia is not rooted deeply enough. The act by the physician to lethally inject a coma patient was incorrectly presented as a case of euthanasia. There was no former confirmation of the presence of an informed consent from the patient in before his coma (Hoshino, 1996). In this case, the family's decision was crucial and the physician was influenced by the family member's words "Please let him die in peace!"

In Japan, if someone in the family becomes terminally ill, the doctor would firstly disclose this to the head of the family (usually the first son), sustained by other family members (mostly brothers and sisters, sometimes other relatives). The doctor would ask them whether they would allow the patient to be told about the real severity of the illness. In most cases, the family would refuse to tell the patient the truth. The doctor would tell the patient in such a case not the real illness (for example, stomach cancer) but a much lighter condition (for example, stomach ulcer). The patient would have the illusion that he may recover soon. So, until now this has been the habitual pattern of reaction by family members. The doctor's action is largely governed by the weight of the family's decision and not by the patient's own decision (Hoshino, 1996). This cultural factor may play a role in the patient's suicide risk; for example the ill person may know about own illness, but no one will speak overtly about it.

Development of Passive Euthanasia

Along with the influences of the individualistic thinking from western countries, today there is a movement called "The Japanese Society of Death with Dignity", established since the year 1976. This society was firstly called "Japanese Society of Euthanasia". However, they renamed the society from 1983 in the above mentioned way, because of the fear that the name "euthanasia" would be misunderstood and be equalled with the one of "assisted suicide". The membership of the society increasing rapidly and in the year 1995 they had 72,000 members (Sakai, 1996). The reasons for such an increase in the membership could be identified in the following factors: 1) a growing consciousness of the right of self-decision and self-selection of the type of death, 2) a growing awareness of the different ways of dying, due to the increase in the number of nuclear families that nurtures individualism; 3) the problem of the financial burden associated with high technology medicine; 4) medical care for prolonging life; and 5) a growing awareness about life and death issues due to a general improvement in living conditions and education. The so-called "living will" is more and more respected as a means to express one's own desire and decision (Kuroyanagi, 1994). Such tendency reflected also on the message of the Japanese Medical Association (1992) that terminal patients should have the right to decide whether they will accept the treatment or not after receiving a detailed explanation by doctors. Once patients are able to clearly express this will, doctors should respect the will and stop the treatment, thus letting the patient dying by natural death (dying with dignity). In that case doctors would not be responsible for stopping life sustaining apparatuses. This message is in general welcomed. However it has still few problems: 1) a verbal expression of the will is also accepted; 2) if the patient is not able to express his/her own will, the family can decide on it; and 3) it is also valid for patients under the age of 15. Here we could clearly identify the centrality of the role of the family in the decision-making process of ending life (Sakai, 1996).

The Standpoint of Buddhism

The influence of Buddhism is difficult to measure. Consider, for instance, the Buddhist reflection upon "What virtually is dignity?" With regard to the elderly, perhaps there is a struggle with this notion of dignity. From Buddhist philosophy, if we can not use hands, we still have voice, and if we lose our voice, we have our eyes to remind us of life, and if we lose our eyes we still have ears to listen to nature's sound, etc. Mind and body are embedded within the movements of the universe. They are always changing. Within the natural order is the process of living, aging, getting ill and dying, and this is a precious reality. No one can change this reality (Hoshino, 1996).

The Meaningful Life Therapy

Finally, some consideration on the so-called "Meaningful Life Therapy", which is actually based on the Japanese psychotherapy called "Morita Therapy." Morita Therapy was established by Masatake Morita (1874–1938) in the early 1900's. The main concept could be reduced to two factors. One is called "Obedience to Nature" and the other is called "Subordination to Circumstances." We, human beings, are namely part of Nature and its movements. Then what is nature? Nature means psychological and physiological fact. It is natural that we feel hot in summer and cold in winter. "One is not in accordance with reality if he/she tries not to feel the summer's heat or the winter's cold" It is natural that we have feelings of both comfort and discomfort. It is also unrealistic to try to have only comfort feelings. It is natural that we fear death, dislike discomfort, lament calamities, and complain about what we cannot control. All these are natural human responses and emotions. Also, one gets heaviness in the head after oversleeping, discomfort in the stomach after overeating, and heart palpitations when startled. So the important thing is to accept these realities as they are. The treatment goal is also to move patients from unnatural thoughts and feelings to natural ones. They are unnatural because they tend to want to experience only comfort or happiness (Morita, 1998). Such a therapy could also apply to the state of terminal illness or the issues of euthanasia.

Typical Japanese sentiments towards both suicide and euthanasia may be gathered from the following story. The tragic story called "Narayama Bushikou" is a masterpiece of Shichiro Fukazawa which is based on a legend of abandoning the elderly in the mountains. Similar legends were abundant in many areas of Japan when the country was poor. Orin, the heroine, was 69 years old. She ordered her son to carry her on his back to the mountain "Narayama" and abandon her as a way to decrease the burden for the family so that other family members could have something more to eat. Orin was a very hard working old woman and it was an astounding thing that she declared the will to end her life; although she was loved by her son and his spouse and children. Such kind of self sacrificial thoughts and behavior fill the minds of many Japanese people and it was regarded as a tragic and yet irresistible and understandable deed (Ohi, 1995). Buddhist influences, parables and folk stories require more investigation regarding their influence on elderly peoples' thoughts and actions regarding suicide.

References

Beck., A.T., Kovacs, M., & Weissman, A. (1979). Assessment of Suicidal Intention. The Scale of Suicidal Ideation. *Journal of Counsulting and Clinical Psychology, 47*, 343–352.

Conwell, Y., Olsen, K., Caine, E. D., Flanney, C. J. (1991). Suicide in Later Life: Psychological Autopsy Findings. *International Psychogeriatrics, 3*, 59–66.

Dorpat, T. L., Anderson, W. F., Ripley, H. S. (1968). The Relationship of Physical Illness to Suicide. In H. P. L. Resnik (Ed.), *Suicidal Behaviors: Diagnosis and Management* (pp. 209–219). Boston: Little Brown.

Endler, N. S., & Parker, J. D. A. (1990). Multidimensional Assesment of Coping. A Critical Evaluation. *Journal of Personality and Social Psychology, 58*, 844–854.

Erdman, P. (1975). The status and integration of the aged in Japanese Society. *Journal of Gerontology, 30*, 199–208.

Hoshino, K., & Tanaka, S. (Ed.). (1996). *Dignity of Death-Bioethics in Japan and America.* Kyoto: Onbunkaku. [In Japanese]

Ishihara, O., Naitou, K., & Nagashima, K. (1992). Trial for making the QOL Evaluation Scale based on Psychological Traits due to Subjective Scale. *Pohnen Shakai Kagaku* [Social Science on Elderly], 14, 43–51. [In Japanese]

Itami, J. (1990). Application of Morita Therapy for Cancer and Intractable disease. *Journal of Morita Therapy, 1* (2), 239–241.

Kuroyanagi, Y. (1994). *On Death with Dignity*. Tokyo: Iwanami-Shoten.Tokyo. [In Japanese]

Minami, H. (1985). *Japanese Ego*. Tokyo: Diwanami Shoten. [In Japanese]

Morita, M. (1998). *Morita Therapy and the True Nature of Anxiety Based Disorders*. New York: State University of New York Press.

Nakagawa, Y. (1995). Death with Dignity in the Japanese Culture. *Psychiatry and Clinical Neuroscience, 49(*Suppl. 1), S161–163.

Nakakuki, M. (1994). Normal and Developmental Aspects of Masochism: Transcultural and Clinical Implications. *Psychiatry 57*, 244–257.

Ohi G.(1995): Ethical Orientations and dignified death. *Psychiatry and Clinical Neuroscience, 49*, Suppl.1, S155-159.

Rachels, A. (1975). Active and Passive Euthanasia. *New England Journal of Medicine, 292,* 78–80.

Sakai, A. (Ed.). (1996*). Euthanasia or Dignified Death?* Sapporo: Hokkaido University Books Publishing Society. [In Japanese]

Seemann, T., & Berkmann, L. (1988). Structural Characteristics of Social Networks and their Relationships with Social Support in the Elderly: Who provides Support. *Social Science and Medicine, 26,* 737–749.

Sheik, J. I., Yesavage, J. A. (1986). Geriatric Depression Scale (GDS) Recent Evidence and Development of a Shorter Version. *Clinical Gerontologist, 5,* 165–173.

Takahashi, Y. (1998). *Senile Depression*. Tokyo: Nihon Hyouronsha. [In Japanese]

Takahashi, Y., Hirasawa, H., Koyama, K., Asakawa, O., Kido, M., Onose, H., Udagawa, M., Ishikawa, Y., & Uno, M. (1995). Suicide and Aging in Japan: An Examination of Treated Elderly Suicide Attempters. *International Psychogeriatrics, 7*, 239–252.

Tamura, K. (1979). Life Value and Death of the Japanese. – Case study on the elderly suicide in the area of population decrease in rural area. In K. Tamura, *Suicide Prevention and Death and Life Concept* (pp. 159–164). Tokyo: Seiwa Shoten. [In Japanese]

Watanabe, N., Hasegawa, K., & Yoshinaga, Y. (1995). Suicide in Later Life in Japan. *International Psychogeriatrics, 7* (2), 253–261.

Whitlock, F. A. (1986). Suicide and Physical Illness. In A. Roy (Ed.), *Suicide* (pp. 151–170). Baltimore: Williams & Wilkins.

Appendix

The health questionnaire for older people contained the following items:

1) Personal variables (age, sex, study career, occupation career, existence of spouse, etc.);
2) Family variables (number of generations and their dimensions, etc.);
3) Health variables (use of alcohol, smoking, illnesses and the use of medical services);
4) Geriatric Depression Scale (Short Version). The full score is 15 points (Sheik, et al., 1986);
5) Coping Inventory for Stressful Situation Scale for older adults (CISS-O): characteristic coping behaviors of the individuals might be classified as: a) task-oriented coping, b) emotion-oriented coping and c) avoidance-oriented coping. The full score was for each coping 40 points (Endler et al., 1990);
6) QOL-Assessment Scale: mixed with PGC-morale scale and Life-Satisfaction Index (LSI-A). The Scale is divided into 3 categories with each one having a full score of 8 points (Ishihara et al., 1992).
    a) Present Life Satisfaction,
    b) Psychological stability
    c) Energy for living.
7) Social Support Inquiry: About support from spouses, other family members living together, children or relatives living outside the family and friends or neighbors. It is divided into 3 categories, namely
    a) positive support
    b) physical support
    c) negative support.
8) Suicide Ideation Questionnaire (SIQ): Beck's Suicide Intent Scale were shortened into following 5 questions (Beck et al., 1979):
    a) Within one month did you have an intention to die?
    b) Within one month did you want to kill yourself?
    c) How long did your wish to kill yourself last time?
    d) Have you ever written your suicide note?
    e) Do you think of suicide and its method now?

Loss experiences within one year: Bereavement and separation from spouses, brothers and sisters, children, friends, work, economical loss, loss of the social role and bereavement from pets.

Suicide in Elderly and Youth Populations – How Do They Differ?

Kerryn Neulinger and Diego De Leo

Australian Institute for Suicide Research and Prevention, Griffith University, Brisbane, Australia

Introduction

Generally, the highest suicide rates in countries reporting to the World Health Organisation have been for those aged over 75 years (Figure 1), and with the increase in the world's older population, this rate of suicide was predicted to increase even more (De Leo, 1997). Actually, in recent years suicide in the elderly has declined in many countries and currently more suicides (57%) are realised by people below the age of 45 than by those aged 45 years and over. This is based on global mortality data (WHO, 1999). An increase in youth suicide has also contributed to this decline in elderly suicide, especially in Western (and particularly Anglo-Saxon) countries

Figure 1. Global suicide rates (per 100,000), by gender and age, selected countries, 1995 (WHO, 1999).

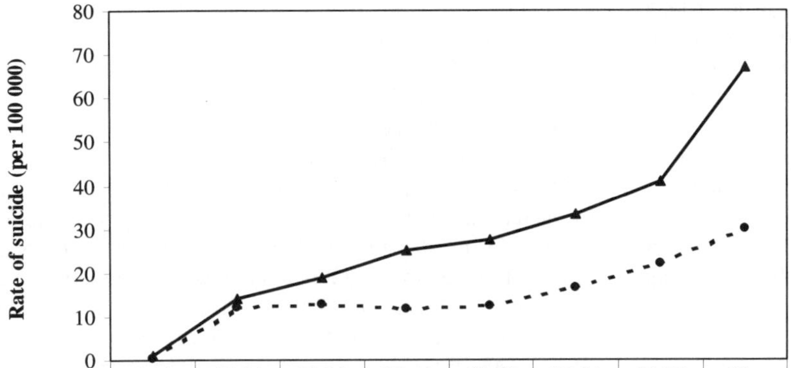

	5-14	15-24	25-34	35-44	45-54	55-64	65-74	75+
males	0.9	14.2	18.9	24.9	27.6	33.3	41	66.9
females	0.5	12	12.6	11.6	12.4	16.4	22.1	29.7

Age group

(De Leo, 2000). The reasons for the decline in suicide rates of older adults and an increase in those of youth remain unclear. The elderly were not the special target on any national prevention program, and they only benefited from the general improvement in health care and living conditions that affected the general population as a whole. In addition, especially in western countries, more managed care interventions, such as the reduction of hospital beds and stays, could have an adverse impact on suicide rates, especially in old age (De Leo, 2000).

In the past, suicide rates in Australia have increased with age, with the lowest rates in the youth and highest in the elderly (Goldney & Harrison, 1998). More recently, rates for the elderly have decreased and youth rates have increased, so that the most recent data shows little discrepancy between these age groups. This is true for both genders, with rates for Australian males aged 15–24 (26.6 per 100,000) slightly higher than rates for the elderly (aged 75+) males (25.5 per 100,000) in 1998; and female youth suicide rates (6.3 per 100,000) almost equivalent to female elderly rates (6.4 per 100,000) (ABS, unpublished data).

In a comparison of 23 Western countries by age and gender for mean rates from 1991–1994 (Cantor et al., 1999), all mainland European countries had higher rates for both elderly males and females than their youth counterparts. New Zealand was the only Western country listed that did not experience greater rates in the elderly, with Canada demonstrating this trend in males only and Scotland, Ireland and Northern Ireland in females only (see Table 1).

With suicide rates greatest in the elderly, it is interesting to note a general marked difference between those aged 65–74 years and those 75+. In the Cantor et al. study (1999), rates were greater in 75+ compared to 65–74-year-olds across both genders for 14 of the 23 countries. Ireland was the only country in which 65–74-year-olds had higher rates and in Denmark, Finland, USA, Norway, Canada, New Zealand, Scotland and Northern Ireland only males showed higher rates for those aged over 75 years. In 1998, the rates of Australian males aged 65–74 were 22.0 per 100,000 and 6.0 per 100,000 for females. However, this difference between the young-old and old-old groups has generally been much greater during the 1970s to mid 1990s and it was only this most recent data (1998, in ABS, 1999) that showed a closing of this gap. In fact, this may be a fluctuation that may not be continued in future years.

A further point of interest is the gender ratio differences within these three age groups (see Table 2). In all countries the gender ratio was greater for those aged 75+ than for those aged 65–74 years. In some cases, notably USA and Finland, these ratios were markedly different, whereas for Australia the ratios were quite similar. This is discerning because for most countries there is a greater female population in the over 75 age group and thus the male rate may be overly inflated due to a smaller population. The differences between the youth and 75+ rates vary, with about half the countries having highest ratio differences in the elderly (for example, USA, Belgium, Portugal) and the rest having highest gender ratios in the youth (for example, Ireland, England & Wales, Denmark).

With the recent changes occurring in elderly and youth suicide rates, the fact that these groups have the greatest suicide rates in Australia, and the obvious differences in developmental issues between these populations, a comparison between these age groups seemed warranted to determine how these groups differed or were similar.

Table 1. Rank ordering of mean elderly (aged 75+) to youth (aged 15–24) suicide ratios for 23 Western countries by gender, 1990–1994 (for latest available years)

	Males		**Female**	
Rank	**Country**	**Elderly:Youth**	**Country**	**Elderly:Youth**
1st	Portugal	10.2:1	Hungary	10.9:1
2nd	Hungary	9.1:1	Denmark	9.2:1
3rd	Italy	7.3:1	Germany	7.5:1
4th	Spain	6.8:1	Spain	7.0:1
5th	France	6.7:1	France	5.6:1
6th	Belgium	6.3:1	Portugal	5.5:1
7th	Germany	6.2:1	Italy	5.2:1
8th	Denmark	5.8:1	Greece	4.9:1
9th	Austria	4.9:1	Belgium	4.7:1
10th	Greece	4.0:1	Austria	4.6:1
11th	Sweden	3.9:1	Switzerland	4.0:1
12th	Netherlands	3.8:1	Netherlands	3.3:1
13th	Switzerland	3.5:1	England & Wales	2.8:1
14th	USA	2.5:1	Sweden	2.4:1
15th	Finland	1.7:1	Norway	1.7:1
16th	England & Wales	1.5:1	Australia	1.6:1
17th	Australia	1.3:1	Scotland	1.6:1
18th	Norway	1.3:1	USA	1.6:1
19th	Canada	1.1:1	Finland	1.3:1
20th	Ireland	0.8:1	Ireland	1.2:1
21st	Northern Ireland	0.8:1	Canada	1.0:1
22nd	New Zealand	0.8:1	Northern Ireland	1.0:1
23rd	Scotland	0.8:1	New Zealand	0.7:1

Through such a comparison, a greater understanding of risk factors for these populations may be established which could lead to better and more specific prevention strategies. Several international studies have been conducted in which comparisons have been made between youth and older populations. However these studies usually either focus on youth and so compared their focus group (for example, 15–24, 13–19, etc) with the remaining suicide population (Rich et al., 1986; Eisele et al., 1987), or focused on elderly comparisons (for example, 65+ with the rest of the population) (Vassilas & Morgan, 1994; Heikkinen & Lönnqvist, 1995).

Therefore, the aim of this study was to compare suicides of youth (aged 15–24) specifically with those occurring in the elderly (aged 65+) to determine differences between these two populations. This information can then be used to make meaningful comparisons with more distinct age groupings that could potentially suggest better preventative measures.

In conjunction, a comparison within the elderly age group between 65–74-year-olds and 75+-year-olds was also conducted to determine if differences are unique within the 65+ age group. This seemed pertinent, with the greater rates of suicide in the 75+ compared to 65–74-year-olds, although to ensure greater numbers for analyses, 65+ are usually used in comparisons.

Table 2. Rank ordering of mean youth and elderly suicide ratios for 23 Western countries by gender, 1990–1994 (for latest available years)

Rank	15-24		65-74		75+	
1st	Ireland	7.3:1	USA	5.0:1	USA	9.2:1
2nd	Northern Ireland	7.3:1	Portugal	3.7:1	Finland	7.5:1
3rd	New Zealand	6.3:1	Australia	3.7:1	New Zealand	6.9:1
4th	USA	5.8:1	Canada	3.6:1	Canada	6.1:1
5th	Greece	5.7:1	Greece	3.6:1	Northern Ireland	5.3:1
6th	Finland	5.5:1	Finland	3.5:1	Portugal	4.8:1
7th	England & Wales	5.3:1	Austria	3.3:1	Italy	4.8:1
8th	Canada	5.1:1	Northern Ireland	3.3:1	Greece	4.6:1
9th	Scotland	5.1:1	New Zealand	3.2:1	Ireland	4.6:1
10th	Australia	5.0:1	Italy	2.9:1	Austria	4.1:1
11th	Germany	4.0:1	Ireland	2.9:1	France	4.1:1
12th	Norway	4.5:1	France	2.6:1	Belgium	4.1:1
13th	Switzerland	4.4:1	Spain	2.6:1	Australia	4.1:1
14th	Spain	4.1:1	Hungary	2.5:1	Spain	4.0:1
15th	Austria	3.9:1	Sweden	2.5:1	Switzerland	3.9:1
16th	Denmark	3.9:1	Norway	2.5:1	Sweden	3.7:1
17th	France	3.4:1	Switzerland	2.4:1	Norway	3.5:1
18th	Italy	3.4:1	England & Wales	2.3:1	Germany	3.3:1
19th	Hungary	3.2:1	Scotland	2.2:1	Netherlands	2.9:1
20th	Belgium	3.1:1	Belgium	2.1:1	England & Wales	2.9:1
21st	Portugal	2.6:1	Germany	2.1:1	Hungary	2.7:1
22nd	Netherlands	2.5:1	Netherlands	1.9:1	Scotland	2.7:1
23rd	Sweden	2.3:1	Denmark	1.5:1	Denmark	2.5:1

De Leo and Scocco (2000) suggested that the higher rates in the latter group are possibly due to a greater concentration of more unfavourable life circumstances than those who are younger. Thus, the comparison of the young-old/old-old groups was made.

Method

Data were obtained from the Queensland Suicide Register (QSR) maintained by the Australian Institute for Suicide Research and Prevention (AISRAP). The QSR records all suspected suicides which are committed in Queensland, compiling information from Coroner's reports, Police reports and psychology autopsies designed by AISRAP and completed by police officers (specifically trained for the purpose) during their investigation of a possible suicide. Data were restricted to those people whose usual residence was Queensland and died from suicide during 1994–1996.

Comparisons were made between young elderly (65–74 years) and old elderly (75+ years); and youth (15–24 years) and elderly (65+ years). Due to higher numbers of suicides in youth compared to those aged 75+, the elderly group was extended to include those aged 65+ to enhance the numbers. There were 89 suicides (64 males, 25 females; mean age = 69.69, SD = 2.88) for those aged 65–74; 82 suicides (69 males, 13 females; mean age = 80.65, SD = 4.58) for those aged 75+; 306 suicides (264 males, 42 females; mean age = 20.65, SD = 2.44) for those aged 15–24. There were 171 suicides (133 males, 38 females; mean age = 74.94, SD = 6.67) recorded in total for those aged 65+.

Variables considered for all age groups were gender, alcohol consumption prior to their suicide (yes/no); positive blood alcohol content as shown in post mortem (yes/no); suicide note or other recorded intention of death (yes/no); living alone (yes/no); marital status (married or de facto/divorced or separated/never married/widowed); threat of suicide within last 12 months of their death (once or twice/several times/no times); suicide attempt within last 12 months of their death (yes/no); and psychiatric treatment (yes/no).

Method of suicide was used for both age group comparisons and ICD–9 classifications employed. However, because numbers were insufficient in some age groups, some codes were collapsed or omitted in analyses. For the comparison between youth (15–24) and elderly (65+), methods were categorised as: poisoning by solids/liquids (E950), other gases and domestic gases (E952 and E951), hanging (E953), drowning (E954), firearms (E955), jumping (E957) and all other methods (E958 and E956). For the comparisons between the two elderly groups the jumping and all other methods categories were omitted (due to small numbers).

Place of suicide was also used for both comparisons and was collapsed into three categories. The first category "at residence or with family/friends" encompassed anywhere at own residence or residence of people they knew and was utilised to indicate those people who were likely to be found by someone they knew. Second category "institutions" included prison, hospital or nursing home; and "elsewhere" included bodies of water, in a car other than at residence, hotel, bushland or parks, etc.

The presence of a physical illness was used for both age comparisons but collapsed differently due to small numbers in the older ages. This variable was measured as whether the person had seen a doctor within three months prior to their death for any complaints regarding physical illness. For the youth/elderly comparison, distinctions were made between severity of illness so that the categories were "yes (mild illness)", "yes (serious illness)", "yes (unknown severity of illness)" and "no illness." For the elderly comparison no division was made between the yes categories and thus was collapsed as yes/no.

In addition, five other variables were used to make comparisons between youth and elderly. These were alcohol habit which caused problems (yes/no); suicide attempt made greater than 12 months prior to their death (yes/no); legal trouble about which they were concerned (yes/no); someone in the family or close friend who had attempted or died from suicide (yes/no); and information through the media (newspapers, music, movies etc) which recently caught their attention (yes/no).

Comparisons between age groups and variables were conducted with crosstabs analyses, using the chi-square statistic, through the statistical package SPSS 10.0.5 for Windows. Due to lower numbers in the two elderly groups, some variables were not included in analyses between these age groups.

Logistic regression was conducted on the youth/elderly comparison, as numbers were larger in these groups to accommodate this analysis. Variables included in this analysis were method, gender, alcohol consumption, alcohol habit, suicide note, household composition, threat of suicide, suicide attempt within last 12 months, previous psychiatric treatment, legal trouble and suicide in social group.

Results

Youth (15–24-year-olds) with Elderly (65+-year-olds) Age Groups

A significant difference was found when comparing methods across age groups [$\chi^2(6) = 36.11$, $p < .0005$] (see Table 3 for distributions). Hanging accounted for almost half of the youth suicides, but less than 1/3 of the elderly suicides. The proportion of suicides by poisoning in the elderly was more than twice the percentage of that occurring in youth suicides.

A significant difference was found when comparing gender across the age groups: $\chi^2(1) = 5.67$, $p < .05$. Male suicide in the youth group accounted for 86% whereas 78% of the elderly suicide group were male.

Age group varied significantly by place of suicide [$\chi^2(2)=13.40$, $p<0.001$]. For youth, 62% suicided at place of residence compared to 75% of elderly. In contrast, 33% of youth suicided "elsewhere" and only 17.5% of elderly did the same.

Table 3. Percentage and number of suicides by method and age group, Queensland 1994–1996

Method	Aged 15-24		Aged 65+	
Poisoning by solid/liquids	7.2%	(22)	16.4%	(28)
Other gases (inc. domestic gases)	12.1%	(37)	11.7%	(20)
Hanging	45.1%	(138)	27.5%	(47)
Drowning	1.6%	(5)	8.8%	(15)
Firearms	24.2%	(74)	30.4%	(52)
Jumping	3.6%	(11)	2.9%	(5)
All other methods	6.2%	(19)	2.3%	(4)

Marital status differed significantly by age group, $\chi^2(3) = 216.34$, $p < .0005$. As would be expected the greatest percentage of youth fell into the "never married category" (81%) with only 12% being in married/de facto relationships, and 6.6% separated or divorced. Conversely, 50% of the elderly were married/de facto, 31.5% widowed, 10% never married and 9% divorced/separated.

No significant difference was found between the two groups fof having made a threat of suicide: $\chi^2(2) = 0.73$, $p > .05$. A suicide threat made once or twice within the last 12 months was reported in 30% of the youth and 26% of the elderly. Threats made several times were reported for 24% of the youth and 26% of the elderly and no threats occurred in 46% of the youth and 49% of the elderly.

When analyzing the two age groups for recent physical illness, a significant difference was found [$\chi^2(3) = 101.47$, $p < .0005$]. Percentage distributions were fairly similar between the two groups for "mild" (15% for youth and 19% for elderly) and for "unknown severity" (7% for both youth and elderly). However, greater discrepancies were found within the "none" and "serious" categories, with 73% of the youth having been indicated as having no illness and 5% having a serious illness, while 17% of the elderly were reported to have no illness and 58% a serious illness. The percentage, number and chi-square statistic for the remaining variables are in Table 4.

The logistic regression used those variables that produced significant differences between the two age groups. A positive blood alcohol content was not included, as the results were too similar to alcohol consumption, which was included. Likewise, only suicide attempt within 12 months was included as this variable had less missing data and is more reliable than suicide attempt greater than 12 months. Marital status was also excluded due to its potential for confounding effects as it easily discriminates between the two groups for categories of "widow" and "never married." The analysis was conducted on those subjects who had no missing data across all variables, making a total sample of 138.

Table 4. Variables of suicide – percentage and chi-square statistic by age group (15–24 and 65+), Queensland, 1994–1996

	Aged 15–24		Aged 65+		Chi square Statistic*
Variable	**Yes**	**No**	**Yes**	**No**	
Alcohol consumption	47% (125)	53% (143)	19% (26)	81% (111)	χ^2=29.67 p<0.0005
Alcohol habits caused problems	38% (70)	62% (115)	8% (8)	92% (89)	χ^2=27.85 p<0.0005
Positive blood alcohol content	43% (101)	57% (136)	23% (26)	77% (87)	χ^2=12.72 p<0.0005
Suicide note	36% (104)	64% (187)	42% (69)	58% (94)	χ^2=1.93 n.s.
Lived alone	12% (24)	88% (179)	39% (45)	61% (71)	χ^2=31.68 p<0.0005
Suicide attempt < 12 months	27% (56)	73% (155)	15% (18)	85% (102)	χ^2=5.87 p<0.05
Suicide attempt > 12 months	20% (38)	80% (156)	7% (8)	93% (103)	χ^2=8.45 p<0.01
Psychiatric treatment	44% (86)	56% (109)	53% (60)	47% (54)	χ^2=2.10 n.s.
Legal troubles	37% (72)	63% (122)	5% (5)	95% (103)	χ^2=38.54 p<0.0005
Social group attempted/ completed suicide	19% (37)	81% (162)	8% (10)	92% (108)	χ^2=6.01 p<0.05
Media informed about suicide	10% (19)	90% (170)	5% (6)	95% (107)	χ^2=2.10 n.s.

*degrees of freedom = 1

Table 5 shows the logistic coefficients for the variables that were included in the final regressive model equation. Applying this model, the overall percentage of correctly predicted subjects was 79%, with 13% of the youth incorrectly classified as elderly and 30% of the elderly incorrectly classified as youth.

Young-Old (65–74-Year-Olds) Compared with Old-Old (75+-Year-Olds)

No significant differences were found when comparing the two elderly groups across gender, method of suicide (see Table 6), place of suicide or threat of suicide. However, marital status did differ significantly, $\chi^2(3) = 8.51$, $p < .05$. Similar percentages were found between the two groups for married/defacto (54% and 45%, respectively) and divorced/separated (9% for both groups), with greater percentage discrepancies found between never married (14.5% versus 4.5%, respectively) and widowed (22% versus 42%, respectively).

Table 5. Logistic coefficients with variables in the equation

Variables	Coefficient (B)	S.E.	Wald statistic	df	significance	R	Exp (B)
Alcohol habit	-1.34	0.65	4.21	1	0.04	-0.11	0.26
Lived alone	1.97	0.67	8.61	1	0.00	0.19	7.19
Legal trouble	-1.45	0.74	3.84	1	0.05	-0.10	0.23
Physical illness			22.78	3	0.00	0.30	
1	-2.11	0.97	4.74	1	0.03	-0.12	0.12
2	-0.49	1.04	0.22	1	0.64	0.00	0.62
3	0.59	1.02	0.33	1	0.57	0.00	1.80
Suicide site			7.66	2	0.02	0.14	
1	1.58	0.57	7.63	1	0.01	0.17	4.85
2	0.91	1.30	0.49	1	0.48	0.00	2.49
Constant	-0.25	0.95	0.07	1	0.79		

Table 6. Percentage and number of suicides by method and age group, Queensland 1994–1996

Method	Aged 65–74		Aged 75+	
Poisoning by solid/liquids	22.0%	(18)	12.5%	(10)
Other gases (inc. domestic gases)	11.0%	(9)	13.8%	(11)
Hanging	26.8%	(22)	31.3%	(25)
Drowning	8.5%	(7)	10.0%	(8)
Firearms	31.7%	(26)	32.5%	(26)

The distribution and chi-square statistic for the remaining comparisons between the two elderly groups are in Table 7. Previous psychiatric treatment was the only variable to reach significance. Frequency distribution was considered for psychiatric diagnosis for those people who had received psychiatric treatment to determine if there may have been differences between the age groups according to diagnosis. A greater percentage of the 75+-year-olds were diagnosed with depression (73%), compared with the 65–74-year-olds (64%). However, all of those classified as having multiple diagnoses were also diagnosed with depression, thus percentages for those with depression overall were 75% for 65–74-year-olds and 77% for those aged 75+.

Discussion

A direct comparison between youth (15–24-year-olds) and elderly (65+) age groups using the psychological autopsy method had not previously been conducted. Differences between age groups have, in the past, generally been made between the targeted age group and the rest of the suicide population. By making more distinct groups of elderly and youth, comparisons seem to be more meaningful. Further, subdividing the 65+ group into young-old (ages 65–74) and old-old (75+) was done to gain a greater understanding in this highly at risk age group.

There has been some concern about the quality of psychological autopsy studies on elderly populations. However, Younger et al. (1990) found that in an examination of 145 suicides in Cook County, Illinois, approximately 90% of suicides were identified by medical examiner's records as having informants who had recent contact and knew about the suicide victim. Nevertheless, the use of the psychological autopsy method to older age suicide is a relatively recent occurrence (Pearson et al., 1999).

Youth (15–24) Compared with Elderly (65+) Age Groups

Within the comparison between youth and elderly, many significant differences emerged. A significant difference for youth and elderly persons in relation to gender

Table 7. Variable of suicide – percentage and chi-square statistic by age group (65–74 and 75+), Queensland, 1994–1996

	Aged 65–74				Aged 75+				Chi-square Statistic*
Variable	**Yes**		**No**		**Yes**		**No**		
Alcohol consumption	21%	(15)	79%	(56)	17%	(11)	83%	(55)	χ^2=0.44 n.s.
Positive blood alcohol content	30%	(18)	70%	(42)	15%	(8)	85%	(45)	χ^2=3.53 n.s.
Suicide note	45%	(37)	55%	(46)	40%	(32)	60%	(48)	χ^2=0.35 n.s.
Lived alone	33%	(20)	67%	(40)	45%	(25)	55%	(31)	χ^2=1.56 n.s.
Suicide attempt < 12 months	16%	(10)	84%	(52)	14%	(8)	86%	(50)	χ^2=0.13 n.s.
Psychiatric treatment	62%	(37)	38%	(23)	43%	(23)	57%	(31)	χ^2=4.15 $p<0.05$
Physical illness	78%	(51)	22%	(14)	88%	(57)	12%	(8)	χ^2=1.97 n.s.

* degrees of freedom = 1

distribution was found. However, it was thought that this difference may reflect population figures, of which 51% of 15–24-year-olds and 45% of 65+-year-olds were male (and closely resembled the 86%/78% split of youth/elderly male suicides).

A post hoc chi-square test showed no difference between the distributions of the suicides and populations [$\chi^2(1) = 4.13$, $p > .01$], suggesting that the association between gender and age was similar to that in the general population. Due to the large population numbers necessary in this calculation, the p value was taken at 0.01 to avoid type I error. Gender differences were not found either when comparing 13–19-year olds with those aged 20+ in a study of teenage suicide in King County Washington (Eisele et al., 1987).

The more violent methods of hanging and firearms were most popular in both populations, although hanging accounted for almost half of the youth and less than 1/3 of the elderly. The lower lethal methods of poisoning by solids and liquids and drowning were also more common in the elderly, accounting for 23.2% of elderly suicides compared with only 8.9% in the youth age groups. This may be due to elderly people being less able to be revived from such methods, due to poorer health and less resilience. This is in contrast to other research which has found that elderly populations are more likely to use lethal methods than youth (Lester, 1994; Harwood & Jacoby, 2000). This claim is further supported by a lower incidence of suicide attempts in the elderly (Pearson et al,, 1997). Our data does support this later concept, with a significantly greater proportion of suicide attempts in the youth age groups within 12 months prior to the suicide as well as greater than 12 months prior to the death.

Age groups differed significantly regarding alcohol consumption prior to the suicide. Almost half of the youth group (47%) had consumed alcohol before their death, whereas, less than 1/5 of the elderly group (19%) had done so. This was further demonstrated by a significant difference being found between the two age groups for having a positive blood alcohol content at the time of their death with 43% of the younger group having a positive blood alcohol content compared to 23% of the older group. The differences in percentages between these two variables is due to larger numbers of missing data for "positive blood alcohol content" as a result of no toxicology screens conducted for these cases. However, the similar percentages and significant differences offers some reliability to the finding that younger persons are more likely to have consumed alcohol, and have possibly been intoxicated, prior to their death.

Further, a significantly greater proportion of the youth group (38%) were identified as having an alcohol habit which caused problems than the elderly group (8%). Therefore, the consumption of alcohol at the time of death may have been due to the person's regular intake or use of such means as a solution to problems.

The age groups did not differ in regards to having left a suicide note. A suicide note was left by 36% of the youth group and 42% of the elderly. Other studies have also found little differences between age groups and suicide notes (Eisele et al., 1987; Quan & Arboleda-Florez, 1999).

In much of the literature, elderly suicides have typically been associated with living alone and being isolated. Although studies have refuted this concept (Younger et al., 1990; Clark, 1993), current study lends some support to this idea, with a significantly greater amount of elderly people (40%) living alone than youth (12%). It must be considered that the greater percentage of elderly suicides living alone may be associated with widowhood [which has often been associated with high suicide rates (ABS, 1994; Cantor & Slater, 1995)]. Not surprisingly, marital status differed significantly across the two age groups, mainly due to the vast differences between youth and elderly for the "widowhood" and "never married" categories. Although over 80% of the youth were classified as never married, only 10% of those never married were living alone. This contrasts with the elderly group who were widowed (33%) having 66% living alone. Thus, this loss may have been more influential to the suicide, than living alone per se. However, many studies have found interpersonal loss to be related to youth rather than older age group suicide (Rich et al., 1988; Heikkinen & Lönnqvist, 1995).

In addition, a greater percentage of elderly people were found to have suicided at their place of residence. This could reflect the greater percentage of elderly people living alone which makes discovery and the chances of prevention/resuscitation less likely.

Elderly suicides were significantly more likely to have a recent physical illness than youth age groups (measurement based on whether the person had seen a doctor 3 months prior to their death for any complaints regarding physical illness). Physical illness is often cited as more common in elderly suicides (Vassilas & Morgan, 1994; Quan & Arboleda-Florez, 1999). However, Clark (1993) stated that most elderly persons who die from suicide are not in worse health than their peers. It would seem reasonable that the elderly group would have been significantly more likely to have attended a doctor than the youth group as an older population is more prone to illness. However, there were little differences between the two age groups when analyzed for illnesses which were categorised as mild or of an unknown severity. Indeed the most profound differences occurring between the groups for those who had not attended a doctor were 73% for youth, 17% for elderly, and differences for those with a serious illness were 8% for youth and 59% for elderly). This makes the finding more reliable in suggesting that illness may have played a contributing role in the elderly person's suicide.

No differences were found between the two age groups when examining the data for previous psychiatric treatment. Approximately 44% of the youth and 53% of the elderly age groups had been identified as ever having had previous psychiatric treatment. It has been reported that elderly people rely more often on GPs when feeling depressed than mental health services (Pearson et al., 1997). Although the previous psychiatric treatment variable does not preclude self-referral to a GP, it is inevitably more difficult to ascertain whether a person went to their GP for psychological or physical reasons. Indeed, ambiguity surrounding the nature of a person's visit to their GP may well contribute to an underestimation of the true amount of psychiatric care received by elderly people. This may be further evidenced by the greater percentage of elderly seeking medical treatment prior to their death, as mentioned above.

Significantly more of the youth group (37%) were identified as having been worried about legal trouble compared with only 5% of the elderly. Similarly, Rich et al. (1988) found greater numbers of youth (aged under 30) who had legal problems when compared with those aged over 30.

Almost 20% of the younger age group were identified as having known someone in the family or close friend who had attempted or completed suicide compared with 8.5% of the elderly age group. A comparison study of teenage suicides versus suicides in people aged over 20 by Eisele et al. (1987), found no significant differences when analyzing for family history of suicide. However, the percentage of family suicide was similar in their age groups (16% versus 20%, respectively) when compared with our youth group. The idea of modelling behaviour in the youth cannot be discounted, although no firm conclusions can be made without more detailed investigations regarding completed versus attempted suicide, relationship to the person, and length of time from known person's suicide to their suicide. In general however, no differences were found between the age groups when examining the data for modelling behaviour effects brought about through recent media.

A logistic regression was conducted to try and quantify the probability of predicting the age group of suicide deaths. Five variables were extracted which were good predictors: Alcohol habit, living alone, legal trouble, physical illness and suicide site. Using these predictors, almost $^4/_5$ of the sample were correctly classified according to their age group. Physical illness had the highest partial contribution to the model (as seen in Table 5). This confirms our initial findings and that of many other studies, which have found physical illness to be a significant factor of elderly suicide (see above discussion).

Young-Old (65–74) Compared with Old-Old (75+) Age Groups

The two elderly age groups were found to differ in relation to previous psychiatric treatment. A greater percentage (62%) of the 65–74-year-olds had a history of psychiatric treatment than the 75+-year-olds (43%). This could reflect a greater percentage of 75+-year-olds going to GPs rather than psychiatrists, perhaps indicating that relatives were less aware of their psychological well-being, as was discussed with youth-elderly comparisons. However, it may be a true reflection of the age groups with the oldest group not having sought treatment either because they were less in need, or less inclined to seek treatment due to associated (or perceived) stigma, not knowing how to access appropriate help, or financial concerns. In Quan & Arboleda-Florez's study of elderly suicide (1999), 17.4% of men aged 55–64 had a mental illness compared with 6.9% of 75+ men, suggesting that perhaps our sample of 75+-year-olds were indeed less in need of psychiatric care.

Depression was the major diagnosis for both age groups, with approximately ¾ of those people who had had psychiatric treatment receiving this diagnosis. Depression is frequently cited as more often associated with older suicides than younger suicides (Conwell et al., 1996) and it often goes unrecognised or untreated (De Leo et al., 1999). This latter point may add credence to the previous finding of differences between psychiatric treatment, with the oldest age group less inclined to seek treatment.

Marital status was also found to differentiate the two groups, with a greater percentage of the 75+-year-olds, understandably, having been widowed and more surprisingly, a greater percentage having never been married than those aged 65–74. However the numbers in the never married category (11 for 65–74-year-olds, and 3 for 75+) were too small to make any firm conclusions about this influence on suicidal behaviour.

Limitations of the Study

There are several limitations inherent in the psychological autopsy. Firstly, it is a retrospective exercise, gathering second-hand information (Cohler & Jenuwine, 1995). Knowing that the death resulted from suicide may influence the responses given to the police by informants, as they may shape their answers to fit with what they believe the profile of a suicide should be. This is especially true for elderly suicides in which dementia may be attributed to the suicide, as younger people may perceive this to be a situation which would lead to suicide (De Leo, 1996). However, many studies have shown that suicide rates are low in people with Alzheimer's and other related diseases (see for example, Harris & Barraclough, 1997).

Secondly, because the data for the QSR is gathered by police officers, this may also influence the quality of the information as police may be more inclined to record the information which they perceive to be the most useful. However, with the structured questionnaire and the training and experience which police officers have in completing these questionnaires, this may not be as great a concern.

Thirdly, missing data is inevitable when using outside sources (police) to gather data and relying on informants with varying degrees of knowledge about the person who had died. No matter how well the informant knew the person, if the person had become more withdrawn due to depression or was generally a secretive person, information regarding psychiatric and medical care, for example, may not be fully known. However, all analyses were conducted on data with ample numbers to render the statistics reliable.

Fourthly, our results showed and confirmed those of previous studies, namely that living alone, being widowed and physical illnesses were risk factors for elderly suicide and further, were statistically more so than for youth age groups. However, all of these situations are common occurrences in later life (Pearson et al., 1999). Thus, without comparisons to the general elderly population or a control group of deaths of elderly people due to causes other than suicide, then firm conclusions about elderly suicide cannot be easily made.

Recommendations and Further Research

Due to the many differences found between the elderly and youth age groups, it is evident that these populations are not the same, and thus should not be treated as such when constructing and implementing, prevention and intervention strategies. Previous suicide attempts, problematic alcohol consumption and illegal behaviour were all variables which youth had significantly greater incidence of than elderly age groups. Therefore, programs aimed at youth groups should be more focussed toward their outward behaviour. Suicide prevention strategies could be implemented at the first signs of legal or alcohol problems with young people, with intervention strategies definitely needed after suicide attempts. De Leo and Scocco (2000) inicated that suicide prevention schemes aimed at elderly suicide attempters are not as affective as when implemented for youth, because with less suicide attempters in the elderly, these schemes would be acting on a smaller risk population.

Preventative and intervention strategies for elderly people could be focussed on GP involvement. Strategies aimed at increasing GP awareness of depression and suicidal ideation in the elderly can be justified in light of the greater number of elderly people visiting GPs within 3 months prior to their death, and the reticence of the elderly towards seeking psychiatric treatment. A study in Gotland found that after an educational program to increase the knowledge about diagnosis and treatment of patients with affective disorders was introduced to all GPs on the Swedish island the suicide rate decreased significantly in the following year (Rutz et al., 1989). There may be many implications for such an approach in relation to elderly suicide in Australia.

Further research may consider comparing elderly suicides with control groups of elderly deaths by other means. This would help determine if the risk factors, which we found to be more distinct in elderly versus youth suicides, are particular to this suicide population or simply general factors that discriminate between elderly and youth age groups, regardless of the reason for death.

In addition, with suicide rates in Australian youth being comparable if not greater than that of elderly suicides, differences between youth and elderly (with distinct age groupings) should be considered in other countries where elderly rates are much greater than those of youth age groups.

Conclusion

In conclusion, the elderly appear to be more at risk of suicide due to a higher incidence of physical illness. Additionally, the elderly age group reveals a clear division that suggests that the younger elderly age groups have a greater history of mental illness compared with their older elderly counterparts (75+-year-olds). In contrast, youth age groups are more at risk due to problematic behaviour, such as alcohol and legal problems, and have a more extensive history of suicide attempts and knowledge of associates who have attempted or completed suicide.

Although missing data and informant bias can make data obtained from psychological autopsies unreliable, several variables were considered separately to increase the reliability of the general findings (for example, variables for alcohol consumption). These findings confirm that although high suicide rates in both youth and elderly age groups require effective intervention and prevention strategies, these strategies need to be distinct to provide for the differences in risk factors related to suicide in the different age groups. Further, comparisons between age groups in suicide research needs to consider more distinct age groupings rather than comparing the focus age group to "everyone else."

References

Australian Bureau of Statistics. (1994). *Suicides, Australia 1982–1992* (ABS Catalogue no. 3309.0). Canberra: Government Printing Office.

Australian Bureau of Statistics. (1999). *Causes of Death, Australia* (ABS Catalogue no. 3303.0). Canberra: Government Printing Office.

Cantor, C. H., Neulinger, K., & De Leo, D. (1999). Australian suicide trends 1964–1997: Youth and beyond? *Medical Journal of Australia, 171,* 137–141.

Cantor, C. H., & Slater, P. J. (1995). Marital breakdown, parenthood and suicide *Journal of Family Studies, 1,* 91–102.

Clark, D. C. (1993). Narcissistic crises of aging and suicidal despair. *Suicide Life-Threatening Behavior, 23,* 21–26.

Cohler, B. J., & Jenuwine, M. J. (1995). Suicide, life course and life story. *International Psychogeriatrics, 7,* 199–219.

Conwell, Y., Duberstein, P. R., Cox, C., Herrmann, J., Forbes, N. T., & Caine, E. D. (1996). Relationships of age and axis I diagnosis in victims of completed suicide: a psychological autopsy study. *American Journal of Psychiatry, 153,* 1001–1008.

De Leo, D. (1997). Suicide in late life at the end of the 1990s: a less neglected topic? *Crisis, 18,* 51–52.

De Leo, D. (2000). *Suicidal Behaviours at the Dawn of the New Millennium.* Inaugural Professorial Lecture. Griffith University Public Lecture Series, 8th June, Brisbane, Australia.

De Leo, D., Hickey, P. A., Neulinger, K., & Cantor, C. H. (1999). *A Hidden Problem: Suicide in Older Men in Queensland* (DFYCC Publication No. 99–0270). Brisbane: Queensland Government.

De Leo, D., & Scocco, P. (2000). Treatment and prevention of suicidal behaviour in the elderly. In K. Hawton & K. van Heeringen (Eds.), *The International Handbook of Suicide and Attempted Suicide.* Oxford: John Wiley & Sons, pp. 555–570.

De Leo, D. (1996). Dementia, insight and suicidal behavior. *Crisis, 17,* 147–148.

Eisele, J. W., Frisino, J., Haglund, W., & Reay, D. T. (1987). Teenage suicide in King County, Washington. II. Comparison with adult suicides. *American Journal of Forensic Medicine and Pathology,* 8, 210–216.

Goldney, R. D., & Harrison, J. (1998). Suicide in the elderly: Some good news. *Australasian Journal on Ageing, 17,* 54–55.

Harris, E. C., & Barraclough, B. M. (1997). Suicide as an outcome for mental disorders. *British Journal of Psychiatry, 170,* 205–228.

Heikkinen, M. E., & Lönnqvist, J. K. (1995). Recent life events in elderly suicide: A nationwide study in Finland. *International Psychogeriatrics, 7,* 287–300.

Lester, D. (1994). Are there unique features of suicide in adults of different ages and developmental stages? *Omega: Journal of Death and Dying, 29,* 337–348.

McCall, P. L. (1991). Adolescent and elderly white male suicide trends: Evidence of changing well-being? *Journal of Gerontology, 46,* S43–S51.

Pearson, J. L., Caine, E. D., Lindesay, J., Conwell, Y., & Clark, D. C. (1999). Studies of suicide in later life: Methodologic considerations and research directions. *American Journal of Geriatric Psychiatry, 1,* 203–210.

Pearson, J. L., Conwell, Y., Lindesay, J., Takahashi, Y., & Caine, E. D. (1997). Elderly suicide: A multi-national view. *Aging and Mental Health, 1,* 107–111.

Quan, H., & Arboleda-Florez, J. (1999). Elderly suicide in Alberta: difference by gender. *Canadian Journal of Psychiatry, 44,* 762–768.

Rich, C. L., Fowler, R. C., Fogarty, L. A. & Young, D. (1988). San Diego suicide study. *Archives of General Psychiatry, 45,* 589–592.

Rich, C. L., Young, D., & Fowler, R. C. (1986). San Diego suicide study. *Archives of General Psychiatry, 43,* 577–582.

Rutz, W., von Knorring, L., & Wålinder, J. (1989). Frequency of suicide on Gotland after systematic postgraduate education of general practitioners. *Acta Psychiatrica Scandinavica, 80,* 151–159.

Vassilas, C. A., Morgan, H. G. (1994). Elderly suicides' contact with their general practitioner before death. *International Journal of Geriatric Psychiatry, 9,* 1008–1009.

WHO (1999). *Figures and Facts About Suicide.* Geneva: Author.

Younger SC, Clark DC, Oehmig-Lindroth R, Stein RJ. (1990) Availability of knowledgeable informants for a psychological autopsy study of suicides committed by elderly people. *Journal of the American Geriatric Society* 38: 1169-1175

Suicide in the Canadian Elderly

Antoon Leenaars

Windsor, Ontario, Canada, and University of Leiden, The Netherlands

Introduction

Older adults have consistently had the highest rate of suicide in many countries across the world (Gulbinat, 1996). It is a leading cause of death for people over the age of 55 in the United States (U.S.) and Canada. Given the extent of the problem, the paucity of integrated and sound empirical information is remarkable. This paucity is even greater in Canada than the U.S.

Our intent here is to present an overview of what is known about suicide in the Canadian elderly. The following will be discussed: i) Suicide rates in Canada in comparison with the United States, with specific reference to the elderly/older adult; ii) An outline of what is known about suicide in older adults in Canada, with special reference to the federal report, *Suicide in Canada* (1987); iii) A model for understanding suicide in older Canadians (and Americans), with focus on differences in older adults compared with other adults; iv) A note on Canadian research on intervention with older Canadians, with special discussion on means restriction; and v) Finally, we will address what needs to be done in Canada.

Suicide Rates in the Elderly in Canada and the United States: Are They the Same or Different?

It is often assumed that Canada is quite similar to the United States since these two countries share not only close proximity but also similar languages and cultural backgrounds. However, despite a vast number of commonalities, there is remarkable divergence between them. Differences between the United States and Canada have been observed in such areas as recognition of authority, patterns of deviance, achievement motivation, and patterns of association and marriage (Hiller, 1982; Spencer, 1985). Most comparative studies, however, between Canada and the United States have little relevance to suicidal behaviors.

Suicide is also often assumed to be similar in Canada and the United States. Labovitz and Brinkerhoff (1977) had pointed out in the 1970's that the rates of suicide were the same. Leenaars (1989), in the mid 1980's, questioned whether the suicide rates are similar today in Canada and the United States. Leenaars and Lester

(1992) designed a study to empirically explore the rates and patterns of suicide between Canada and the United States, for 1960–1988, a period for which comparative data were available. This is not only important for its own sake, but also because a number of suicidologists have emphasized the importance of understanding the suicidal act in the culture within which it occurs (Counts, 1991; Shneidman, 1985). Such comparisons allow one to take a perspective on suicide and suicidal phenomena that is different from the one within one's own country. In addition, such an approach has a direct implication for prevention and/or service delivery.

The Leenaars and Lester study (1992) will be augmented here with more current data, for 1950 to 1992 in the U.S. and 1993 in Canada. To make our study more meaningful than just comparing rates, we decided to present the following: i) rates (defined as incidence per 100,000) by year, 1950–1990's for both sexes; and ii) patterns by chronological age for both sexes, 1960 and 1990.

The data for the United States were obtained from the annual volumes published by the National Center for Health Statistics, *Vital Statistics of the United States*, 1950–1988. The data for Canada were obtained from Canada's Health and Welfare's report, *Suicide in Canada* (1987), supplemented with the more current data from Statistics Canada, (annual). *Suicide in Canada* represented the final report of Canada's National Task Force on Suicide.

These data sources are the official statistics on suicide in both countries. It may be argued that the use of such official data is problematic, because data collection and death certification procedures in the United States and Canada may differ. There is, however, no evidence for or against this hypothesis, and no study is likely to be forthcoming on it. Moreover, time trends *within* each nation are not going to be affected by differences in death certification *between* the nations.

A more general problem is the use of national mortality statistics themselves. Suicide statistics are collected, compiled, and published from governmental agencies. Although such suicide statistics have been criticized with respect to bias and underreporting (Leenaars, 1989; McIntosh, 1992), the evidence is not undisputed (e.g., Sainsbury & Jenkins, 1982). It is likely that although such governmental figures do not present a totally accurate picture, they may be viewed as the most conservative estimates (McIntosh, 1992). It should also be pointed out that they are the only systematically available data in Canada and the United States.

From the epidemiological data (see Figure 1) the annual suicide rates for men and women for Canada and the United States show that up to 1971, the reported suicide rates for both sexes were lower in Canada than the United States. However, from 1977 on, the suicide rates in Canada were greater than the suicide rates in the United States. It is likely that Labovitz and Brinkerhoff's conclusion (1977) that the rates are similar is dated. The rates of suicide in Canada are different, and higher since 1977, than in the United States. Thus, Canadians suffer one type of violence more, that is, suicide.

For men in both nations, the trend has been for an increasing suicide rate since 1960, with the suggestion of ongoing fluctuation in Canada since 1983. For women, the suicide rates in both nations appear to be decreasing slightly since the 1980's. It would appear that predictions that the suicide rate of women would increase in recent years as women supposedly gained more equal social and economic equality with men (Lester, 1979) are not borne out by the data in both countries.

Figure 1. Suicide rates for males and females for Canada and the United States

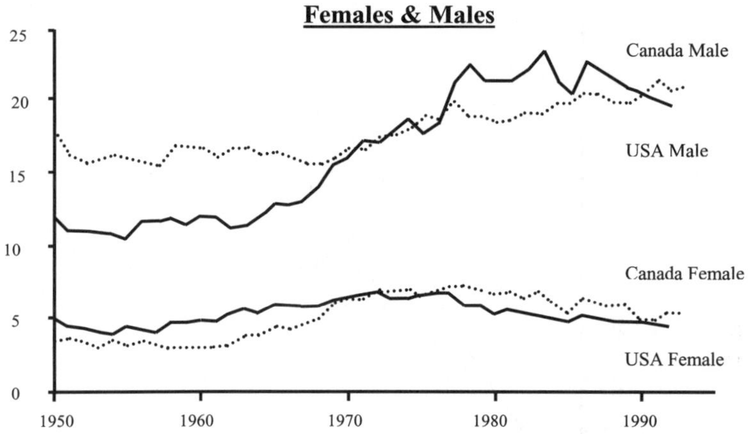

Figure 2. Suicide rates for females in Canada and the United States

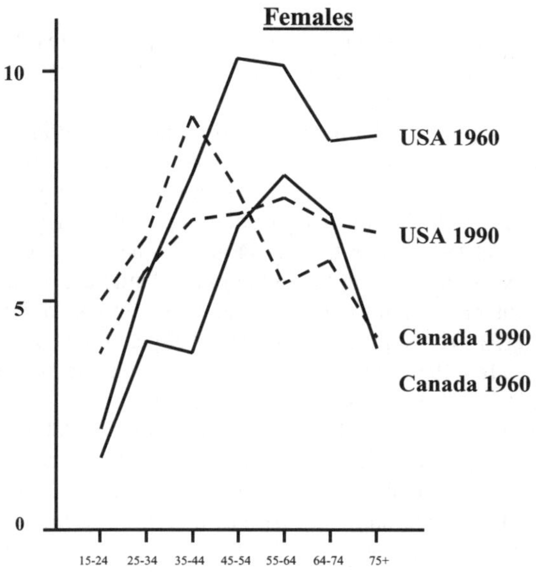

Figure 3. Suicide rates for males in Canada and the United States

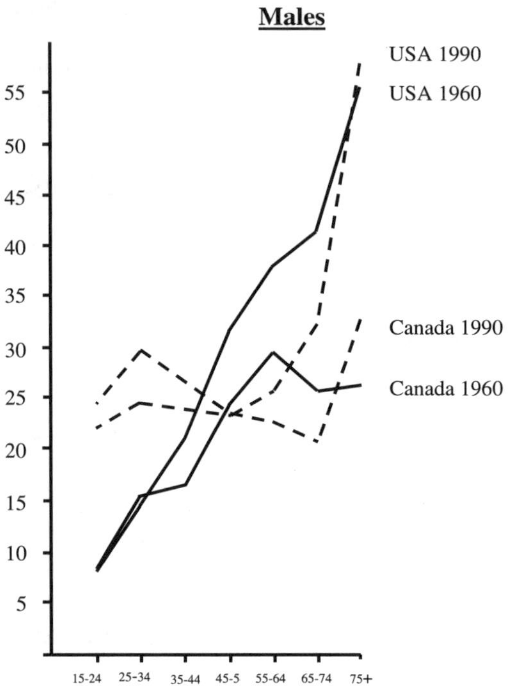

One way of viewing the current patterns is by age. Figures 2 and 3 present the changing patterns of suicide by age for Canada and the U.S. For both nations, rates for 1960 and 1990, thirty years apart, are presented.

For women (see Figure 2), the patterns have remained overall unimodal (i.e., one peak), with a peak in middle age, for both nations and both eras. However, in Canada, the peak appears to be moving toward a younger age group, not the elderly. The peak now is in the 35–44 age group, whereas in 1960 it was 55–64. In the U.S., the peaks in 1960 and 1990 are in the 45–54 and 55–64 age range. Thus, since 1960 to 1990, differences are not only noted in the rates of suicide, but also the age groups at risk. In 1980, this pattern, not the rates, was more similar in the U.S. and Canada (Leenaars & Lester, 1992), suggesting that the changes in female suicides in Canada occurred by 1990, after 1980. Yet, it is of note with the topic at hand that the elderly females in both nations, are not the highest risk group.

For men (see Figure 3), both Canada and the United States experienced a tremendous increase in the suicide rates of men aged 15–34 during this thirty year period. The rise was especially notable for those aged 20–24 (i.e., young adults) whose rates shifted from the unimodal pattern in 1960 to a bimodal (i.e., two peak) pattern in the early 1980's (Leenaars & Lester, 1992a). In 1990, the bimodal pattern is especially evident in Canada. Peaks occur in the younger group and the elderly. The results concur with observations and predictions by McGinnis (1987) and Leenaars (1989a, 1991) that young adult males are and will be a very high-risk group for suicide in both countries, warranting greater prevention and/or service delivery.

The data, thus, show a very important phenomenon; namely, that the suicide rates of late adolescents and young adults for both sexes in both countries have increased dramatically since 1960, especially in Canada. The rate of suicide, in fact, for Canadian males, ages 15–19, has been 50 to 60% higher than the United States today. Young adults of both sexes, however, have an even higher rate than late adolescents. It is the males in this age group that are at very high risk. However, although older adults have a very high rate of suicide in both nations, it is the age group with the highest rate in the U.S., even slightly higher in 1990 than 1960. Be that as it may, as noted by Leenaars (1989a), young adult males in Canada now have a very high rate of suicide across the life span in that country. The females equally show an increase since 1960. Alarmingly, the data indicate that the rates of suicide are continuing to increase for these age groups.

The results clearly show that Canada has its own unique problem. It appears that currently the suicide rate is higher in Canada than the United States, with the shift occurring around the early 1970's. The elderly are one of the highest risk groups, along with the young, in males, but not females. In the U.S., the elderly males are clearly the highest risk group. They are not *the* highest at-risk group in Canada. Females in middle age are the highest risk group in Canada (and the U.S.).

Our results clearly show that the rates and patterns of suicide in Canada and the United States are different. It appears that currently the suicide rates of the elderly males are high in both nations. However, the rates for the elderly are lower in Canada. In the U.S., the older adult males are the highest at-risk group; whereas, in Canada, in males it is both the young and old. For females in Canada and the U.S., the highest at-risk group is those in middle age. Lepine (1982) had presented earlier a detailed outline of the rates of suicide in the elderly in Canada. Mishara (1991) has also made recent observations on the high rates of the elderly males. The study of the epidemiology, however, warrants greater focus in Canada since this has been largely neglected in Canada compared with the United States, especially with regard to the elderly. We believe, on a different note, that caution is warranted about generalizing research on suicide in the elderly from the United States to Canada, and probably, by implication, any nation. A cultural approach is needed in the epidemiology of suicide across the globe.

As a footnote, it should be noted that Canada and the United States are not homogeneous countries. Statistics for Canada and the United States show considerable variation; for example, provinces, and states. Even within both countries, there are high risk groups (e.g., Aboriginal people). Yet this should not obscure the fact that comparisons between nations are meaningful by themselves.

What Is Known about Suicide in Canada?

To begin, there is little known about suicide in the Canadian elderly. The National Task Force report, *Suicide in Canada* (1987), identifying Canadian older adults as a high risk group, provided little content that was unique to Canadia. In fact, the title of that document should be, "Suicide in Canada from American data." Studies by Sakinofsky (1976a, 1976b, 1982, 1983), and Syer-Solursh and Wyndowe (1981) are the exceptions. The problem in Canada is that we simply do not know much about suicide in the Canadian elderly; this government document reflects that fact.

The early studies by Sakinofsky (1976 a & b, 1982, 1983) focused on the rates of suicide in Canada. He showed then already that the risk for suicide peaks in the post-70 age group in Canada, particularly for the males; that increase in the rate of suicide in the elderly has ceased, after a particular rise after the 1950's; and that the high rate of suicide in older Canadians may be associated to the choice of lethal methods in this age group. Syer-Solursh and Wyndowe (1981), however, have cautioned Canadians about the accuracy of mortality data in Canada, noting that underreporting may well have been a major problem for this age group. Of course, accuracy of data is a global issue, not uniquely a Canadian issue. A recent update on the federal report reflects a no better situation than the first issue.

An on-line bibliographic citation list generated by SIEC (Suicide Information and Education Centre), Canada's foremost literature retrieval service, together with our own recent publications, produced only 8 additional professional articles on the Canadian elderly, not cited in the first edition of the document *Suicide in Canada*. Of course, it is possible that we may have omitted some publications. There are no known peer-review articles in the French language in Canada (R. Boyer, personal communication, March 13, 1999). The eight articles located, provide the following: various information on provincial (regional) rates, a study of attempts in the elderly, a study of the association between social factors and suicide, a study on the poor knowledge of the elderly about suicide, a note on the attitudes toward suicide by the elderly in Canada and a note on the association of poverty to suicide.

Agbayewa (1993) reported that in British Columbia the elderly had a disproportionately high rate of suicide in that province. However, he noted considerable variation within the province with regions that did not show that trend. Agbayewa (1993) showed that the variation was consistent with population size, with rural areas having higher rates. He speculated that economic factors may account for the trends.

Jarvis and Boldt (1980) reported a study on a another province, Alberta. Alberta, like British Columbia, has a high rate of elderly suicide. Jarvis and Boldt (1980) suggested that physical illness may be associated to the rates, but mainly in men. For women, they offered a closer association to mental illness. Drugs and alcohol were less frequently associated with the suicide of older Albertans than younger Albertans. Jarvis and Boldt (1980) also suggested that the use of lethal means was highly related to the rate of suicide in older people in Alberta.

Bagley and Ramsay (1993), studying the elderly in Calgary, Alberta, suggested that suicide in the elderly was less associated to mental illness in the elderly than in younger people.

Sendbuehler and Goldstein (1977) reported that the rate of attempted suicide in the elderly was low. Among the elderly, suicide attempt groups were found to have more physical illness. They also found a high rate of organic brain syndrome. Mental illness was also cited.

Leenaars and Lester (1995) studied the association of social factors (divorce, birth rates, marriage rates) and economic factors (unemployment) to suicide. For older males, suicide rates were higher in times when unemployment was higher, divorce was more common, and birth rates were lower. For older women, rates of suicide were associated with divorce and birth rates. However, of note, they also reported that the power of the social and economic variables in predicting was less in the elderly than in the young in Canada.

Leenaars, Saunders, Balance, Wenckstern and Galgan (1991) studied the level of knowledge of Canadian elderly on facts and myths about suicide. They found that older people in Canada know much less about basic facts than the general population.

Evans, Fogle and McDonald (1987) reported that the prevailing attitude towards suicide by the Canadian elderly was a permissive one.

Finally, Leenaars and Lester (1998) examined suicide rates and socio-economic factors in the elderly in each province of Canada. They found that suicide rates were higher in provinces where elderly people had higher incomes, yet where a greater percentage of elderly had low incomes. The question that they, thus, raised is whether elderly people living in poverty in the wealthier provinces have the highest suicide rates.

Of course, the above studies have methodological concerns. For example, older adult and related terms, were used differently. This and other concerns warrant caution about how accurate of a picture the research on suicide in the Canadian elderly to date actually is. Be that as it may, the few studies cited so far – and one to be discussed later – is the extent of our professional knowledge of suicide in older adults in Canada. Simply asked: Is the current knowledge on suicide in the Canadian elderly an accurate picture? The answer is most likely, "no."

How Can We Understand Suicide in the Older Adults in Canada?

Concerning the document *Suicide in Canada*, like most literature this document attributes suicide in the Canadian elderly singularly to one or two factors, such as aging or inadequate income. But as with suicide at all stages of the life span, suicide in the elderly is probably better understood as a multi-dimensional malaise (Leenaars, 1988, 1996; Shneidman, 1985). Research in Canada shows that this is as true in Canadians as in Americans (Leenaars, 1992).

Suicide is a multidimensional malaise in older adults. It is not simply a psychopathological entity in the DSM-IV (American Psychiatric Association, 1994). We do not agree with those who point to an external stress as the cause of suicide. We also do not agree that it is only pain. We tend to place the emphasis on the multideterminant nature of suicide. Suicide is *intrapsychic*. It is not simply the stress or even the pain, but the person's inability to cope with the event or pain. The issue of any schema about human personality, that is, personology (Murray, 1938), is one that makes an individual an individual. It should be the study of the whole organism, not only the stress or pain. People, for example, do not simply complete suicide because of old age, but because it is unbearable; they are mentally constricted; they cannot cope, and much more.

However, from a psychological view, suicide is not only intrapsychic, it is also *interpersonal*. Individuals are interwoven. We live in a world. We disagree with those who point to only some intrapsychic aspects such as anger turned inward or primitive narcissism. Suicide occurs between people (or relationships to some similar ideal). Metaphorically speaking, suicide is an intrapsychic drama on an interpersonal stage.

To begin, suicide can be clinically understood in older adults from at least the following concepts (Leenaars, 1988, 1996).

Intrapsychic

Unbearable Psychological Pain

The common stimulus in suicide is unendurable psychological pain (Shneidman, 1985). The suicidal person is in a heightened state of perturbation, a *psychache* (Shneidman, 1993). Although, as Menninger (1938) noted, other motives (elements, wishes) are evident, the person primarily wants to flee from pain experienced in a trauma, a catastrophe. The suicide, as Murray (1967) noted, is functional because it abolishes pain.

Cognitive Constriction

The common cognitive state in suicide is mental constriction, rigidity in thinking, narrowing of focus, tunnel vision, and concreteness (Shneidman, 1985). The person is figuratively "intoxicated" or "drugged" by the constriction. The suicidal person exhibits at the moment before his/her death only permutations and combinations of a trauma (e.g., poor health, death of a spouse). This constriction is one of the most dangerous aspects of the suicidal mind.

Indirect Expressions

The suicidal person is ambivalent. There are complications, concomitant contradictory feelings, attitudes and/or thrusts, often toward a person and even toward life. The person experiences humility, submission, devotion, subordination, flagellation and sometimes even masochism. Yet, there is much more. What the person is conscious of is only a fragment of the suicidal mind; there are vast unconscious processes (Freud, 1917/1974; Leenaars, 1988, 1993).

Inability to Adjust

People with all types of problems, pain, losses, and so forth, are at risk for suicide. Depressive disorders, manic-depressive disorders, anxiety disorders, schizophrenic disorders, panic disorders, borderline disorders, psychopathic disorders, have been related to suicides (Sullivan, 1962, 1964; Leenaars, 1988). Depressive disorders may well be the most frequent. Suicidal people, in fact, see themselves as unable to adjust. Their state of mind is incompatible with accurate discernment of what is going on.

Ego

The ego, with its enormous complexity (Murray, 1938), is an essential factor in the suicidal scenario. The Oxford English Dictionary (OED) defines ego as "the part of the mind that reacts to reality and has a sense of individuality". Ego strength is a protective factor against suicide. Suicidal people, however, frequently exhibit a relative weakness in their capacity to develop constructive tendencies and to overcome their personal difficulties (Zilboorg, 1936). The person's ego has likely been weakened by a steady toll of traumatic life events (e.g., loss, rejection, abuse, failure). This implies that a history of traumatic disruptions – *pain* – placed the person at risk for suicide.

Interpersonal

Interpersonal Relations

The suicidal person has problems in establishing or maintaining relationships (object relations). There frequently is a disturbed, unbearable interpersonal situation in which psychological needs are frustrated, thwarted or unfulfilled. Suicide appears to be often related to an attachment need, although other needs, often more intrapsychic, may be equally evident, for example, autonomy, dominance, honor (Shneidman, 1985).

Rejection-Aggression

The rejection-aggression hypothesis was first documented by Stekel in the famous 1910 meeting of the Psychoanalytic Society in Freud's home in Vienna (Friedman, 1910/1967). Loss is central to suicide; it is, in fact, often a rejection that is experienced as an abandonment. It is an unbearable narcissistic injury. Within the context of a deep ambivalence, suicide may become the turning back upon oneself of murderous impulses (wishes, needs). Suicide may be murder in the 180th degree (Shneidman, 1985).

Identification-Egression

Freud (1917/1974, 1920/1974, 1921/1974) hypothesized that intense identification with a lost or rejecting person or, as Zilboorg (1936) showed, with any lost ideal (e.g., health, youth, employment, freedom) is crucial in understanding the suicidal person. Identification is defined as an attachment (bond), based upon an important emotional tie with another person (object) (Freud, 1920/1974) or any ideal. If this emotional need is not met, the suicidal person experiences a deep pain (discomfort) and wants to egress, that is, to leave, to be gone, to be elsewhere.

The question that here arises is whether this schema is applicable to the elderly? Shneidman and Farberow (1957), in the first controlled study of suicide notes, indicated that psychological aspects of suicide vary with age, implying that a developmental perspective is essential in suicidology. Leenaars (1989) designed a study to investigate if the schema, using 60 suicide notes, was applicable to specific adult age ranges (Young Adulthood, Middle Adulthood, Older Adulthood). He found that there were more similarities on the psychological dimensions across the adult life span than differences. However, differences were also noted. About the intrapsychic drama, we learned that people in young and middle adulthood are more indirect and ambivalent in their suicide (Indirect Expression). Or the converse, the elderly are more direct, showing less redirected aggression, complications, and unconscious implications. Maybe older adults are less confused about their suicide, having a stronger ongoing wish to die. Leenaars (1989) reported other differences, many not associated to the elderly. Young adults, for example, appear to be less able to cope with life's demands (Inability to Adjust) and appear to exhibit more often a weakened ego (Ego).

The interpersonal stage differs also in some ways. We learned that Interpersonal Relations are more often critical in young adulthood although it is pivotal to remember that "object relations" are common in all suicides. There are, however, gender differences in the elderly. Of note, however, in the elderly, males equally often make note of loss, abandonment than the younger adults, not the older females.

We can, thus, tentatively conclude that the perspective outlined, including validation with a Canadian sample (Leenaars, 1992), is applicable across the adult life span. These are some probable commonalities or similarities. The specific differences, however, may reflect age-specific stressors or concerns that may be important in understanding suicide, including in the elderly. Specific differences across the adult life span, of course, are an issue of more or less, not presence or absence (Leenaars, 1988; Bauer, et al., 1997).

Our main conclusion is in support of the theory that there may be more psychological similarities in suicide than differences. It may be useful to look at the core psychological aspects, both intrapsychic and interpersonal, from an older adult developmental perspective, but the underlying commonalities across the life span appear equally meaningful (Shneidman, 1991). Indeed, greater psychological commonalities than differences are to be expected in all suicidal events, by virtue of their human quality (Shneidman, 1991). Yet, as predicted by developmental theory (Erikson, 1963, 1968; Leenaars, 1991) and as the studies show, there may be aspects that are distinctly age specific. Each suicide, including of the elderly, must still be understood with awareness that some of the distinctiveness between suicide may well be a reflection of developmental age. The psychological as well as social study of suicide in the elderly is necessary.

Intervention: What Have We Learned in Canada about the Elderly?

To answer the question: Almost nothing is known about intervention with the suicidal elderly in Canada, with one important exception. Although suicide intervention in Canada predates the arrival of the white man (Leenaars et al., 1997), the two common tactics in this century for preventing suicide have been individual treatment (with medications and psychotherapy) of suicidal individuals and the establishment of suicide prevention centers/programs. Canada has in modern times developed both approaches to prevention. Psychiatric emergency services were already established in the late 1960's by Isaac Sakinofsky (Howe & Sakinofsky, 1979; Miller, Sakinofsky & Steiner, 1979). A distress centre was established in 1967 in Toronto with the first, we believe, established in Sudbury by Rev. Bruce McDougall (Leenaars et al., 1997). Recent research (Leenaars & Lester, 1995) shows positive trends of such centres in reducing the rates of suicide in Canada. Specific programs, which are truly Canadian, have been in place for decades; for example, Canadians have developed special efforts to address suicide in youth (Wenckstern, Leenaars & Tierney, 1995). However, little has specifically focused on the elderly, and nothing on effectiveness of the two traditional approaches. A third avenue, which has been suggested to prevent suicide, is to restrict the availability of lethal means (Clark & Lester, 1989). It is research on the third tactic that is the important exception.

In the last couple of decades, a popular proposal for reducing the incidence of suicide has been restricting the availability of methods for committing violence (i.e., means restriction), which is simply called controlling the environment. Stengel (1964) was one of the first to propose this as a means for decreasing the incidence of suicide, noting that the detoxification of domestic gas (from coal gas with a high carbon monoxide content, to natural gas) might have reduced the suicide rate in the nations where the switch had taken place. Subsequent research on the detoxification of domestic gas in England supported Stengel's proposal (Kreitman, 1976), and the research has been extended to the detoxification of car exhaust and to the restriction of firearms (Clarke & Lester, 1989).

Countries differ in the most popular method for suicide, but firearms are the preferred method in some, including Canada and the United States. In the United States, Lester (1984) found that states with the stricter gun control laws had lower rates of suicide using guns but similar rates of suicide by other methods, suggesting that strict gun control laws reduced the suicide rate and that people did not switch to any great extent to other methods for suicide when guns were less readily available.

An opportunity for studying the effects of strict gun control laws on their use for suicide in Canada is provided by Canada's Criminal Law Amendment Act of 1977 (Bill C-51), enforced since 1978. This Act required acquisition certification for all firearms, restricted the availability of some types of firearms to certain types of individuals, set up procedures for handling and storing firearms, required permits for those selling firearms, and increased the sentences for firearm offenses.

Lester and Leenaars (1993) reported on the preventive effect on suicide from the Act on suicide in Canada as a whole, with no evidence that switching to alternative methods for suicide took place. This result was supported by Carrington and Moyer (1994) who analyzed the impact of the Act in each of the Canadian provinces.

Lester (1994), in reviewing suicide prevention tactics, suggested that many of these tactics may not be effective in people of different ages. For example, the elderly do not typically contact suicide prevention and crisis intervention services, and educational programs on suicide are usually directed at school children rather than adults. This raises the question, therefore, of whether the restriction of firearms in Bill C-51 in Canada had a preventive impact for those of various ages or only for some ages. Specifically, we can ask, did Bill C-51 impact on the elderly? Leenaars and Lester (1997) designed a study to answer this question.

Data were obtained from Statistics Canada (annual) for the period 1969 to 1985 on suicides committed in Canada by each method. Suicide rates for the total Canadian population were calculated for ten-year age groups, permitting a comparison of the period 1969–1976 prior to the passage and enforcement of Bill C-51 with the period 1978–1985 after its passage.

The data and results on suicide rates prior to and after the passage of Bill C-51 show that the firearm suicide rate of the total population increased after the passage of the Act, from 4.27 per 100,000 per year to 4.72; the suicide rate by all other methods increased also, from 7.85 to 9.40. However, the percentage of suicides decreased after passage of the Act, from 35.2% to 33.4%. Furthermore, whereas prior to the passage of the Act, the firearm suicide rate was increasing (the slope of the regression line was 0.16), after passage of the Act the firearm suicide rate began to decrease (the slope of the regression line was -0.13).

The effect of passage of the Act as a function of the age of the suicide, however, shows that the firearm suicide rate decreased after passage of the Act only for suicides aged 35–64, whereas the firearm suicide rate increased for those aged 15–34 and 64+. The percentage of suicides using firearms decreased only for those aged 15–64, while it increased for those aged 65+. Thus, the general conclusion seems to be that the impact on suicide of making the gun control laws stricter in Canada was not apparent in those over the age of 65.

Stengel (1964) predicted that, although the restriction of guns would lead to a lowering of the overall rate of suicide, it may lead to a compensating use of other methods (e.g., drugs). Our study provides an interesting comment on Stengel's (1964) speculation. For the overall suicide rate in Canada, whereas the results indicated a lower percentage of suicides used guns for suicide after the passage of the Act, there was no significant reduction in the absolute firearm suicide rate or the total suicide rate. There was, however, a suggestion that, after passage of the Act, there was the beginning of a decline in the firearm suicide rate. When the age of the suicides was taken into account, the limited beneficial impact of passage of the Act was present only for those under the age of 65. Canadians over the age of 65 showed no reduction in the use of firearms for suicides.

This result appears consistent with clinical observations about suicide in the elderly. Shneidman and Farberow (1957) and, more recently, Leenaars (1992) have argued that the suicidal elderly have a stronger intent to die than younger adults and are less ambivalent about the death. Older people more often appear to have a chronic course in their suicidal intent. Perhaps individuals with less ambivalence in their suicidal actions are less inclined to be dissuaded by increased difficulty in obtaining their preferred method for suicide?

This result, in connection with other research (see Lester, 1992), suggests that three of the major tactics presently in operation for preventing suicide are less effective with the elderly than with younger adults – suicide education programs, telephone-oriented suicide prevention, and crisis intervention services, and restriction of the availability of lethal means for suicide, although whether this is true in all nations is not known. Yet, it can be concluded that much more thought must be given to devising tactics for preventing suicide in the elderly in Canada and elsewhere (see Leenaars et al., 1992; Richman, 1993).

What are the Views on the Right-to-Die in Canada?

In Canada, as elsewhere, there are questions about whether suicide and assisted suicide are the same and/or different? The right-to-die debate is, in fact, a critically important issue in Canada. It is controversial. There is growing support for the right-to-die process; in fact, more so in Canada than in the United States (Leenaars & Domino, 1993). As recognized by the 1995 report of the Special Senate Committee on Euthanasia and Assisted Suicide, there is a strong belief in Canada that the issue must be reflected on and discussed. There are numerous questions in Canada such as, given the increasing limitations in available health services, “Are we willing to provide the services that terminally ill people need?” We already know that the poorest elderly in Canada are at greatest risk for suicide (Leenaars & Lester, 1998).

Attempted suicide was a crime in Canada until 1972. Currently the Criminal Code of Canada (Criminal Code R.S.C 1985, C46, as amended) states that assisted suicide and euthanasia are, however, illegal. Canada’s law holds that societal rights predominate over individual ones, although the right-to-die debate has begun to question such a law. There have been test cases, the most noteworthy was Sue Rodrigues (Young, 1998). Mrs Rodrigues had Amyatrophic Lateral Sclerosis (ALS) and asked that a medical doctor provide her with the means to end her life, if she wished. In *Rodrigues vs British Columbia* (1994), Mrs Rodrigues’s motion was denied; yet, the minority opinion strongly supported the sanctity of life; Justice Sopinka for the majority stated:

> The long standing blanket prohibition is S.241(b), which fulfils the government's objective of protecting the vulnerable, is grounded in the state interest in protecting life and reflects the policy of the state that human life should not be depreciated by allowing life to be taken. (Quoted in Young, 1998, p. 437).

The minority opinion, however, supports the act, if certain "strict conditions" were met (such as applicant be fully disabled) and called for Canada's parliament to rewrite the law. A subsequent Senate hearing was equally controversial, although it suggested that a separate definition of euthanasia, assisted suicide and suicide be made in Canada. This is, in fact, a critical issue in Canada; What is a suicide and what is not? (Leenaars, 1998) As elsewhere, there is a needs for clear definition and understanding. Indeed, years ago, the case of Nancy B (*Nancy B v. Hotel Dieu de Quebec*, 1992) brought forward the issue of the right of refusal of medical treatment. In that case, the court ruled that Nancy B could refuse treatment – a significant change in Canada's view on the right-to-die, as there had been strong opposition to withdrawal and refusal, until that decision.

A persistent question that has been raised in Canada is whether Canadians have sufficient understanding of the issues (Leenaars, 1998). The issues are not only controversial but evasive and complex. Be that as it may, the views are clear about some matters. America's Jack Kevorkian killed one Canadian, Austin Bastable (Leenaars & Diekstra, 1997), a person who did not suffer from a terminal illness. There is no – or little – acceptance of such murders in Canada. Yet, as the minority opinion at both the provincial British Columbia level and federal Supreme Court level, there is support for the right-to-die, under strict conditions. In all probability, Canada's view will develop, especially as medical intervention continues to prolong life, well beyond Nature's intent.

What Are the Needs in Canada?

Where do we begin? The needs are so obvious, all too many Canadian older people, especially males, are dying by their own hands. Yet, despite the need, little is going to be done in Canada – at least, in this way, the United States has more resources available for its elderly. Canada lacks in its support for research of the elderly, as across the life span, in suicidology (Leenaars, 1989).

From a research perspective, there is a lot of research to do in suicide in the elderly and across the life span in Canada; yet, it is unlikely to occur. Maris (1993) has noted that very little funding for research is available in the U.S. Canada's problem is even worse. There is a lack of research, productive universities and private funding institutions (Lipset, 1990). Government funding bodies refuse to support research in suicide; yet, this is a reflection of Canada's refusal to support research in general. Canada's support for research is on a per capita basis and is among the lowest in the major countries reporting to the Organization for Economic Cooperation and Development (Lipset, 1990). Support is less in the 1990's than in the 1980's. Support in the 1980's was lower than in the 1970s. Canada lacks a history of support for research. This is as true about the elderly as in all age groups. We know little about suicide in the elderly in Canada. In all probability, this will also be true in the next century.

References

Agbayewa, M. (1993). Elderly suicide in British Columbia: An exploration of regional variation and related factors. *Canadian Journal of Public Health, 84,* 231–236.

American Psychiatric Association. (1994). *Diagnostic and statistical manual of mental disorders* (DSM-IV) (4th ed.). Washington, D.C.: Author.

Bagley, C., & Ramsay, R. (1993). Suicidal ideas and behavior in contrasted generations: Evidence from a community mental health survey. *Journal of Community Psychology, 21,* 26–34.

Bauer, M., Leenaars, A., Berman, A., Jobes, D., Dixon, J., & Bibb, J. (1997). Late adulthood suicide: A life span analysis of suicide notes. *Archives of Suicide Research, 3* (2), 91–108.

Carrington, P., & Moyer, S. (1994). Gun availability and suicide in Canada. *Studies on Crime and Crime Prevention, 3,* 168–178.

Clarke, R., & Lester, D. (1989). *Suicide: Closing the exits*. New York: Springer-Verlag.

Colarusso, C., & Nemiroff, R. (1981). *Adult development*. New York: Plenum.

Counts, D. (1991). Suicide in different ages from a cross-cultural perspective. In A. Leenaars (Ed.), *Life-span perspectives of suicide*. New York: Plenum.

Domino, G., & Leenaars, A. (1995). Attitudes toward suicide among English-speaking urban Canadians. *Death Studies, 19* (5), 489–500.

Erikson, E. (1963). *Childhood and society* (2nd ed.). New York: W.W.Norton.

Erikson, E. (1968). *Identity: Youth and crises*. New York: W.W. Norton.

Evans, A., Fogle, D., & McDonald, C. (1987). Cultural attitude toward suicide of the aged. *Proceedings of the 20th annual conference of the American Association of Suicidology* (pp. 90–91). Denver: American Association of Suicidology.

Freud, S. (1974). A case of homosexuality in a woman. In J. Strachey (Ed. & Trans.), *The standard edition of the complete psychological works of S. Freud*, Vol. XVIII (pp. 147–172). London: Hogarth. (Original published in 1920)

Freud, S. (1974). Group psychology and the analysis of the ego. In J. Strachey (Ed. & Trans.), *The standard edition of the complete psychological works of S. Freud*, Vol. XVIII (pp. 67–147). (Original published in 1921)

Freud, S. (1974). Mourning and melancholia. In J. Strachey (Ed.), *The standard edition of the complete psychological work of S. Freud*, Vol. XIV (pp. 239–260). London: Hogarth. (Original published in 1917)

Friedman, P. (1967). *On suicide*. New York: International Universities Press. (Original published in 1910)

Gulbinat, W. (1996). The epidemiology of suicide in old age. *Archives of Suicide Research, 2,* 31–42.

Health and Welfare, Canada. (1987). *Suicide in Canada*. Ottawa: Department of National Health and Welfare.

Hiller, H. (1982). *Society and Change: S.D. Clark and the Development of Canadian Sociology*. Toronto: University of Toronto Press.

Howe, A., & Sakinofsky, I. (1979). A short-stay intensive care multi-disciplinary unit for parasuicides. *Proceedings 10th international congress of suicide prevention and crisis intervention, 2,* 34–38.

Jarvis, G., & Boldt, M. (1980). Suicide in later years. *Essence, 4,* 145–158.
Kimmel, D. (1974). *Adulthood and Aging*. New York: Wiley.
Kreitman, N. (1976). The coal gas story. *British Journal of Preventive & Social Medicine, 30,* 86–93.
Leenaars, A. (1988). *Suicide notes*. New York: Human Sciences Press.
Leenaars, A. (1989). *Rates and patterns of suicide for Canada and the United States: Their implications for socio-political action*. Presidential address presented at Canadian Association for Suicide Prevention Conference, Toronto, Ontario.
Leenaars, A. (1992). Suicide notes from Canada and the United States. *Perceptual and Motor Skills, 74,* 278.
Leenaars, A. (1993). Unconscious processes. In A. Leenaars (Ed.), *Suicidology: Essays in honor of Edwin Shneidman* (pp. 127–147). Northvale, NJ: Aronson.
Leenaars, A. (1996). Suicide: A multidimensional malaise. *Suicide and Life-Threatening Behavior, 26,* 221–236.
Leenaars, A. (Ed.). (1991). *Life span perspectives of suicide*. New York: Plenum.
Leenaars, A., & Lester, D. (1992). A comparison of rates and patterns of suicide in Canada and the United States, 1960–1988. *Death Studies, 16,* 433–440.
Leenaars, A., & Lester, D. (1995). The changing suicide pattern in Canadian adolescents and youth, compared to their American counterparts. *Adolescence, 30,* 541–547.
Leenaars, A., & Lester, D. (1997). The impact of gun control on suicide and homicide across the life span. *Canadian Journal of Behavioural Science, 29,* 1–6.
Leenaars, A., & Lester, D. (1998). Predicting suicide rates among elderly persons in Canadian provinces. *Psychological Reports, 82,* 1202.
Leenaars, A., Boldt, M., Connors, E., Harnisch, P., Harrington, G., Litofsky, K., Kiddy, K., Krawll, M., Osberg, B., Ramsay, R., Sakinofsky, I., & Winch, G. (1997). History: Vignettes of the development in suicide prevention. In A. Leenaars., S. Wenckstern., I. Sakinofsky., R. Dyck., M. Krawl., & R. Bland (Eds.), *Suicide in Canada*. Toronto: University of Toronto Press.
Leenaars, A., Maris, R., McIntosh, J., & Richman, J. (Eds.). (1992). *Suicide and the older adult*. New York: Guilford.
Leenaars, A., Saunders, M., Balance, W., Wenckstern, S., & Galgan, R. (1991). Knowledge about facts and myths of suicide in the elderly. *Gerontology & Geriatrics Education, 12,* 61–68.
Lepine, L. (1982). *Suicide among the aged in Canada*. Ottawa: Dept. of National Health & Welfare.
Lester, D. (1984). *Gun control*. Springfield, IL: Charles Thomas.
Lester, D. (1992). *Why people kill themselves* (3rd ed.). Springfield, IL: Charles Thomas.
Lester, D. (1994). Are there unique features of suicide in adults of different ages and development stages? *Omega, 29,* 337–348.
Lester, D., & Leenaars, A. (1993). Suicide rates in Canada before and after tightening firearm control laws. *Psychological Reports, 72,* 787–790.
Lipset, S. (1990). *Continental divide*. New York: Routledge.
Maris, R. (1993). The evolution of suicidology as a professional discipline. In A. Leenaars (Ed.), *Suicidology: Essays in honor of Edwin S. Shneidman* (pp. 3–21). Northvale, N.J.: Aronson.
McIntosh, J. (1992). Epidemiology of suicide in the elderly. In A. Leenaars., R. Maris., J. McIntosh., & J. Richman (Eds.), *Suicide and the older adult*. New York: Guilford.
Miller, J., Sakinofsky, I., & Steiner, D. (1979). The family and social dynamics of adolescent parasuicide. *Proceedings 10th international congress of suicide prevention and crisis intervention, 2,* 122–134.
Mishara, B. (1991). Suicide in the elderly. In B. Wigdor., & S. Fletcher (Eds.), *Mental health and aging,* (pp. 85–95). Ottawa: National Advisory Council on Aging.
Murray, H. (1938). *Explorations in personality*. New York: Oxford University Press.

Murray, H. (1962). Death to the world: The passions of Herman Melville. In E. Shneidman (Ed.), *Essays in self-destruction* (pp. 3–29). New York: Science House.
Nancy B v. Hotel Dieu de Quebec, 69 C.C.C. (3d) 450 (1992)
National Center for Health Statistics. (annual). *Vital statistics of the United States*. Washington, D.C.: United States Government Printing Office.
Neugarten, B., Moore, J., & Lowe, J. (1965). Age norms, age constraints, and adult socialization. *American Journal of Sociology, 70,* 710–717.
Richman, J. (1993). *Preventing elderly suicide*. New York: Springer.
Rodrigues vs British Columbia, 85 C.C.C. (3d) 15 (Attorney General, 1994)
Sainsbury, P., & Jenkins, J. (1982). The accuracy of officially reported suicide statistics for purposes of epidemiological research. *Journal of Epidemiology and Community Health, 36,* 43–48.
Sakinofsky, I. (1976a). *Depression in the elderly*. Paper presented at the Coming of Age conference, Toronto, ON.
Sakinofsky, I. (1976b). *Suicide and depression in the elderly*. Paper presented at the Canadian Association on Gerontology conference, Toronto, ON.
Sakinofsky, I. (1982). Review of Lepine's "Suicide among the aged in Canada." *Canada's Mental Health, 30,* 16–17.
Sakinofsky, I. (1983). *The relationship between provincial suicide rates in men and women in Canada to social and demographic factors*. Hamilton: McMaster University.
Sendbuehler, J., & Goldstein, S. (1977). Attempted suicide among the aged. *Journal of the American Geriatrics Society, 25,* 245–248.
Shneidman, E. (1985). *Definition of suicide*. New York: Wiley.
Shneidman, E. (1991). The commonalities of suicide across the life span. In A. Leenaars (Ed.), *Life span perspectives of suicide* (pp. 39–52). New York: Plenum.
Shneidman, E. (1993). *Suicide as psychache*. Northvale, NJ: Aronson.
Shneidman, E., & Farberow, N. (Eds.). (1957). *Clues to suicide*. New York: McGraw-Hill.
Spencer, M. (1985). *Foundations of modern sociology*. Scarborough, Ontario: Prentice-Hall, Canada.
Statistics Canada. (annual). *Mortality data of Canada*. Ottawa: Author.
Stengel, E. (1964). *Suicide and attempted suicide*. Baltimore, MD: Penguin.
Sullivan, H. (1962). Schizophrenia as a human process. In H. Perry., N. Gorvell., & M. Gibbens (Eds.), *The collected works of Harry Stack Sullivan*, Vol. II. New York: Norton.
Sullivan, H. (1964). The fusion of psychiatry and social sciences. In H. Perry., N. Gorvell., & M. Gibbens (Eds.), *The collected works of Harry Stack Sullivan*, Vol. II. New York: Norton.
Syer-Solursh, D., & Wyndowe, J. (1981). *How coroners' attitudes towards suicide affect certification procedures*. Toronto: Ontario Ministry of the Solicitor General.
Wenckstern, S., Leenaars, A., & Tierney, R. (Eds.). (1995). *Suicide prevention in Canadian schools: A resource*. Calgary, AB: Canadian Association for Suicide Prevention.
Zilboorg, G. (1936). Suicide among civilized and primitive races. *American Journal of Psychiatry, 92,* 1347–69.

Euthanasia: The Australian Experience

Robert Goldney

Adelaide University and The Adelaide Clinic, South Australia, Australia

Introduction

For nine months in the Northern Territory of Australia in 1996/1997 euthanasia was legally sanctioned. Considerable emotional and political activity were aroused, leading to it being overturned by Australian Commonwealth legislation. It is now time to reflect on this experience in order that we may learn from it.

After providing definitions of actions that are sometimes subsumed under the broad term euthanasia, this review examines attitudes of health professionals to euthanasia in Australia over the last twelve years in order to give an indication of the social/medical environment in which this law arose. Then it provides a chronology of events, both leading to the enactment of the law and to its overturn. Clinical information about those who died under this law will then be provided. Finally, comment will be made about the whole experience, focusing particularly on the question posed recently by Battin (1998): "Physician-Assisted Suicide: Safe, Legal, Rare?"

Definitions

Euthanasia is a deceptively simple term, but a term which can have different meanings for different individuals, a fact eloquently stated by Kelleher (1998) in his article entitled "Humpty Dumpty and the language of euthanasia." In the Australian context, Kuhse et al. (1997) have noted that euthanasia has traditionally been defined broadly using the Vatican's definition of "an action or an omission which of itself or by intention causes death, in order that all suffering may in this way be eliminated" (Catholic Church, 1980). However, this broad definition encompasses at least five clinical situations which have been more precisely elucidated by van der Maas et al. (1991, 1996).

Euthanasia can be considered specifically as "the administration of drugs with the explicit intention of ending the patient's life, at the patient's request"; physician-assisted suicide is "the prescription or supplying of drugs with the explicit intention of enabling the patient to end his or her own life"; ending of life without the patient's explicit request is "the administration of drugs with the explicit intention of ending the patient's life, without a concurrent, explicit request by the patient"; alleviation of pain and symptoms with opiods is "the administration of doses large enough so that there was a probable life-shortening effect"; and a decision not to treat is "the withholding or withdrawing of potentially life-prolonging treatment."

Such a delineation of actions appears to have face validity, certainly from the clinical point of view, but, as will become apparent, few Australian studies have examined anything other than the broader definition.

The Australian Context

One of the first studies in Australia to examine medical attitudes to euthanasia was conducted in 1987, although not reported until 1998 by Baume. In a survey of 2,000 doctors in New South Wales and The Australian Capital Territory, of those 63.6 percent who responded, 56.1 percent thought a change in the law regarding "voluntary euthanasia" was desirable and 44.6 percent thought that a request to hasten death was sometimes rational. It was of note that at that time, 10.5 percent of doctors acknowledged that they had hastened death in some manner which they were not required to specify.

A more recent survey of doctors' attitudes to "euthanasia" was conducted in 1993 by Hassan (1995) and involved a 10 percent sample of all doctors practicing in South Australia. There was a 68 percent response rate and 48 percent acknowledged that they had received a request from patients to withdraw treatment and 33 percent had received a request for active steps to be taken to hasten the patient's death. Of those doctors surveyed, 44 percent considered that active steps "could ever be right" and, with regards to the withdrawal of treatment ever being right, 65 percent of doctors considered that that was the case. In contrast to the 10.5 percent of New South Wales and Australian Capital Territory doctors who had acknowledged having taken active steps to hasten a patient's death in 1987, 19 percent of doctors in South Australia acknowledged having done so by 1993.

Another important group of professionals who inevitably are intimately involved in decisions about euthanasia is the nursing profession. In a recently published survey of 2,000 nurses, of whom 61 percent responded, Kitchener (1998) reported that 71 percent considered that "active voluntary euthanasia" was "sometimes right", and 67 percent thought that the law should be changed to allow that. In the perhaps more pertinent question of whether or not they would be involved in euthanasia, 66 percent said that they would be involved in a general sense; 30 percent said that they would give a patient drugs in order that the patient could take them him or herself; and only 14 percent indicated that they would administer such medication.

A more detailed Australian study by Kuhse et al. (1997), was modelled on the methodology reported by van der Maas et al. (1991, 1996), with the previously noted clear delineation of different interpretations of euthanasia. However, there was an important difference in that the Australian study was an anonymous postal survey, whereas the Netherlands study was a face to face interview. Kuhse et al. (1997)

indicated that that was necessary as euthanasia was neither legal nor officially condoned in Australia and therefore anonymity was required. It could also be argued that anonymity would allow practitioners to respond in a more open manner than would a face to face interview.

Using the clearly defined criteria, Kuhse et al. reported that 1.8 percent of deaths in Australia could be considered euthanasia; 0.1 percent could be considered physician-assisted suicide; 3.5 percent could be considered an end of life decision by the doctor without the patient's request; and no less than 30.9 percent and 28.6 percent of deaths respectively could be considered related to the alleviation of pain with drugs in high enough doses to hasten death or a decision taken not to treat the patient. They noted that the figures for euthanasia and physician-assisted suicide were similar in Australia to those in the Netherlands, but that the decision of a doctor to end a patient's life without the patient's request was taken more often in Australia, as were the decisions to use high doses of drugs which would hasten death and not to treat, thereby hastening death. Kuhse et al. noted that these figures tended to support the view that the liberalization of euthanasia in the Netherlands had not been associated with an increase in deaths in the broader euthanasia sense, and in fact the ostensibly less liberal Australian environment resulted in more such deaths.

These reports reflect the clinical situation in Australia at the time of the introduction of the Northern Territory legislation. It is also fair to note that euthanasia had received a considerable degree of general publicity as well as professional interest. It was in such a climate of professional and public opinion that legislation had been mooted in a number of different States, but it was only in the Northern Territory that such legislation was enacted.

The Northern Territory Legislative Process

The legislative process, both in terms of the development of the Northern Territory Act and its overturn by the Parliament of the Commonwealth of Australia, have been described in detail by Quirk (1998). However, the basic facts are as follows.

On February 1st, 1995 the Chief Minister of the Northern Territory announced that an Act, which was to be known as the Rights of the Terminally Ill Act, would be introduced to parliament. This was done initially on the 22nd of February and on May the 24th, 1995 it passed its second reading by the narrowest of margins, 12 votes to 11. The following day it passed its third reading and on June 16th, 1995 it became law. However, subsequent legal challenges and private members bills in the Northern Territory led to uncertainty about the validity of the Act and it was not until those challenges were defeated that the Act came into operation on July 1st, 1996.

Requirements of the Act

There were a number of requirements which had to be met before euthanasia could be legally undertaken. Thus the person had to be over the age of 18 and of "sound mind"; that person had to be experiencing pain and suffering; and two doctors, one of whom had to be a psychiatrist, and each of whom had to have had more than five years experience, had to have assessed the patient.

For the purposes of the Act the definition of terminally ill was: "an illness which in reasonable medical judgement will, in the normal course, without application of extraordinary measures or of treatment unacceptable to the patient, result in the death of the patient."

Other requirements included the patient being aware of the nature and course of his or her illness with treatment; the patient must have had no treatable depression; there must have been advice on palliative care; the patient had to have considered family implications; and if the patient had not been a native English speaker an interpreter had to have been provided. There was also a "cooling off" period of seven days before the initial signature of authorisation by the patient and doctors and then a further "cooling off" period of 48 hours before euthanasia could be undertaken. Finally, the doctors participating under the Act could not benefit financially from the patient's death.

Those who Died

Four patients died under the Act and the deaths of a further three patients received considerable publicity. Clinical details about these deaths have been published recently (Kissane et al, 1998).

The first person was a 66-year-old male who had had cancer of the prostate from 1991. He had had a history of depression with suicidal thoughts, but he was said to be not currently depressed. It is of interest that his palliative care team were not aware of him being assessed for euthanasia, and it was reported that "the news of it came as a shock to those involved." Although this person's wife was present and provided support, his sons were said to be unaware of events until after his death on September the 22nd, 1996.

The second person was a 52-year-old woman who had the dermatological condition, mycosis fungoides. There was doubt about the terminal nature of her illness, and one physician who assessed her considered that she was not terminally ill. Eventually an orthopaedic surgeon completed the required documentation. It was noted that she was on 150 mgm daily of the anti-depressant, Doxepin, as well as Lorazepam and Flunitrazepam, and it was also recorded that a dermatologist had suggested various medications, including the psychotropic drugs, Haloperidol, Pimozide and Fluoxetine. There was no indication that there had been further manipulation of psychotropic medication, and she was said to be suffering from depression and pruritis. She was accompanied by her husband and child when she died on January 2nd, 1997.

The third person was a 69-year-old male who had never married and who had no relatives in Australia. He had carcinoma of the stomach and was reported to be emaciated, jaundiced and weak, with constant nausea and intermittent vomiting. His prognosis was considered to be hopeless and over a period of two months, during which time he was indecisive, he finally elected to undergo euthanasia on January 20th, 1997.

The fourth patient was a 70-year-old woman with cancer of the breast and widespread metastases. Her sister had died recently from a similar condition and she had been distressed about that. She had received palliative care, during which time she had become weaker and bedridden. She was accompanied by her family when euthanasia was undertaken on March 1st, 1997.

Subsequent Commonwealth of Australia Legislation

Even prior to the formal commencement of euthanasia in the Northern Territory on July 1st, 1996, on June 19th, 1996 a member of the Commonwealth Parliament in Canberra in the Australian Capital Territory announced that he would introduce a Bill to overturn the Northern Territory Act. On September, 9th, 1996 the Euthanasia Laws Bill was introduced and on December, 10th, 1996 the lower House of Representative passed that Bill 88 votes to 35. The upper house, the Senate, also passed the Bill, 38 votes to 33, on March the 25th, 1997. Two days later, on March 27th, 1997, Royal Assent was given to that Bill and from that time on the Northern Territory Rights of the Terminally Ill Act was no longer valid. The Rights of the Terminally Ill Act of the Northern Territory of Australia had been in operation for nine months.

Discussion

These deaths provoked widespread interest and comment, not only in Australia, but also around the world (The Times, 1996; New York Times, 1996). Typical of reporting in Australia were National press headlines such as "The euthanasia divide: first legal death splits the nation" (1996). There were also detailed descriptions of the infusion device built by Dr. Nitschke, the doctor who had conducted euthanasia under the law, whereby the patient made the final decision to go ahead with the lethal injection (The Times, 1996). Indeed the use of such a mechanism could, in terms defined by van der Maas et al. (1991, 1996), delineate the deaths more as assisted suicide than euthanasia.

The recently published clinical records are of great value in assessing the functioning of the legislation. Whilst it is probably fair to say that the legislative requirements embodied the majority of safeguards most proponents of euthanasia would require, reservations about the propriety of what occurred in the first two persons must be expressed. For example, in the first his palliative care team were apparently unaware of the assessment for euthanasia, as were his sons, both of which factors raise doubts about compliance with the full requirements of the law.

Perhaps of more concern was the second person, where doubts about the terminal nature of her illness were expressed; her acknowledged depression does not appear to have been treated vigorously (in fact the suggestion for the use of Fluoxetine was made by a dermatologist); and the final medical authorisation was given by an orthopaedic surgeon when other medical specialists, ostensibly more appropriately qualified for the task, had declined to do so.

It is acknowledged that it is easy to criticise from a distance, but these issues need to be raised. It is also on record that it is acknowledged that palliative care services in the Northern Territory were not well developed, and it was reported that Dr. Nitschke conceded that he had had limited experience in palliative care (Kissane et al, 1998).

In contrast to the first two patients, the latter two appeared to fit more comfortably with the scenario described cogently by Battin (1998), who in endorsing euthanasia refers to the concept of viewing life longitudinally, with the final few days or weeks being sacrificed with the intention of providing a more dignified and acceptable death.

In this regard it is pertinent to explore further the terminology in this contentious area. The broad definition of euthanasia provided by The Vatican appears to encompass what could be interpreted as traditionally good palliative care, and the delineation provided by van der Maas et al. (1991, 1996) appears to be of heuristic value. However, the distinction between narrowly defined euthanasia and assisted suicide is blurred, as is illustrated by the actual mechanism of death in these Australian examples.

It could also be argued that the term assisted suicide has connotations which are not necessarily in the best interests of either the patient, the health professionals involved, or indeed regulatory authorities. Although "suicide" may etymologically strictly be correct, it hardly conveys the overall context in which death occurs in these situations. Indeed, it may be more pragmatic, and in fact more accurate to speak of "assisted death" or "assisted dying" in these circumstances, rather than "assisted suicide."

When the Northern Territory law was overturned by the Australian Commonwealth Government the issue of euthanasia remained very much in the public view. For example, a woman who had been assessed as fulfilling the requirements for the Act, but who had chosen not to undergo euthanasia by the time the Act was overturned, subsequently died under the care of Dr. Nitschke. With a considerable degree of publicity, she was treated at home with an infusion which "contained morphine, 1440 mg plus Midazolam, 15 mg over 24 hours, and the doses increased to morphine, 4800 mg plus Midazolam, 200 mg plus Ketamine, 400 mg per 24 hours over the next 3 days, supplemented by boluses of phenobarbital and Chlorpromazine when the patient was restless" (Kissane et al, 1998). On the information provided it is not clear which of the categories of van der Maas et al. (1991, 1996) this death would conform to. After her death the Coroner decided to take no further action.

What does this Northern Territory of Australia experience offer in response to Battin's question: "Physician-Assisted Suicide: Safe, Legal, Rare?" For reasons noted immediately above, the word "suicide" could perhaps be replaced by the more neutral words "death" or "dying." With regard to the operation of the legislation being safe, one can simply note that even with ostensibly strict guidelines embodying most issues considered by proponents of euthanasia to be important, as a result of the clinical details provided there exist reservations about what occurred with two of the four persons who died under the Northern Territory legislation. This is hardly a reassuring record for examples of euthanasia which would inevitably be subjected to the most intense public scrutiny.

The issue of legality has been resolved in the negative, at least for the present time in Australia. However, it is perhaps even more complicated than might immediately be apparent, particularly when considering the more detailed distinctions provided by van der Maas et al. (1991, 1996). Thus, in a comprehensive review of "fundamental legal issues" in the Australian perspective, Robertson (1996) observed that "the distinction between acts of commission and acts of omission is a distinction with no moral significance", and he went on to state that "Anglo-Australian jurisprudence has also traditionally not distinguished between acts of commission and acts of omission when the intention is to cause a termination of life." The complexity of such an interpretation of the law is further illustrated by the recent comments of an Australian anti-euthanasia advocate, Archbishop Rayner (1998), who supported the introduction of a law to protect doctors from prosecution if medications used for pain caused premature death. When one adds these observations to the results of the Kuhse et al. (1997) work, the legal situation remains anything but clear.

Finally, with regards to its rarity, depending on one's interpretation of the Kuhse et al. (1997) survey of the practices of doctors in making end of life decisions, if one considers the broad Vatican definition of euthanasia, or even the more narrow doctor assisted death definition, it appears to be anything but rare in Australia.

Conclusion

Experience gained in Australia during the nine month operation of the Northern Territory Rights of the Terminally Ill Act, coupled with other Australian research, has provided a unique opportunity to add to the debate on euthanasia. As a result, reservations remain about the safety of euthanasia, no matter how it is defined; it is no longer legal and in fact the legal complexities have, if anything, been brought into more prominence; and finally, depending on its delineation, it does not appear to be rare.

Whether or not the overall experience has been a success depends on individual interpretation of the data. For example, even two of the three co-authors of the recently published clinical details have disagreed publicly about their interpretation of the effectiveness of the legislation, with Kissane reporting it a failure, and Nitschke, who supervised the deaths, claiming it a success and vowing to establish a euthanasia clinic in another city (The Advertiser, 1998).

In the meantime the present assessment of the Australian experience can be added to an increasing body of data, such as that which is being collated by the ongoing Oregon experience (Chin et al, 1999), in order to provide further information to clinicians, the general community and legislators in this important issue of contention.

References

Battin, M. P (1998). Physician-Assisted Suicide: Safe, Legal, Rare? In M. P. Battin., R. Rhodes., & A. Silvers (Eds.), *Physician-Assisted Suicide: Expanding the Debate* (pp. 11-27). New York and London: Routledge.

Baume, P. (1998). Voluntary euthanasia: responses of medical practitioners in New South Wales and the Australian Capital Territory to six open-ended questions. *Australian and New Zealand Journal of Public Health, 22,* 269–270.

Catholic Church. (1980). *Sacred Congregation for the Doctrine of the Faith: Declaration on Euthanasia* (No. 6). Vatican City: Author.

Chin, A. E., Hedberg, K., Higginson, G. K., & Fleming, D. W. (1999). Legalized physician-assisted suicide in Oregon – the first year's experience. *The New England Journal of Medicine, 340,* 577–583.

Hassan, R. (1996). Euthanasia and the medical profession: an Australian study. *Australian Journal of Social Issues, 31,* 239–251.

Kelleher, M. J. (1998). Humpty Dumpty and the language of euthanasia. *Crisis, 19,* 100–101.

Kissane, D. W., Street, A., & Nitschke, P. (1998). Seven deaths in Darwin: case studies under the Rights of the Terminally Ill Act, Northern Territory, Australia. *Lancet, 352,* 1097–1102.

Kitchener, B. A. (1998). Nurses' attitudes to active voluntary euthanasia: a survey in the A.C.T. *Australian and New Zealand Journal of Public Health, 22,* 276–278.

Kuhse, H., Singer, P., Baume, P., Clark, M., & Rickard, M. (1997). End-of-life decisions in Australian medical practice. *Medical Journal of Australia, 116,* 191–196.

New York Times. (1996, September 26). Australian man first in world to die with legal euthanasia.

Quirk, P. (1998). Euthanasia in the Commonwealth of Australia. *Issues in Law and Medicine, 13,* 425–446.

Rayner, K. (1998, October 16). *Radio Comments*. Australian Broadcasting Commission.

Robertson, D. (1996). The withdrawal of medical treatment from patients: fundamental legal issues. *Australian Law Journal, 70,* 723–746.

The Advertiser. (1998, October 6). N.T. right-to-die law "a failure."

The Advertiser. (1996, September 26). The euthanasia divide.

The Times. (1996, September 26). Man opts for death at push of a button.

Van der Maas, P J., van Delden, J. M. M., & Pijnenbourg, L. (1991). Euthanasia and other medical decisions concerning the end of life. *Lancet, 338,* 669–674.

Van der Maas, P. J., van der Wal, G., Haverkate, I., de Graaff, C. C., Kester, J. G., Onwuteaka-Philipsen, B. D., van der Heide, A., Bosma, J. M., & Willems, D. L. (1996). Euthanasia, physician-assisted suicide, and other medical practices involving the end of life in the Netherlands, 1990-1995. *New England Journal of Medicine, 335,* 1699–1705.

Family Factors in the Wish to Hasten Death and Euthanasia

Robyn Leigh and Brian Kelly

Department of Psychiatry, University of Queensland, Brisbane, Australia

Introduction

In this chapter consideration will be given to assisted suicide, euthanasia and the wish to hasten death in the context of the western family. There is very limited literature on the family in this context, but this chapter will attempt to draw together literature that may inform the request to hasten death when terminally ill from a family perspective.

End of life decision-making has received increasing attention from medical, social, and ethical perspectives. This issue has become increasingly relevant to the elderly. As advances in medical treatments in some cultures greatly increase life expectancy, a complex environment has developed in which medical treatments (and the withdrawal of these treatments) are negotiated (Battin, 1998; Cicirelli, 1997). Increasing attention to quality of life in medical decision-making has occurred, although the parameters, meaning, and application of the "quality of life" dimension across differing cultural settings is contentious. The perception of quality of life considerations and their place in decision-making may vary significantly between patients and their doctors (Uhlman & Pearlman, 1991). These issues confront some of the basic underpinnings of medical care, the approach to suffering, illness and disability (Cassell, 1982) and the difficulties modern medicine has with confronting death and chronic disease (Annas, 1993). It is notable there is very little published systematic research assessing the issue of assisted suicide and euthanasia in relation to the family.

The contemporary dilemma of medical decision-making and end of life care has focussed on the place of individual autonomy in such decisions. The cultural bias in the emphasis on autonomy has been challenged (Glick, 1997). Others have highlighted the limitations of this selective focus on autonomy, when illness, disability, and age may affect an individual's physical and social autonomy (Mann, 1998). The interpersonal, social and cultural context of illness must question the sole reliance on individual autonomy as the key ethical principle used to navigate the complex environment of medical decision-making.

The question of assisted suicide contains within it the complex meanings of illness, death and dying across cultures. The meaning of death and the bereavement rituals of any society reflect the deeply held cultural and spiritual foundations. Suffering is reported and acknowledged differently across cultures (Kleinman & Kleinman, 1995). Within any pluralistic society, consideration must therefore be given to the divergent sets of meaning and cultural perspectives. On a societal level, significant concerns exist regarding the potential for marginalised, disadvantaged, and disenfranchised groups to be vulnerable to potential abuses from such any legislation that enables assisted suicide (Arras, 1998). Access to comprehensive health care, particularly palliative care, is limited for many individuals (Arras, 1998). For the elderly there are particular concerns about coercion and abuse (Francis, 1998). As the containment of health care costs becomes an increasing political and social concern (Caine & Conwell, 1993), the potential for such coercion towards assisted suicide needs to be recognized.

The examination of the wish to hasten death from a family or systems perspective is far more complex than it initially appears to be. To be able to examine this issue many questions arise. Questions such as; How do families function when a family member is seriously ill and dying? What is family systems theory, and how is it relevant to a person wishing to hasten death? What is the family process in dealing with loss and death issues? What happens to both the average family and the most vulnerable family when a member becomes ill? And finally what is occurring in the family when a dying member requests assisted suicide or euthanasia?

To examine this topic it is important to have an understanding of theories of family functioning, an overview of which is beyond the scope of this chapter, but the model we endorse using is that of family systems theory. The next important area to understand is what is written about families when a member is ill and dying, and literature on families and bereavement. The next task is to then look at the complex topic of euthanasia, which will be examined from the clinical perspective. From there it is possible to draw together ideas about these broad areas: family functioning, families and loss, and euthanasia and consider hypotheses about what could be happening in a family when a member requests to hasten their death. It also becomes clear that it is possible, though difficult, to be scientific about areas of our life that are highly existential, and that science is not the only paradigm from which to look at these areas.

Despite the subjective and existential nature of family life and the dying process one can still pose hypotheses about mental illness and health, psychological and psychodynamic factors and their relevance to families and euthanasia. It is also relevant to use psychodynamic and other psychological theories and tools to help to understand the topic further, in an attempt to augment the clinical role of psychiatrists helping dying patients and their families.

Euthanasia and the factors surrounding euthanasia are highly relevant to psychiatry. Psychiatrists have become integral members of the treatment team in providing integrated care for medically and surgically ill and dying patients, most formally developed in an academic role is that of the psycho-oncologist. Psychiatrists are commonly called upon in this setting when there are high levels of anxiety in the patient, family or team, when there is existential despair and when there are ethically challenging decisions to be considered as well as when there is recognized psychopathology to be referred. In such a position the psychiatrist may often find referral of the patient requesting euthanasia or suicide.

Clinical Issues in Euthanasia

The areas most relevant to the clinical situation of the terminally ill patient requesting to hasten their death include:

- The understanding of psychiatric co-morbidity in the terminally ill.
- The empirical research data on the wish to hasten death among the terminally ill and the request for physician assisted suicide.
- The contribution of psychiatry in understanding a terminally ill patient requesting to hasten their death.
- The importance of unrelieved suffering in the terminally ill in the consideration of euthanasia

The consideration of the issues for families in euthanasia has been conducted from a position of suspending an opinion of support or opposition to euthanasia, but rather with the approach of a "why, in whom and in which situation does the request to die occur." Additionally the issue of how this is relevant to clinical psychiatry becomes more apparent. Regardless of the legality of euthanasia, we as psychiatrists must be able to respond to terminally ill patients who wish to hasten death, and understand the broad number of factors that may contribute to this situation.

Using the definitions discussed by Sawyer et al. (1993) and used by Chochinov and Wilson (1995), euthanasia and assisted suicide are defined as:

- *Euthanasia*, being positive acts of commission, such as lethal injections, which are undertaken deliberately by physicians to end the lives of patients who have explicitly asked to die.
- *Assisted suicide,* being the provision of advice or the means for an individual to commit suicide.

In considering the request of a terminally ill patient for euthanasia, as doctors and psychiatrists, it should primarily be considered from a broader framework than the perspective of individual "rights" or autonomy (Mann, 1998). Additionally, rather than considering the request arising, as an individual autonomous request, we should see this as occurring in an ill individual with prominent physical and emotional needs living and interacting in a family and medical system. Therefore a range of factors within the patient, the family and the medical system need to be considered as to their contribution in this request. Chochinov and Wilson (1995) conclude that, "As a special case of suicide, euthanasia and physician assisted suicide are of particular relevance to mental health professional."

The views about the "right to die", "rational decision making", and the need to determine if the patient is "competent" to make a decision about ending his/her life when terminally ill are, all expressed as being important legal and ethical decisions in the euthanasia debate (Conwell & Caine, 1991). These are undoubtedly of importance but from a clinical perspective, need to be considered alongside a more detailed understanding of the suffering for patients with terminal illness, and the medical and psycho-social processes that affect the wish to die (Chochinov et al., 1995).

In approaching the issue of why a terminally ill person makes a request to hasten their death we need to consider:

- The incidence of psychiatric co-morbidity in serious medical illness and at the end of life, including the incidence of suicidality, depression and delirium and the impact these may have on the wish to hasten death;
- Who are the patients asking to hasten their death and in what ways do they differ from patients who do not wish a sooner death?
- What is known about suffering and the relief of suffering at the end of life, and;
- What are the roles of the psychiatrist and other mental health professionals?

As Zalcberg and Buchanan (1997) suggest: "By asking patients why they wish to die rather than accepting such statements at face value, it becomes clear that requests to help them die are made in the context of either unrelieved, debilitating symptoms, or in circumstances in which they are experiencing helplessness, loneliness, depression or marked anxiety."

Psychiatric Co-morbidity in Terminal Illness

Psychiatric co-morbidity in the setting of terminal illness is exceptionally high with:

- Rates of delirium in cancer and AIDS ranging from 25–85% (Brietbart et al., 1995, 1998; Massie et al., 1983);
- Rates of clinically significant depression of 25–50% reported in the terminally ill (Brietbart et al., 1998; Shuster et al., 1998; Chochinov et al., 1994, 1995; Grassi et al., 1996, Brown et al., 1986). For diagnostic purposes a single item question of "Are you depressed ?" was found to be a valid method of screening for depressed patients who are terminally ill (Chochinov et al., 1997);
- Among broader groups of patients with cancer, rates of severe depression have been estimated at levels of up to 24% (McDaniel et al,1995)
- 47% of 215 randomly assessed cancer patients were found to have a DSM III diagnosis, with 85% of those manifesting a psychiatric complaint having a disorder with depression or anxiety as a central symptom (Derogatis et al., 1983);

- The prevalence of depression was found to be much greater in cancer patients with high pain than low pain symptoms, with 33% of patients with high levels of pain having depression versus 13% of patients with low pain having depression. Additionally the patients with high pain levels were significantly more anxious and emotionally distressed than the low pain group. Pain intensity and frequency also correlated with mood disturbance as well as vigor and fatigue (Spiegel et al., 1994), and;
- Relatively few cancer patients commit suicide, but they are at increased risk (Holland, 1991).

Psychiatric illnesses at the end of life are common but often are not recognized or treated. There are a number of contributing factors to this, firstly the difficulty diagnosing psychiatric disorders that are co-morbid with physical illness due to the over-lap in symptoms (Shuster et al., 1999). Additionally, many patients, families and physicians hold the belief that psychiatric symptoms, especially depression are normal at the end of life, and they do not know that these symptoms can respond well to treatment (Shuster et al., 1999). Other barriers that preclude these psychiatric symptoms and illnesses being seen by psychiatrists are the lack of psychiatric consultation in many hospice teams and lack of consultation to psychiatry by physicians caring for terminally ill patients. Stigma about psychiatric diagnosis by patients, families and physicians makes physicians less likely to make a psychiatric diagnosis or referral (Shuster et al., 1999).

Who Are the Patients Who Wish to Hasten Death?

Hendin and Klerman (1993) suggest that terminally ill patients who wish to hasten their death are not significantly different from other people who face other crises with the desire to end their lives. Medical illness plays a role in suicide in 25% of cases and this contribution rises with increasing age (Hendin, 1999). Hendin (1999) notes that the overwhelming majority of terminally ill patients fight for life to the end, and only 2–4% of suicides occur in the setting of terminal illness.

In keeping with the idea of the wish to hasten death being a response to crisis, of the patients making a request for assisted suicide, at repeat interview two weeks later, two thirds showed a significant decrease in the desire to die (Emmanuel et al., 1996). Patients who attempt suicide show ambivalence about death and so too do patients requesting assisted suicide (Hendin, 1999). The idea of the desire to hasten death being ambivalent and unstable is an important concept since if euthanasia were offered, it is assumed that patients who request to die would not want to withdraw their request at a later time. Chochinov et al. (1999) investigated the important concept of the temporal instability of the wish to hasten death in the terminally ill. This is obviously important since once the act is performed it can not be reversed. It was found that thoughts of a desire for death are common in the terminally ill, with 44.5% of patients having at least a fleeting desire to hasten their death (Chochinov et al., 1995). In their study (Chochinov et al., 1999) assessing 168 patients admitted to a palliative care facility, the will to live or the wish to die was found to be highly unstable over time in the terminally ill. Factors impacting on the will to live were depression, anxiety, dyspnoea and a sense of well being

Mental illness raises the risk of suicide even more than does physical illness, with up to 90% of people who kill themselves having a psychiatric illness in the months before suicide (Barraclough et al., 1974). In the elderly, such findings are also confirmed, with physical illness and objective health indices having less influence on the wish to die than psychosocial factors (Cicirelli, 1997).

It could be imagined that as disease progresses and physical circumstances worsen the desire to hasten death would increase. This is not the case; in fact the reverse has been found (Owen et al., 1992). It has been suggested that this counter-intuitive response may be a function of human hope, with the fact that as each day passes with symptoms being able to be kept under some sort of control each day becomes more precious and suicide less considered (Owen et al., 1992).

If we look to the population of terminally ill patients who wish to hasten death who have been systematically studied it may come as little surprise to some that these patients do indeed have a high rate of psychiatric illness especially depression. The prevalence of depression in terminally ill patients with a wish to hasten death is eight times higher than in those who do not want to hasten their death (Chochinov et al., 1995). Depressive syndromes are found in 58.8% of patients with a wish to hasten death versus 7.7% in patients who did not have this wish (Chochinov et al., 1995). One of the earliest reports of the incidence of depression in patients with a wish to hasten death was by Brown et al., (1986) who found depression in all 10 palliative care patients who endorsed a wish to hasten death. Depression is the strongest determinant of suicidal ideation and the wish to hasten death in those with a serious or terminal illness (Chochinov et al., 1994 1995, Grassi et al., 1996)

Among 200 patients recruited from a palliative care facility, 8.5% of the group reported an unequivocal desire for death to come soon and held this consistently over time (Chochinov et al., 1995). In this group depression emerged as a unique predictor of the desire for death. Pain and family support measures were found to exert more indirect influences (Chochinov et al., 1995). The findings of this study suggested that prolonged pain may increase the risk of depression and family support may protect against it, with depression then being a more direct forerunner to the wish to die.

In a depressed terminally ill patient who has a wish to hasten death, it is not known whether by treating the depression the wish to die resolves. However, in a study of a depressed geriatric population, 25% who initially refused life-sustaining treatment showed an increase desire for life sustaining treatments once their depressive symptoms had improved (Ganzini et al., 1994)

The psychodynamic literature suggests that the request to die may have a number of possible meanings. Some of the thoughts and feelings the patients may have include the request being a communication in itself, a way of taking control over life even though it is illusory and paradoxical, a split in the experience of the self with the fantasy of killing "the medically sick part of the self" (Muskin, 1998). Additionally, the wish to die may be a way of expressing rage and revenge, with this being rage felt towards themselves, their doctors, their god and the world, with revenge being sought through their own death (Muskin, 1998). For some patients the request to die may also express hopelessness, suffering, pain, sadness and, depression. For some patients, being ill may be associated with guilt with the need for punishment and atonement via death, for others in view of past traumatic experience they may already feel dead, the so called "living dead" and may just want it over quickly (Muskin, 1998).

In contrast to the concept of defining the request to render the acting upon it necessary, one argument posed is that many of our choices in life are motivated in part by irrational considerations and why should the choices involving our death be less so? (Lester, 1996).

The Issue of Unrelieved Suffering

At the core of the euthanasia debate is the relief of suffering, loneliness, and helplessness in the terminally ill (Zalcberg & Buchanan, 1997). "Ending patient's lives relieves their suffering, but in ending a life we do not deal with the reality that most patients desperately want to live, even in the most difficult of circumstances" (Zalcberg & Buchanan, 1997).

Cherny (1996) posed the issue of euthanasia as one of unrelieved suffering. He believes that the truth of the perception that patients need to be killed or assisted to kill themselves to have relief of suffering, depends on the availability of methods to relieve suffering. He goes on to suggest that it is the failure to appreciate, or to effectively address the full diversity of contributing factors that may render therapeutic strategies to relieve suffering, less effective. He believes that we need to assess in each of the three parties of the patient, family and medical team, any suffering related to medical variables, psychological variables and social/financial variables.

Grassi (1995) notes that though death invokes extreme anxiety, it is the dying process with the uncontrollable symptoms such as pain, which take anguish to a level that makes the last stages of life unlivable. In this situation the impulse to seek death arises from the impossibility of the subject to accept a new identity in the face of the losses and changes due to the illness (Pajusco & De Leo, 1993).

From the Dutch experience, in the case of requests for euthanasia, physicians reported the reasons why patients wanted euthanasia were: loss of dignity, pain, "unworthy dying", being dependent on others and "tiredness of life" (van der Maas et al., 1991). This supports Cherny's concept of euthanasia reflecting unrelieved suffering and highlights the need to look at the situation more carefully. Cherny et al. (1994) discuss that it is often the combination of factors of uncontrolled physical symptoms, depression or anxiety, severe existential distress, and family member and health care provider fatigue, that contribute to the request. They then go on to suggest that these factors exist in combination, such as "the patient with uncontrolled pain who is attended by frustrated, distressed relatives and an exhausted, exasperated physician." These ideas provoke questions such as; whose suffering is being discussed? The patient's? The family's? The doctor's? (Goodwin, 1991). Additionally, the complex question of how the patient's suffering is being affected by their interaction with the family and the doctor, needs to be asked. This then brings us back to the principal of patient autonomy and the need to consider patient autonomy in the context of a range of influences acting on the patient, including a powerful social and cultural bias towards autonomy as an ideal to be achieved and maintained (Mann, 1998).

Considering the importance of suffering in the terminally ill, the comment that, "uncontrolled suffering in a dying patient is a medical emergency" (Wanzer et al., 1989) can be seen to be an appropriate suggestion.

The Clinical Role of the Psychiatrist in Terminally Ill Patients who Wish to Hasten Death

There is much literature on euthanasia but much less on the role of the psychiatrist in this important clinical situation. From what literature there is on the clinical issues in euthanasia, it has been proposed that psychiatrists could help optimize the adequacy of symptom control, aid the patient in addressing relationship difficulties with family, friends and health care workers, and help deal with psychological disturbances, especially grief, depression, organic mental disorders and personality disorders (Chochinov, 1995). Psychiatrists bring the potential for expert exploration and understanding of the issues involved in the request to die, including elucidation of psychodynamic issues and diagnosis of psychiatric disorder (Muskin, 1998). Additionally there is a significant role for the psychiatrist who, through the psychotherapeutic process, may relieve psychological suffering in the terminally ill patient (Eissler, 1955).

The reason psychiatrists are an important member of the treating team in the setting of end of life care is due to the importance of treating psychiatric and psychological symptoms, which often go unrecognized and untreated. Bloch et al. (2000) summarises why it is important to treat these symptoms at the end of life:

> Psychological distress impairs the patient's capacity for pleasure, meaning, and connection; erodes quality of life; amplifies pain and other symptoms; reduces the patient's ability to do the emotional work of saying good-bye; and causes anguish and worry in family members and friends. Finally, psychological distress, particularly depression, is a major risk factor for suicide and for requests to hasten death.

Additionally, differentiating "normal" distress associated with grief and existential issues from that which is related to psychiatric disorder, or a pre-existing problem such as a personality disorder, requires an appreciation of the clinical characteristics of psychiatric syndromes. The psychiatrist is then in the best position to help develop a treatment plan to address suffering arising from psychological and psychiatric problems in the terminally ill person.

Why the Family is an Important Consideration in End of Life Care

This, may be seen as a two part phenomenon, the first consideration being the family and their importance for the dying patient, and the second being the importance of the family's well being as they confront their family member's dying and then living beyond their family member's death. These two phenomena are of course intimately related.

All death and dying occurs in an intrapsychic, interpersonal, family, social, cultural and religious/spiritual context. The family context of death and dying is important and is a framework that the medical profession has been moving further from in modern day medicine. It seems the medical profession's reluctance to look at the family context may relate to modern day societies prominent valuing of autonomy and self-determinism, especially with respect to health issues (Steinberg et al., 1998). It may also relate to the relative devaluing of the emotional world of the patient and their family, in favour of offering the patient a scientifically and technologically advanced opinion with respect to treatment of his/her illness (Nordquist, 1999). This in turn may relate to the fact that both the society and the medical practitioner have come to view science as reality rather than one paradigm of viewing the world. When viewed from this paradigm the disease becomes more important than the experience of living through the illness.

Despite increasing involvement of the family in cancer care, the impact of cancer or other terminal illnesses on the well-being of family members remains under-researched and under addressed clinically. This occurs at the same time that the trend in medical care is for early discharge of the patient from hospital to the family, and for much treatment to be performed at day hospital and on an outpatient basis, with much of the nursing and ancillary care being provided by the family. Hospital-based care has always included containment of anxiety and despair, and this now rests more and more on the shoulders of the family.

If we turn to the literature and examine the impact of a person with cancer on their family, (and extrapolate to dying in general), we find high rates of emotional distress in the patient and family, and that emotional distress felt during the palliative and terminal phases of illness reverberates throughout the whole family (Kissane et al., 1994). Many studies suggest that one family member's psychological functioning during the end of life period is highly influential on the psychological functioning of other member's (Cassileth et al., 1985; Northhouse, 1984).

Another aspect of the importance of the family in end of life care, is maximizing the families' ability to grieve effectively after the death has occurred. From the literature on families and bereavement we do have much sound information about which families are vulnerable (Walsh & McGoldrick, 1991). Recurrently discussed in the literature on families and loss are the transgenerational consequences of unresolved grief (Walsh & McGoldrick, 1991; Rosen, 1991).

The family is a central consideration in end of life care because of; high rates of distress and psychopathology in the patient and family during the end of life period, the potential for psychopathology in the family from unresolved grief *and* the chance of this psychopathology becoming transgenerational. The idea of the family having a central role in end of life care is valid and as such is a factor worthy of consideration in the terminally ill patient who requests to hasten their death.

The Family System in End of Life Care

Family systems theory acknowledges that the dying or deceased person was involved in a shared life cycle (Rosen, 1991). Rosen (1991) states that "the medical model concerns itself with the dying patient's basic needs for comfort, pain control, and palliation; the family systems model, on the other hand, addresses the effect of illness on the entire family." He suggests that important questions to ask are; how is the daily functioning of the family being affected by this illness? What coping skills are family members using to care for themselves and their ill family member? Who is assuming the ill member's functions in the family, not only the visible functions, such as providing income or preparing meals, but also the more subtle, emotional functions? Does anything in this family's behaviour suggest the possibility of a complicated bereavement?

Bowen suggested that life-threatening illnesses such as cancer creates considerable anxiety in the family system and stresses or alters communication patterns, roles, and relationships among family members (Bowen, 1976). It could be considered that when communication patterns, roles and relationships need to be most stable and containing, that is when you or a family member is dying, they are the most stressed and unstable.

If we consider the complexity of concomitant tasks the patient and the family are dealing with during the end of life period from the systems perspective, we could suspect that the dying patient encumbered with physical symptoms such as pain, fatigue and nausea and managing their own loss issues, would be highly influenced by how well the family is coping. The interrelatedness of how the family and patient cope then starts to be visible.

Families and End of Life Decision-Making

The processes of aging and dying have become complicated by medical technological advances over the past half a century (Cicirelli, 1997; Mann, 1998). We now have the technology to control the timing of death and the capacity in some instances to decide when to prolong or shorten life (Steinberg & Younger, 1998).

The area of end of life decision-making has many facets. These include the influence of high technology medicine, the ethical and legal issues of regard for patient autonomy and the question of how autonomous any patient is at this stressful time. Additionally, there is the legal and clinical/ethical issues about competency of a patient to decide about life sustaining treatments, the validity of surrogate decisionmakers and the underlying economic drive to rationalize services in the face of "medical futility" of low benefit, high expense treatments.

The social and legal position on end of life decision-making see:

- A clear endorsement of the competent patient to accept or reject medical treatment as the gold standard for making end of life decisions (Steinberg & Younger, 1998), and;
- Some advocacy for a shared decision-making process involving the physician, the patient and the family (Steinberg & Younger, 1998).

There is a difference between the involvement of the family in the care of the patient in current day western medicine versus non-western medicine. The contrast is between the depiction of the family as an important carer, integral in the team of people caring for the sick person (as in non western medicine) versus the family as an appendage relegated to the waiting room, seen as an afterthought by the physician and treatment team (Rothchild, 1998). The major focus of the treatment team is seen as being exclusively on treating the patient (Rothchild, 1998) or at times treating only the patient's disease (as in current day western medicine).

Families generally comply with the competent patient's wishes, but the family's own interests such as fear, denial, guilt and other emotions may intrude (Rothchild, 1998). A family member who is guilty or denying the hopelessness of the situation may pressure the patient to continue with treatment (Rothchild, 1998). The family member who is feeling emotionally, physically or financially burdened may pressure the patient to discontinue treatment. Sometimes surrogate decision-makers base decisions on what is best for themselves rather than what is best for the patient or what the patient would want (Rothchild, 1998).

Family responses to end of life decisions are shaped by factors both intrinsic and extrinsic to the family. Rothchild (1998) outlined these as being:

- The patient's role in the family;
- Developmental stage of the patient and the family, for example, the tendency to let go of the elderly more easily than the young;
- Degree of family cohesion;
- Structural characteristics of the family, for example, age or gender may determine a hierarchy for decision making, their may be rules about sharing feelings outside the family, a "closed family system" may share little information with staff. Members of enmeshed families may have exaggerated needs to depend on one another and to project anger outside the family;
- Individual psychopathology;
- Denial, anger or guilt;
- Communication of treatment wishes to proxies. It has been shown that neither patients nor their families are good at predicting the wishes of patients, with families choosing more treatment than the patient, and the physician choosing less than the patient (Danis et al., 1991; Seckler et al., 1991).
- Ethnicity and Religion;

- Economic pressures, and;
- Illness variables with some illnesses being more readily perceived to have a poor prognosis.

Rothchild (1998) describes that issues that need to be addressed in the future include:

- Effects of treatment decisions on family, for example, what happens later to those experiencing regret over treatment decisions;
- Identifying high risk families or family members, who may experience problems with end of life decision-making;
- Development and testing of intervention strategies. There is a heightened awareness of the need to foster communication between staff and families. The question of what interventions, with what families, made when, during the end of life decision making needs addressing, and;
- Effects of changes in the healthcare system. Change in the health care system may have effects on end of life decision-making and on family's involvement in end of life care and need to be monitored and researched.

The issue of deciding whether to accept CPR (cardiopulmonary resuscitation) or to have a DNR (do-not-resuscitate) order has become one of the basic elements in end of life decision-making for patients or families (Larsen, 1999). Guidelines for DNR orders now exist and include, that patients should decide their own DNR status and that for an incompetent patient consent from the next of kin is necessary for DNR status (Rowland & Rowland, 1990).

Despite the encouragement of advanced health directives, the fact that many patients don't have an advanced health directive and that advanced health directives may lack clarity in direction, means that family will continue to be asked to make decisions for an incompetent, terminally ill family member (Larsen, 1999). In reality, therefore, it is the family that makes the decision about resuscitation, rather than the patient (Gleeson & Wise, 1990).

A qualitative study by Larsen (1999) looked at the family experience of making DNR decisions for an incompetent, terminally ill family member. They found that the family's frame of reference was almost always motivated by ethical and emotional values such as quality of life and dying with dignity. Family members also considered basic ethical principals such as autonomy and beneficence and they analyzed the situation in a holistic manner (Larsen, 1999).

The process a family goes through to make the decision to forgo life support for an incompetent, terminally ill family member, was studied by Swigart et al. (1996) in 30 family members of 16 critically ill patients. They identify that the "letting go" or "becoming willing to let go" of life support involves three complex and interrelated processes:

- Family members obtaining and trying to understand information about the critical illness;

- Reviewing the life story of the patient, seeking meaning in the patient's life and the critical illness, and;
- Struggling to maintain family roles and relationships.

In this study, for most families, interpersonal and intrapsychic work created a reframing of the issues related to the critical illness, towards:

- Believing that they had done all that could be done and were able then to relinquish the goal of recovery for acceptance of a peaceful death;
- Reviewing of the patient's life with the belief that the patient would not want to continue on life support, and;
- Coming to the sense that they were "doing the right thing" and that forgoing life support for their relative would not destroy important family relationships.

Overall the family may be considered to be a vital participant in the care of the patient at the end of life. The social and legal role of being involved in end of life decision-making or the more extreme responsibility of being a surrogate decision-maker when a loved one is unable to advocate for themselves, is testament to the central position the family holds at this most important time of life…being one's death.

The information on families and terminating life sustaining treatments, especially the work by Swigart et al. (1996), suggests that decision making at the end of life with respect to terminating life is a process that often demands family collaboration. One could wonder whether the patient wishing to hasten their own death might in some way "check this idea out" with their family, before making a final decision about it. We then need to understand this potential interaction between the terminally ill patient and their family as one of the factors that may be acting on them in deciding whether or not to hasten their death.

Families and Coping with Cancer

Chronic incurable illness in a family member impacts on the entire family (Smith, 1990). Factors that contribute to family distress include:

- Empathic suffering of the family with the distress felt by the patient;
- Grief and bereavement as the family attempt to process multiple losses as they occur, and await the ultimate loss in the death of their member;
- Role changes, and;
- The burdens of care including physical, financial and psychological (Davies et al., 1990).
- Family fatigue can relate to a number of situations, as described by Cherny (1996), including:
- Persistent inadequately relieved suffering of the patient (Vachon, 1993);

- Inadequate resources to cope with home care with compromise of the overall family welfare (Schachter, 1992);
- Unrealistic expectations by the family members of themselves or professional health workers, and;
- Emotional distress in the family even with relief of patient suffering (Davies et al., 1990).

Our knowledge about the degree and type of psychological morbidity that reverberates throughout the family, and the effect that this morbidity has on psychological functioning has been small. Most research has been focused on the patients themselves, a little on spousal effects and offspring have been fairly overlooked (Kissane et al., 1994). The key findings from this literature are:

- Distress rates in next of kin have been found to be between 18–34% (Ell et al., 1988; Northouse, 1989);
- Distress in families has lasted up to 18 months (Ell et al., 1988; Northouse, 1989);
- In the families of 102 palliative care patients, rates of depression (as defined by the Beck Depression Inventory) were identified as 50% in patients, 33% in spouses and 25% in offspring (Kissane et al., 1994), and;
- In families coping with cancer, hostile (families with high levels of conflict) and sullen families (families with moderate conflict, poor cohesion and limited expressiveness) were found to have higher levels of psychological morbidity and poorer social functioning (Kissane et al., 1994).

Looking beyond the period of terminal illness to after the death of the patient, a prospective study investigating the psychological outcome for family carers, found that psychological symptom scores at the time of referral to palliative care services were the chief predictors of psychological symptoms in carers and severity of grief at follow-up (Kelly et al., 1999).

If we reflect on this literature we can appreciate further that the dying process for the family and the patient is a stressful and highly interactive period. The literature also informs us that we, as a medical profession, have been slow to look at the systems nature of serious and terminal illness and how this affects the well-being of both the patient and family members. It seems this lends support to the importance of examining the levels of psychological symptoms, psychopathology and detail of family relationships, and experience in families of dying patients with and without a wish to hasten death.

Euthanasia and the Family

From the literature on clinical factors in euthanasia it can be said that anguish due to both physical and mental suffering is a factor that fuels the wish to die. In terms of dealing with anguish it is farcical to suggest that it is a purely autonomous problem of the patient's. As in all situations, as the intensity of anguish and affect rises, the importance of system containment and of transference and countertransference issues become increasingly important. This is prominently so in the situation of the terminally ill. This is suggested by Zalcberg and Buchanan (1997) who suggest that the euthanasia debate should be considered from the perspective of the clinical interface between doctors, patients, and their families.

Grassi (1996) comments that the context for considering the issue of euthanasia includes the patient, the family and society with its own cultural models. The idea that the request for euthanasia may be highly influenced by others' distress or the perception the patient has of others' experience is an important one. This has been discussed in terms of the patient-doctor relationship, but we would suggest that the importance of the patient's experience of the family's suffering need to be underscored in the wish to hasten death. Cherny (1996) has described the situation of the patient's distress being contributed to by the family's distress and vice versa as "empathic distress."

Within the patient-doctor relationship the agreement by the doctor to act on the patient's wish to hasten death is influenced by the doctor's own experience and feelings (Varghese & Kelly, 1999). This is an important concept and requires an understanding of countertransference. The modern view of countertransference is of it being a jointly created phenomenon, with contributions from both the patient and the doctor. In this construct the patient draws the doctor into a particular role and encourages particular behaviour that reflects the patient's internal world, but the specifics of the role the doctor plays is coloured by his/her own personality and internal world (Gabbard, 1999).

What the patient projects onto the clinician and what the clinician brings to the situation are both relevant to the end result of the countertransference (Gabbard, 1999). The importance of this dyad in understanding the dynamics that are occurring for the doctor when a patient requests euthanasia have been discussed by Varghese & Kelly (1999). They highlight the importance of the doctor understanding his/her own issues with death. Doctors may feel impotent, frustrated, disgusted with disease or the dying, and hopeless and helpless by being presented with a situation they cannot control, with their omnipotence shattered in the face of death. They comment, "The patient's request for euthanasia may be more than just a reflection of the patient's individual despair; it may be an indication that others have despaired of the patient or have been perceived by the patient as having such despair" (Varghese & Kelly, 1999).

It could be proposed that similar unconscious processes in family dyads may be important, as they are in the doctor-patient dyad. In view of the systems nature of the family, the patient's request to die may be highly influenced by what others in the family are experiencing. This would support the need to further define what others in the family *are* experiencing, both in families of patients who have no desire to hasten death and those who do have a wish to hasten their death.

The assumption that seriously ill or terminal patients who wish to end their lives are in some way different to those who are suicidal for other reasons is strongly challenged by Hendin and Klerman (1993). From this notion we can consider what we already understand about the psychodynamics of suicide and the profound importance of family dynamics in this process. The topic of the family's contribution in suicide is another large body of literature and will not be reviewed currently. It is reasonable to say that family dynamics can play a very significant role in both the development of a patient's suicidal ideation and their risk of acting on such thoughts.

The issue of pathological grief in the families where a member has died by suicide is another factor that cannot be ignored in the topic of families and euthanasia. This is to say that if euthanasia were to be legalized we would have to be vigilant in the need to research whether there are any untoward effects on bereavement in the families of patients who died in this manner.

One may consider that a major emotional task of the dying patient and family is to contain and process the negative affects they are experiencing in response to their losses and stress of role changes and family disequilibrium. The negative affect involves separation anxiety, anger, fear, narcissistic injury, hate, ambivalence, guilt, rage, and depression. As in all systems how one person contains or spills over these feelings, effects how others in the system are able to meet the challenge.

As the family comes into contact with the medical system, which they may look to as the "death experts", they are all too often met with a milieu of unwillingness to discuss these issues and the judgement as being "a difficult family" if they are coping poorly or demanding "too much." We would suggest that the problems the family face in talking about death, may be mirrored in the problems faced by doctors in being able to discuss death with the patient and family.

It could be hypothesized that euthanasia may become a fantasy escape from the negative affect associated with the facing of death. Just as the modern medical system has been able to promote the illusion of escaping death, so too might it provide the illusion of mastery of death and relief of the emotions surrounding death by offering euthanasia.

We know that when people have exhausted their ability to deal with a feeling utilizing their psychological apparatus they then resort to action. One would wonder whether, if once the family is "stuck" and unable to communicate about what is happening to them and feel they can no longer tolerate the emotional burden of the dying, it is time "to act." The medical system, primed by the social taboo of avoiding discussing death and by the omnipotence of always being able to offer some "painless solution", may identify with the family transference and "act" to relieve all members of their suffering.

The question then becomes, does this relieve the family suffering? We don't know how a family grieves a death precipitated by euthanasia. Does the family grieve well? Does the negative affect go unprocessed; causing future adverse consequences of its own? Is this then countertransference acting out on the doctor's part? If it is not, when is it not, and to answer this do we not need to look at a systems model? If euthanasia is performed to relieve suffering, do we not have a duty of care to learn whether or not it is going to harm families, or whether (or not) particular family systems or combinations of family/medical systems "ask for euthanasia" more often than others do? Much is written on the need to determine whether the patient requesting euthanasia has individual psychopathology but ignores the issues of family pathology or the sequelae for the family if euthanasia is the cause of death.

It would be reasonable to look at the family of the dying patient with respect to whether there are identifiable differences in the families of those patients who wish to hasten their death versus those that do not. This may help psychiatrists in assessment and management of patients who make a request to hasten their death and allow us to understand the family context. It may also make a contribution to the legislative debate as it continues in the years ahead.

Conclusion

The issue of euthanasia and the wish to hasten death among the terminally ill is a complex issue that is impacted upon by the broad scope of experience the individual encounters. These influencing experiences range from one's most basic experience of one's self, including the response to physical suffering and pain, to interpersonal and family interactions, to the broader social and cultural milieu with which the patient interacts.

Death, dying and the care of the ill are imbued with the flavour of the surrounding broader culture. In Western communities there is ongoing advancement in the technological aspects of medical care and greater complexity of medical decision-making, while at the same time, the medical system is faced with economic rationalism and the increasing demands of an ageing population. It is this system that the patient/family system interacts with when a member faces a terminal illness and at this interface that the request to hasten death arises.

It is the challenge of medical research to understand further the physical, psychological, social, cultural/subcultural, political/legal and ethical factors that may play a role in a terminally ill person requesting to hasten their death.

This chapter has outlined the clinical issues in euthanasia and highlights the fact that the patient lives out their illness and their dying in a family context. The family has a profound influence on the patient and vice versa, with reverberation of distress felt thoughout the system. In light of the family context it is suggested that the family may have a significant influence upon the patient's wish to hasten death. The families of terminally ill patients who have a wish to hasten death deserve to be systematically examined and compared with families of patients who do not wish a sooner death, to explore the differences in these groups.

References

Annas, G. J. (1993). Physician assisted suicide: Michigan's temporary solution. *New England Journal of Medicine, 328,* 1573–1576.

Arras, J. D.(1998). Physician-assisted suicide: A tragic view. In M. P. Battin., R. Rhodes & A. Silvers (Eds.), *Physician-Assisted Suicide: Expanding the Debate* (pp. 11-27). New York: Routledge.

Barraclough, B., Bunch, J., Nelson, B., & Sainsbury, P. (1974). A hundred cases of suicide: clinical aspects. *British Journal of Psychiatry, 125,* 355–373.

Battin, M. (1998). Physician-assisted suicide: safe, legal, rare?. In M. P. Battin., R. Rhodes & R. Silvers (Eds.), *Physician-Assisted Suicide: Expanding the Debate* (pp. 11-27). New York: Routledge.

Bloch, S. (2000) Assessing and managing depression in the terminally ill patient. *Annals of Internal Medicine, 132,* 209–218.

Bowen, M. (1976). Family reaction to death. In P. Guerin (Ed.), *Family Therapy*. New York: Gardner.

Breitbart, W. (1987). Suicide in cancer patients. *Oncology, 1,* 49–53.

Breitbart, W., Bruera, E., Chochinov, H., & Lynch, M. (1995). Neuropsychiatric syndromes and psychological symptoms in patients with advanced cancer. *Journal of Pain Symptom Management, 10,* 131–141.

Breitbart, W., Chochinov, H., & Passik, S. (1998). Psychiatric aspects of palliative care. In D. Doyle., G. W. C. Hanks & N. MacDonald (Eds.), *Oxford Textbook of Palliative Medicine* (2nd ed). Oxford, UK: University Press.

Breitbart, W., & Krivo, S. (1998). Suicide. In J. Holland (Ed.), *Psycho-Oncology* (pp. 541–547). New York: Oxford University Press.

Brown, J., Henteleff, P., Barakat, S., & Rowe, C. J. (1986) Is it normal for terminally ill patients to desire death? *American Journal of Psychiatry, 143*, 208–211.

Caine, E., & Conwell, Y. (1993). Self-determined death, the physician, and medical priorities: Is there time to talk. *JAMA, 270,* 875–876.

Cassell, E. J. (1982). The nature of suffering and the goals of medicine. *New England Journal of Medicine, 306,* 639–645.

Cassileth, B., Lusk, E., Strouse, T., Miller, D., Brown, L., & Cross, P. (1985). A psychological analysis of cancer patients and their next of kin. *Cancer, 55,* 72–76.

Cherny, N., Coyle, N., & Foley, K. (1994). The treatment of suffering when patients request elective death. *Journal of Palliative Care, 10* 71–79.

Cherny, N. (1996). The problem of inadequately relieved suffering. *Journal of Social Issues, 52,* 13–30.

Chochinov, H., Wilson, K., Enns, M., & Lander, S. (1994). The prevalence of depression in the terminally ill: effects of diagnostic criteria and symptom threshold judgments. *American Journal of Psychiatry, 151,* 537–540.

Chochinov, H., & Wilson, K. (1995). The euthanasia debate: attitudes, practices and psychiatric considerations. *Canadian Journal of Psychiatry, 40,* 593–602.

Chochinov, H., Wilson, K., Enns, M., Mowchun, N., Lander, S., Levitt, M., & Clinch, J. (1995). Desire for death in the terminally ill. *American Journal of Psychiatry, 152,* 1185–1191.

Chochinov, H., Wilson, K., Enns, M., & Lander, S. (1997). "Are you depressed?" Screening for depression in the terminally ill. *American Journal of Psychiatry, 154,* 674–676.

Chochinov, H., Douglas, T., Clinch, J., & Dudgeon, D. (1999). Will to live in the terminally ill. *Lancet, 354,* 817–819.

Cicirelli, V. G. (1997). Relationship of psychosocial and background variables to older adults' end-of-life decisions. *Psychology and Aging, 12,* 72–83.

Conwell, Y., & Caine, E. D. (1991). Rational suicide and the right to die; reality and myth. *New England Journal of Medicine, 325*, 1100–1102.

Danis, M., Southerland, L., Garrett, J., Smith, J. L., Hielema, F., Pickard, C. G., Egner, D. M., & Patrick, D. L. (1991). A prospective stud of advance directives for life-sustaining care. *New England Journal of Medicine, 324*, 882–888.

Davies, B., Reimer, J., & Martens, N. (1990). Families in supportive care-Part I- The transition of fading away: The nature of fading away. *Journal of Palliative Care, 6,* 12–20.

Derogatis, L., Morrow, G., Fetting, J., Penman, D., Piasetsky, S., Schmale, A., Henrichs, M., & Carnicke, C. (1983). The prevalence of psychiatric disorder among cancer patients. *JAMA, 249,* 751–757.

Detmer, C., & Lamberti, J. Family Grief. *Death Studies, 15,* 363–374.

Eissler, K. (1955). *The psychiatrist and the dying patient.* New York: International Universities Press.

Ell, K., Nishimoto, R., Mantell, J., & Hanovitch, M. (1988). Longitudinal analysis of psychological adaptation among family members of patients wit cancer. *Journal of Psychosomatic Research, 32,* 429–438.

Emmanuel, E., Fairclough, D., Daniels, E., & Clarridge, B. R. (1996). Euthanasia and physician assisted suicide: attitudes and experiences of oncology patients, oncologists and the public. *Lancet, 347,* 1805–1810.

Francis, L. P. (1998). Assisted suicide: are the elderly a special case? In M. P. Battin., R. Rhodes, & A. Silvers (Eds.), *Physician-Assisted Suicide: Expanding the Debate* (pp. 11–27). New York: Routledge.

Gabbard, G. (Ed.). (1999). *Countertransference Issues in Psychiatric Treatment.* Washington: American Psychiatric Press.

Ganzini, L., Lee, M., Heintz, R., Bloom, J. D., & Fenn, D. S. (1994). The effect of depression treatment on elderly patients' preferences for life-sustaining medical therapy. *American Journal of Psychiatry, 51,* 1631–1636.

Gleeson, K., & Wise, S. (1990). The do-not-resuscitate order: Still too little too late. *Annals of Internal Medicine, 150,* 1057–1060.

Glick, S. M. (1997). Unlimited human autonomy -A cultural bias? *New England Journal of Medicine, 336,* 954–957.

Goodwin, J. S. (1991). Mercy killing: Mercy for whom? *JAMA, 265,* 326.

Grassi, L., Indelli. M., Marzola, M., Maestri, A., Santini, A., Piva, E., & Boccalon, M. (1996). Depressive symptoms and quality of life in home-care assisted cancer patients. *Journal of Pain Symptom Management, 12,* 300–307.

Hendin, H., & Klerman, G. (1993). Physician assisted suicide: The dangers of legalization. *American Journal of Psychiatry. 150,* 143–145.

Hendin, H. (1999). Suicide, assisted suicide, and euthanasia. In D. Jacobs (Ed.), *The Harvard Medical School Guide to Suicide Assessment and Intervention* (pp. 540–560). San Francisco: Jossey-Bass Publishers.

Jordan, J., Kraus, D., & Ware, E. (1993). Observations on loss and family development. *Family Process, 32,* 425–440.

Kelly, B., Edwards, P., Synott, R., Neil, C., Baillie, R., & Battistutta, D. (1999). Predictors of bereavement outcomes for family carers of cancer patients. *Psycho-Oncology, 8,* 237–249.

Kissane, D. (1994). Grief and the family. In S. Bloch., J. Hafner., E. Harari & G. Szmukler (Eds.), *The family in clinical psychiatry* (pp. 71–91). New York: Oxford University Press.

Kissane, D., Bloch, S., Burns, I., McKenzies, K., & Posterino, M. (1994). Psychological morbidity in the families of patients with cancer. *Psyco-Oncology, 3,* 47–56.

Kissane, D., Bloch, S., Burns, I., Patrick, J., Wallace, C., & McKenzie, D. (1994). Perceptions of family functioning and cancer. *Psycho-Onconolgy, 3,* 259–269.

Kleinman, A., Kleinman, J. (1995). Suffering and its professional transformation. In A. Kleinman (Ed.), *Writing at the Margin: Discourse Between Anthropology and Medicine* (pp. 95–119). Berkley: University of California Press.

Larsen, G. (1999). Family members' experience with do-not-resuscitate (DNR). *Journal of Family Issues, 2,* 269–289.

Lester, D. (1996). Psychological issues in euthanasia, suicide, and assisted suicide. *Journal of Social Issues, 52* 51–62.

Mann, P. (1998). Meanings of death. In M. P. Battin., R. Rhodes & A. Silvers (Eds.), *Physician-Assisted Suicide: Expanding the Debate* (pp. 11–27). New York: Routledge.

Massie, M., Holland, J., & Glass, E. (1983). Delirium in terminally ill cancer patients. *American Journal of Psychiatry, 140,* 1048–1050.

McDaniel JS, Musselman DL, Porter MR, Reed DA, Nemeroff CB. (1995) Depression in patients with cancer. Diagnosis, Biology and Treatment. *Archives of General Psychiatry,* 52, 88-89.

McGoldrick, M. (1991). The legacy of loss. In F. Walsh & M. McGoldrick (Eds.), *Living beyond loss. Death in the family.* New York: W.W. Norton & Co.

Muskin, P. (1998). The request to die. Role for a psychodynamic perspective on physician-assisted suicide. *JAMA, 279* 323–328.

Nordquist, G. (1999). American health care and the medicalization of dying. *The Journal of Applied Sciences, 23* 31–42.

Northouse, L. (1984). The impact of cancer on the family: An overview. *International Journal of Psychiatry in Medicine,14,* 215–242.

Northouse, L. A. (1989). Longitudinal study of the adjustment of patients and husbands to breast cancer. *Oncological Nursing Forum, 16,* 511–516.

Owen, C., Tennant, C., Levi, J., & Jones, M. (1992). Suicide and euthanasia: patient attitudes in the context of cancer. *Psycho-Oncology, 1,* 79–82.

Pajusco, E., & de Leo, D. (1993). The "Rational Suicide". *Giornale Italiano di Suicidologia, 3,* 121–129.

Raphael, B. (1984). *The anatomy of bereavement.* London: Hutchinson.

Rosen, E. (Ed.). (1998). *Families Facing Death. A Guide for Healthcare Professionals and Volunteers.* San Francisco: Jossey-Bass Publishers.

Rothchild, E. (1998). Family dynamics in decisions to withhold or withdraw treatment. In M. Steinberg & S. Younger (Eds.), *End of Life Decisions. A Psychosocial Perspective* (chapter 4). Washington: American Psychiatric Press.

Rowlands, H., & Rowlands, B. (1990). *Hospital legal forms, check lists and guidelines.* Gaithersburg: Aspen.

Sawyer, D., Williams, J., & Lowy, F. (1993). Canadian physicians and euthanasia: Definitions and distinctions. *Canadian Medical Association Journal, 148,* 1463–1466.

Schachter, S. (1992). Quality of life for families in the management of home care patients with advanced cancer. *Journal of Palliative Care, 8,* 61–66

Seckler, A., Meier, D., Mulvihill, M., & Paris, B. E. (1991) Substantiated judgement: how accurate are proxy predictions? *Annals of Internal Medicine, 115,* 92–98.

Shapiro, E. (Ed). *Grief as a Family Process. A Developmental Approach to Clinical Practice.* New York: The Guilford Press.

Shapiro, E. (1996). Family bereavement and cultural diversity: A social developmental perspective. *Family Process, 35,* 313–332.

Shuster, J., Breitbart, W., & Chochinov, H. (1999). Psychiatric aspects of excellent end of life care. *Psychosomatics, 40,* 1–4.

Smith, N. (1990). The impact of terminal illness on the family. *Palliative Medicine, 4,* 127–135.

Speigel, D., Sands, S., & Koopman, C. (1994). Pain and depression in patients with cancer. *Cancer, 74,* 2570–2578.

Steinberg, M., & Younger, S. (Eds.). (1988). *End of Life Decisions. A Psychosocial perspective.* Washington: American Psychiatric Press.

Swigart, V., Lidz, C., Butterworth, V., & Arnold, R. (1996). Letting go: Family willingness to forgo life support. *Heart & Lung, 25,* 483–494.

Uhlmann, R. F., & Pearlman, R. A. (1991). Perceived quality of life and preferences for life-sustaining treatments in older adults. *Annals of Internal Medicine, 151,* 495–497.

Vachon, M., Freedman, K., Formo, A., & Rogers, J. (1977). The final illness in cancer: the widow's perspective. *Canadian Medical Association Journal, 117,* 1151–1153.

Van der Maas, P J., van Delden, J. M. M., & Pijnenbourg, L. (1991). Euthanasia and other medical decisions concerning the end of life. *Lancet, 338,* 669–674.

Varghese, F., & Kelly, B. (1999). Countertransference and assisted suicide. In G. Gabbard (Ed.), *Countertransference Issues in Psychiatric Treatment*. Washington: American Psychiatric Press.

Walsh, F., & McGoldrick, M. (Eds.). (1991). *Living Beyond Loss. Death in the Family*. New York: W.W. Norton and Co.

Wanzer, S., Federman, D., Adelstein, S., Cassed, D., Cranford, R., Hook, W., Lo, B., Moertel, C., & Safar, P. (1989). The physicians responsibility toward hopelessly ill patients- a second look. *New England Journal of Medicine, 120,* 844–849.

Worby, C., & Babineau, R. (1974). The family interview: helping patient and family cope with metastatic disease. *Geriatrics, 27,* 83–94.

Zalcberg, J., & Buchanan, J. (1997). Clinical issues in euthanasia. *Medical Journal of Australia, 166,* 150–152.

Safe, Legal, Rare? Physician-Assisted Suicide and Cultural Change in the Future[1]

Margaret P. Battin

Division of Medical Ethics, University of Utah, Salt Lake City, USA

Introduction

Cultural change is well recognized in the recent history of death and dying in the contemporary world. In the wake of Elizabeth Kübler-Ross' 1969 work *On Death and Dying,* not only has it become socially acceptable to talk about death and dying with someone who is terminally ill, but, as traditional religious and legal strictures loosen, it is becoming possible for a person facing death to consider what role he or she wants to play in the forthcoming death. The United States has seen rapid evolution in attitudes and practices about death and dying over the last several decades, beginning with the early legal recognition in the *California Natural Death Act* (1976) of a patient's right to refuse life-prolonging treatment in the face of terminal illness, to the increased public awareness of issues of personal autonomy in dying, raised by Derek Humphrey's how-to book of lethal drug dosages, *Final Exit,* to new sensitivity to physician roles in aiding dying, both in the maverick social activism of Dr. Jack Kevorkian and a New York grand jury's refusal to indict the respected physician Timothy Quill. This process of cultural evolution has reached legal recognition: in 1997, the U.S. Supreme Court jointly decided the cases Washington v. Glucksberg and Vacco v. Quill, and while it held that physician-assisted suicide is not a constitutional right, it by implication also decided that states are free to make their own laws in this matter. Indeed, Oregon has made it legal for a physician to provide a terminally ill patient who requests it with a prescription for a lethal drug, thus bringing above ground the practical manifestation of a long process of cultural change.

Cultural change like this draws on many factors, including changes in medical technology, in the epidemiology of death, and social and legislative recognition of civil and personal rights in many other areas. Or course, cultural change is not unidirectional; although Oregon legalized physician-assisted suicide, Maryland, among others, made it a felony. But it is possible to discern a pattern of increasing

---

[1]This paper is a reframing of my "Physician-Assisted Suicide: Safe, Legal, Rare?", which appeared in Battin, M. P., Rhodes, R., & Silvers, A. (Eds.). (1998). *Physician-Assisted Suicide: Expanding the Debate.* New York: Routledge.

attention to end of life issues and, I believe, to the issue of individual self-determination in the matter of dying.

The story does not end here. This is the most important fact about cultural change – the fact that it is an ongoing process, one which we view only from some intermediate point. What I want to explore in this paper is the prospect of cultural change in the future, and the possibility that physician-assisted suicide may come to look very, very different from the desperation move that it is taken to be now.

Part One: The Way it Looks Now

Observe the current debate over physician-assisted suicide: On the one side, supporters of legalization appeal to the principle of autonomy, or self-determination, to insist that terminally ill patients have the right to extricate themselves from pain and suffering and to control as much as possible the ends of their lives. On the other, opponents resolutely insist on various religious, principled, or slippery-slope grounds that physician-assisted suicide cannot be allowed, whether because it is sacrilegious, immoral, or poses risks of abuse. As vociferous and politicized as these two sides of the debate have become, however, proponents and opponents (tacitly) agree on a core issue: that the patient may choose to avoid suffering and pain. They disagree, it seems, largely about the means the patient and his or her physician may use to do so.

They also disagree about the actualities of pain control. Proponents of legalization insist that currently available forms of pain and symptom control are grossly inadequate and unsatisfactory. Citing such data as the SUPPORT study,[1] they point to high rates of reported pain among terminally ill patients, inadequately developed pain-control therapies, physicians' lack of training in pain-control techniques, and obstacles and limitations to delivery of pain-control treatment, including restrictions on narcotic and other drugs. Pain and the suffering associated with other symptoms just aren't adequately controlled, proponents of legalization insist, so the patient is surely entitled to avoid them – if he or she so chooses – by turning to earlier, humanely assisted dying.

Opponents of legalization, on the other hand, insist that these claims are uninformed. Effective methods of pain control include timely withholding and withdrawal of treatment, sufficient use of morphine or other drugs for pain (even at the risk of foreseen, through unintended, shortening of life), and the discontinuation of artificial nutrition and hydration. When all other measures to control pain and suffering fail, there is always the possibility of terminal sedation: the induction of coma with concomitant withholding of nutrition and hydration, which, though it

[1] According to the SUPPORT study, about 50% of dying hospitalized patients were reported to have experienced moderate to severe pain at least 50% of the time in their last three days of life.

results in death, is not to be seen as killing. Proponents laugh at this claim. Terminal sedation, they retort, like the overuse of morphine, is functionally equivalent to causing death.

Despite these continuing disagreements about the effectiveness, availability, and significance of current pain control, both proponents and opponents in the debate appear to agree that *if* adequate pain control were available, there would be far less call for physician-assisted suicide. This claim is both predictive and normative. *If* adequate pain control were available, both sides argue, then physician-assisted suicide would be and should be quite infrequent – a "last resort," as Timothy Quill puts it, to be used only in exceptionally difficult cases when pain control really does fail. Borrowing use of an expression used by President Clinton to describe his view of abortion, proponents insist that physician-assisted suicide should be "safe, legal, and rare." Opponents do not believe that it should be legal, but they also think that if it cannot be suppressed altogether or if a few very difficult cases remain, it should be very, very rare. The only real disagreement between opponents and proponents concerns those cases in which adequate pain control cannot be achieved.

What accounts for the opposing sides' underlying agreement that physician-assisted suicide should be rare is, I think, an unexamined assumption they share. This assumption is the view that the call for physician-assisted suicide is what might be called a *phenomenon of discrepant development:* a symptom of the disparity in development between two distinct capacities of modern medicine, the capacity to extend or prolong life and the capacity to control pain. Research, development, and delivery of technologies for the prolongation of life have raced far ahead; those for control of pain lagged far behind. It is this situation of discrepant development that has triggered the current concern with physician-assisted suicide and the volatile public debate over whether to legalize it or not.

The opposing sides both also hold in common the view that what would lead to the resolution of the problem is whatever set of mechanisms would tend to equalize the degree of development of medicine's capacities to prolong life and to control pain. To achieve this equalization, two simultaneous strategies are recommended: cutting back on overzealous prolongation of life (as Dan Callahan, 1987, 1990, 1993, for example, has long recommended, and at the same time (as Hospice and others have been insisting[1]) accelerating the development of technologies, modes of delivery, and physician training for more effective methods of pain control. As life prolongation is held back a bit, pain control can catch up, and the current situation of discrepant development between the two can be alleviated. Thus calls for physician-assisted suicide can be expected to become rarer and rarer, and as medicine's capacities for pain control are finally equalized with its capacities for life prolongation, finally to virtually disappear. Almost no one imagines that there will not still be a few difficult situations in which life is prolonged beyond the point at which pain can be effectively controlled, but these will be increasingly infrequent, it is

[1]See especially the work of Foley. K. (1995). Pain, physician-assisted suicide, and euthanasia. *Pain Forum*, 4 (3), 163-178 and other works.

assumed, and in general, as the disparity between our capacities for life prolongation and for pain control shrinks, interest in and need for physician-assisted suicide will decrease and all but disappear.

Fortunately, this view continues, the public debate over physician-assisted suicide now so intense will not have been a waste, since it has both warned against the potential cruelty of overzealous prolongation of life and at the same time stimulated greater attention to imperatives of pain control. The current debate serves as social pressure for bringing equalization of the disparity about. Yet as useful as this debate is, this view holds, it will soon subside and disappear; we're just currently caught in a turbulent – but fleeting – little maelstrom.

Part Two: The Longer View

That's how things look now. But I think we can also see our current concern with physician-assisted suicide in a longer-term, historically informed view. Consider just three of the many profound changes that affect matters of how we die. First, there has been a shift, beginning in the middle of the last century, in the ways in which human beings characteristically die. Termed the "epidemiological transition,"[1] this change involves a shift away from death due to parasitic and infectious disease (ubiquitous among humans in all parts of the globe prior to about 1850) to death in later life of degenerative disease – especially cancer and heart disease, which together account for almost two thirds of deaths in the developed countries. This means dramatically extended lifespans and also deaths from diseases with characteristically extended downhill terminal courses. Second, there have been changes in religious attitudes about death: people are less likely to see death as divine punishment for sin, or to see suffering as a prerequisite for the afterlife, or to see suicide as a highly stigmatized and serious sin rather than the product of mental illness or depression. Third among the major shifts in cultural attitudes that affect the way we die is the increasing emphasis on the notion of individual rights of self-determination, reinforced in the latter part of this century by the civil rights movement's attention to individuals in vulnerable groups: this shift has affected self-perceptions and attitudes towards the terminally ill, and patients, including dying patients, are now recognized to have a wide array of rights previously eclipsed by the paternalistic practices of medicine.

These three transitions, along with many other concomitant cultural changes, invite us to see our current concern with physician-assisted suicide in a quite different way – not just as a phenomenon resulting from the currently disparate development of life-prolonging and pain-controlling technologies, a temporary anomaly, but as a precursor, an early symptom of a much more substantial sea-change in attitudes about death. We might call this shift in attitudes a shift towards "directed dying", or "self-directed dying", in which the individual who is dying plays

[1]The term originates with Omran (1971) and the theory is augmented in Olshansky & Ault (1987).

a far more prominent, directive role than in earlier eras in determining how and when his or her death shall occur. In this changed view, dying is no longer *something that happens to you* but *something you do.*

To be sure, this shift – if it is one – can be seen as already well under way. Taking its legally visible start with the California Natural Death Act, terminally ill patients have already gained dramatically enlarged rights of self-determination in matters of guiding and controlling their own deaths, including rights to refuse treatment, discontinue treatment, stipulate treatment to be withheld at a later date, designate decisionmakers, and to negotiate with their physicians, or have their surrogates do so, such matters as DNR orders, withholding and withdrawal of ventilators, surgical procedures, nutrition and hydration, the use of opioids, and even terminal sedation. Some patients also negotiate, or attempt to negotiate, physician-assisted suicide or physician-performed euthanasia with their physicians. In all of this, we already see the patient as playing a far more prominent role in determining the course of his or her dying process and in its character and timing, and far more willingness on the part of physicians, family members, the law, and other parties to respect the patient's preferences and choices in these matters.

But this may be just the tip of a looming iceberg. For we may ask whether, much as we human beings have made dramatic gains in control over our own reproduction, particularly rapidly in very recent times (the birth control pill was introduced just thirty years ago), we human beings are beginning to make dramatic gains in control over our own dying, particularly rapidly in the last several decades. We cannot keep from dying altogether, of course. But by using directly caused death, as in physician-assisted suicide, it is possible to control many of dying's features: its timing in the downhill course of a terminal disease, its place, the exact agents which cause it, its observers, and so on. Indeed, as Robert Kastenbaum (1976) has argued, because it makes it possible to control the time, place, manner and people present at one's death, assisted suicide will become the *preferred* manner of dying.

But this conjecture doesn't yet show what could actually motivate such substantial social change, away from a culture which sees dying primarily as *something that happens to you*, to a culture which sees it as *something you do* – a deliberate, planned activity, one's final and cumulative activity. What might do this, I think, is a conceptual change, or, more exactly, a shift in decisional perspective in choice-making about pain, suffering, and other elements of dying. It is the kind of shift in decisional perspective that evolves on a society-wide scale as a populace gains understanding of and control over a matter, a shift in choicemaking perspective from a stance we might describe as immediately involved or "enmeshed", to one that is distanced and reflective (I'll use two Latin names for these stances later). This shift can occur for many features of human experience – it has already largely occurred in the developed world with respect to reproduction – but it has not yet occurred with respect to death and dying. It has not yet occurred – or rather, perhaps it has just begun.

Take a patient, an average man. This particular man is so average that he just happens to have contracted that disease which is the usual diagnosis (as we know from the Netherlands[1]) in cases of physician-assisted suicide – cancer – and he is also so average that this disease will kill him at just the average life-expectancy for males in the United States, 72.8 years. Furthemore, he is also so average that if he does turn to physician-assisted suicide, he will choose to forgo just about the same amount of life that, on average, Dutch patients receiving euthanasia or physician-assisted suicide do, less than 3.3 weeks (Emanuel & Battin, 1998). He has been considering physician-assisted suicide since his illness was first diagnosed (since he is an average man, this was about 29.6 months ago), but now, as his condition deteriorates, he thinks more seriously about it. His motivation includes both preemptive elements, the desire to avoid some of the very worst things that terminal cancer might bring him, and reactive elements, the desire to relieve some of the symptoms and other suffering that he is already experiencing. *It's bad enough now,* he tells his doctor, *and it will probably get worse*. He asks his doctor for the pills. He is perfectly aware of what he may miss – a number of weeks of continued life, the possibility of an unexpected cure, the chance, even if it is a longshot, of spontaneous regression or remission, and – not to be overlooked – the possibility that that the worst is over, so to speak, and that the remainder of his downhill course in terminal cancer won't be so bad. He is also well aware that even a bad agonal phase may nevertheless include moments of great intimacy and importance with his family or friends. But he makes what he sees as a rational choice, seeking to balance the risks and possible benefits of easy death now, versus a little more continuing life with a greater possibility of a hard death. He is making his choice *in medias res*, in the middle of things, as the physical, social, and emotional realities of terminal illness engulf him. He is enmeshed in his situation, caught in it, trapped between what seem like two bad alternatives – suffering, or suicide.

But, of course, he might have done his deciding about how his life shall end and whether to elect physician-assisted suicide in preference to the final stages of terminal illness from a quite different, more distanced perspective, a secular version of the view *sub specie aeternitatis*. This is not just an objective, depersonalized view – anybody's view – but his own, distinctively personal view not confined to a specific timepoint[2]. Rather than assessing his prospects from the point of view he has at the time at which he would continue or discontinue his life – that point late in the course of his illness when things have already become "bad enough" and are likely to get worse – he might have done his deciding, albeit rather more hypothetically, from the perspective of a more generalized view of his life. From this alternative perspective, what he would have seen is the overall shape of his life, and it is with respect to this that he would have made his choices about how it shall end. Of course,

[1]Data on physician-assisted suicide and euthanasia in the Netherlands is provided by what is called the Remmelink Commission Report, (Van der Maas, Johannes, van Delden & Pijnenborg, 1992). A five-year update is available in (Van der Maas, Johannes, van Delden & Pijnenborg, 1996).

[2]The distinction I am drawing here between personal views *in medias res* and *sub specie aeternitatis* is thus not quite the same as that drawn by Thomas Nagel between subjective and objective views, though it has much in common with Nagel's distinction in contexts concerning death. See Nagel (1986), especially Chapter XI, section 3, on death.

he could not know in advance whether he will contract cancer, or succumb to heart disease, or be hit by a bus – though he does know that he will die sometime or other. Consequently, his choices are necessarily conditional in form, "*if* I get cancer, I'll refuse aggressive treatment and use hospice care", "*if* I get AIDS, I'll ask for physician-assisted suicide", "*if* I get Alzheimer's, I'll commit suicide on my own, since no physician besides Jack Kevorkian would help me", and so on. Although conditional in form and predicated on circumstances that may not occur, these may be real choices nonetheless, and, particularly because they are reiterated and repeated over the course of a lifetime, have real motive force.

The difference, then, between these two views is substantial. In the first, our average man with an average terminal cancer, doing his deciding *in medias res*, is deciding whether or not to take the pills his physician has given him now. It is his last possible couple of weeks or a month (on average, 3.3 weeks) that he is deciding about. Even if continuing life threatens pain and other suffering, it is still all he has left, and while it may be difficult to live this life – all he has left – it may also be very difficult to relinquish it.

In contrast, if our average man were doing his deciding *sub specie aeternitatis*, from a distanced though still personal viewpoint not tied to a specific moment in his life, he would have been deciding all along between two different conceptions of his own demise, between two possible lives for himself. One of his possible lives would, on average, be 72.8 years long, the average lifespan for a male in the United States, with the possibility of substantial suffering at the end – on average, as the SUPPORT study finds, a 50% chance of moderate to severe pain at least 50% of the time during the last three days before his death. The other of his possible lives would be about 72.7 years long, foreshortened on average 3.3 weeks by physician-assisted suicide, but with a markedly reduced possibility of substantial suffering at the end. (This shortening of the lifespan is not age-based but time-to-death based, planned for, on average, 3.3 weeks before an unassisted death would have occurred; it occurs in this example at age 72.7 just because our man is so average.) This latter, shortened life also offers our man the opportunity to control the timing, the place, the manner, and so on of his death in the way he likes. Viewed *sub specie aeternitatis*, at any or many earlier points in one's life or from a vantage point standing outside life, so to speak, the difference between 72.8 and 72.7 seems negligible: these are both lives of average length not interrupted by grossly premature death. Why not choose the one in which the risk of agonal pain – as high as 50/50, according to the SUPPORT study – is far, far less great, and the possibility of conscious, cumulative experience, surrounded by family members, trusted friends, and permitting final prayers and goodbyes, is far, far greater?

It may seem difficult to distinguish these two choices in practice. This is because we typically make our decisions about death and dying *in medias res*, not *sub specie aeternitatis*, and our medical practices, our bioethics discussions, and our background culture strongly encourage this. The call for assisted dying, like other patient pleas, is seen as a reaction to the circumstances of dying, not a settled, longer term, preemptive preference (Prado, 1990). True, some independently minded individuals consider these issues in a kind of background, hypothetical way throughout their lives, but this is certainly not the practical norm. We can only really understand this view as involving a substantial cultural shift from our current perspective.

But if this shift occurs, a slightly abbreviated lifespan in which there is dramatically reduced risk of pain and suffering will not only seem to be preferable to one which is negligibly longer but carries substantial risk of pain and suffering in its agonal phase, it will also be seen as rational and normal to plan for this abbreviated lifespan and to plan the means of bringing it about. The way to ensure it, of course, is to plan for direct termination of life. After all, one cannot count on being able to discontinue some life-prolonging treatment or other – refusing antibiotics, disconnecting a respirator – to hasten death and thus avoid what might be the worst weeks at the end. This most likely means planning for physician-assisted suicide. From this distanced perspective, a 72.7-year life with a virtually assured good end looks much, much better than a 72.8-year life that has an even chance of coming to a bad end. Arguably, it would be rational for any individual, except those for whom religious commitments or other scruples rule out suicide altogether, to plan to ensure this. But if it looks this way to one individual, it will look this way to many; and it is thus plausible to imagine that physician-assisted suicide would not be rare but rather a choice viewed as rational and preemptively prudent by many or most members of the culture. Thus it can come to be seen as a normal course of action, not a rarity or a "last resort." To be sure, there are other ways of abbreviating a lifespan to avoid terminal suffering – withdrawing or withholding treatment, overusing of morphine or other pain-relieving drugs, discontinuing artificial nutrition and hydration, and terminal sedation – but these cannot be used unless the patient's condition has already worsened and thus likely to involve that pain or suffering the person might choose to avoid. Thus these other modalities function primarily reactively; it is assisted suicide that can function preemptively.

But, as soon as planning for a normal, slight abbreviation in the lifespan by means of assisted suicide becomes conceptually possible not just for our average man but for actual persons in general, it also becomes possible to imagine a wide range of context-specific cultural practices which might emerge surrounding physician-assisted suicide. After all, that a person understands and expects his lifespan to be one which will end in an assisted death a few weeks before he might otherwise have died, while he is still conscious, alert, and capable of deciding what location he wants it to take place in, what family members, caregivers, clergy, or others he wants to have present, what ceremonies, religious or symbolic, he wants conducted, etc., suggests that more general social practices would grow up around these possibilities. After all, our average man sees his life this way; but it is possible for him to do this partly because the others in his society see their lives this way as well. Attitudes about death are heavily socially conditioned, and so are the perspectives from which choicemaking about death is seen.

This is the precondition for the development of a whole range of social practices supporting such choices. These might include various kinds of practical supports, such as legal, insurance, and other policies which treat assisted dying as acceptable and normal; various sorts of cultural and religious practices which similarly treat assisted dying as acceptable and normal (for instance by developing rituals and rites concerning the forthcoming death); familial supports within the family, including family gatherings, preparing for the death, and sharing reminiscences and goodbyes; pre-death dispositions of wills and life insurance (we already recognize viaticums, pre-death payoffs of life insurance for terminally ill patients); and even such now-inconceivable practices as pre-death funerals, understood as ceremonies of leavetaking and farewell, expressions of both celebration of a life complete and grief at its loss. In turn, such social practices come to function as positive reasons for choosing a somewhat earlier, elective death – formerly and rudely called "physician-assisted suicide," even when pain control is no longer the issue at all, and the new social pattern – so different from our current one – reinforces itself. This has nothing to do with a *Soylent Green* sort of view, in which people are forced into choices they do not genuinely make (this film can be understood only from our current, *in medias res* view); but a world in which their normal choices have genuinely changed, and changed for reasons which seem to them good.

Furthermore, if the culture-wide view of choicemaking about death and dying were more fully held *sub specie aeternitatis* in this distanced, less enmeshed and less merely reactive way, in which earlier, elective death becomes the norm, we could also expect the more frequent practice of "setting a date", as people who have contracted predictably terminal illnesses carry out the plans they had been developing all along for their own demises. Setting a date for one's own death – presumably, a couple of weeks or so before the date it might naturally have been, revisable of course in the light of any changes in the diagnosis or prognosis – would still be both preemptive and reactive in character, but far more preemptive than choices made *in medias res*, where choices will be highly reactive to the then-current circumstances the patient finds himself or herself in. The timing of such choices might always be revised in consultation with the physician; but what would be culturally reinforced would be the general commitment to advance planning for one's own death as well as a commitment to assuming a comparatively autonomist, directive role in it. Self-directed dying would be the norm, though of course different people would direct their deaths in quite different ways.

If the profound changes affecting matters of how we die that are already underway – the epidemiological transition, shifting from parasitic and infectious disease deaths to deaths of predictably degenerative disease; the changes in religious conceptions of suicide so that it is not understood primarily as sin; and the steadily increasing attention to patients' and terminally ill patients' rights of self-determination, it is an open conjecture whether this is where we may be going. Are we in fact experiencing just a temporary aberration in our basic cultural patterns of death and dying, an aberration which is a function of the discrepant development of technologies for life prolongation and for pain control? Or are we seeing the first breaking waves of a sea-change from one perspective on death and dying to another, a far more autonomist and self-directive one?

Obviously, I can't say. But I can say that if this is what is happening, the assumption that physician-assisted suicide would or should be rare, an assumption still held by both sides in the current debate, will collapse. We would have no reason to assume that assisted dying should be rare, whatever the relationship between capacities for life prolongation and pain control. Of course, such a picture is very difficult to envision, since we do not think that way about death and dying now. But if we can at least see what is different about viewing personal choices about one's own death *sub specie aeternitatis* and in our current way, *in medias res,* enmeshed in particular circumstances, we can understand why it might occur.

Would it be a good thing, or a bad thing? I can hardly answer that question here, but let me close with a story I heard somewhere in the Netherlands several years ago. I do not remember the exact source of the story nor the specific dates or names, and it is certainly not representative of current practice in Holland. But it was told to me as a true story, and it went something like this.

> Two friends, old sailing buddies, are planning a sailing trip in the North Sea in the summer. It is late February now, and they are discussing possible dates.
> "How about July 21?" says Willem. "The North Sea will be calm, the moon bright, and there's a music festival on the southern coast of Denmark we could visit."
> "Sounds great", answers Joost, "I'd love to get to the music festival. But I can't be gone then; the 21st is the date of my father's death."
> "Oh, I'm so sorry, Joost," Willem replies. "I knew your father was ill. Very ill, with cancer. But I didn't realize he had died."
> "He hasn't," Joost replies, "That's the day he will be dying. He's picked a date and made up his mind, and we all want to be there with him."

Such a story seems just that, a story, a fiction, somehow horrifying and also somehow liberating, but in any case virtually inconceivable to us. But it was not told to me as a fiction, but as a true story. I've tried to explore the conceptual assumptions that might lie behind such a story, and to consider whether in the future such stories might become more and more the norm. I have not tried to say whether this would be good or bad, but only that this might well be where we are going. In fact, I think it would be good – just as I think increasing personal control over reproduction is good – but I haven't argued for that view here.

Cultural change is an ongoing, long-term process of evolution, one which it is often hard to discern from a particular point in time. We see evolution in the past; but we have little way to think about the future. I've tried to suggest that our current point of view about personal autonomy in death and dying is unduly limited; while we recognize that substantial change has already occurred, we fail to realize that change as great or greater may be coming in the future. Indeed, it could involve a full reversal of earlier cultural attitudes about one's own role in one's own death. Of course cultural change is not unidirectional, and there may be backward as well as forward motion; nor do the attitudes of all members of a culture evolve at the same rate at the same time. Factors like wars, plagues, famines, scientific discoveries, and technological advances have reversed or hastened cultural change in the past, and could of course do so in the future. Just the same, I think it is possible to discern motion beyond the current view that physician-assisted suicide should be rare, a desperation move when nothing else works, toward the view that one's own death at the conclusion of terminal illness may be self-directed, that individuals can and should have the psychological and social freedom to reflect in a longer term way about their own future choices when they embark on the dying process, perhaps making physician-assisted suicide an eventual part of their plans, as well as the practical and legal freedom to plan whatever family gatherings, ceremonies, and religious observances they might wish – not as a desperate last resort or reactive escape from bad circumstances, but as a preemptively prudent, significant, cumulative experience. How long this process of cultural change might take, and what might interrupt it or hasten it, only time will tell.

References

Callahan, D. (1987). *Setting Limits: Medical Goals in an Aging Society*. New York: Simon and Schuster.

Callahan, D. (1990). *What Kind of Life? The Limits of Medical Progress*. New York: Simon and Schuster.

Callahan, D. (1993). *The Troubled Dream of Life: Living with Mortality*. New York: Simon and Schuster.

Connors, A. F., Jr., Dawson, N. V., Desbiens, N. A., Fulkerson, W. J., Jr., Goldman, L., Knaus, W. A., Lynn, J., & Oye, R. K. [SUPPORT Principal Investigators] (1995). A Controlled Trial to Improve Care for Seriously Ill Hospitalized Patients. *Journal of the American Medical Association, 274* , 1951–98.

Emanuel, E. J., & Battin, M. P. (1998). The Economics of Euthanasia: What are the Potential Cost Savings from Legalizing Physician-Assisted Suicide? *New England Journal of Medicine, 339*, 167–172.

K. Foley. (1995). Pain, physician-assisted suicide, and euthanasia. *Pain Forum, 4*, 163-178

Kastenbaum, R. (1976). Suicide as the Preferred Way of Death. In E. S. Shneidman (Ed.), *Suicidology: Contemporary Developments* (pp. 425–441). New York: Grune & Stratton.

Nagel, T. (1986). *The View from Nowhere*. New York: Oxford University Press.

Olshansky, A. J., & Ault, A. B. (1987). The Fourth Stage of the Epidemiologic Transition: The Age of Delayed Degenerative Disease. In T. M. Smeeding (Ed.), *Should Medical Care Be Rationed By Age?* (pp. 11–43). Totowa, New Jersey: Rowman & Littlefield.

Omran, A. R. (1971). The Epidemiologic Transition: A Theory of the Epidemiology of Population Change. *Milbank Memorial Fund Quarterly, 49*, 509–38.

Prado, C. G. (1990). *The Last Choice: Preemptive Suicide in Advanced Age*. Westport, Conn: Greewood Press.

Van der Maas, P. J., Johannes, J. M., van Delden, J. M. M., & Pijnenborg, L. (1992). Euthanasia and other Medical Decisions Concerning the End of Life. *Health Policy, 22* (1,2).

Van der Maas, P. J., van der Wal, G., Haverkate, I., de Graaff, C. C., Kester, J. G., Onwuteaka-Philipsen, B. D., van der Heide, A., Bosma, J. M., & Willems, D. L. (1996). Euthanasia, physician-assisted suicide, and other medical practices involving the end of life in the Netherlands, 1990-1995. *New England Journal of Medicine, 335,* 1699–1705.

Addendum

The Elderly and Their Self-Determined Death in The Netherlands: A Brief Update

Willem J. Schudel and Johanna M. Vroom-Jorgerden

Department of Psychiatry, University of Rotterdam, The Netherlands

In the Netherlands euthanasia and physician-assisted suicide are criminal acts. However, if a number of well defined criteria for careful practice are fulfilled beforehand, physicians are not prosecuted for their involvement in euthanasia or assisted suicide (Griffith et al, 1998; Gevers, 1996).

Procedures for the official notification of assisted suicide were established in 1990 in order to formalise requirements and guidelines for both doctors and public prosecutors. Within the notification procedures and in the amendments to the criminal law, *no* formal distinction is recognised between euthanasia and physician-assisted suicide. Five regional review committees were created in November 1998 after careful assessment and a political debate (Netherlands Ministry of Foreign Affairs, 1998). The membership of these committees comprises specialists in the fields of medicine, law and ethics and are appointed by the Minister of Justice in consultation with the Minister of Health, Welfare and Sport. Their first annual report covered cases in 1999 of which there were 2,216 (Ministerie van Volksgezondheid and Welzijn en Sport 2000), 2,000 were euthanasia, 196 were assisted suicide and 20 were classified as a combination of euthanasia and assisted suicide. The review committees did not report on the age distribution of the cases.

The official Dutch statistics bureau reported a total of 1,519 suicides in 1998, of which just over one third (510) were men and women aged 55 years and older (Hoogenboezerm and Berg, 2000). Suicide rates in the Netherlands have shown a modest decline since 1985. The decline had been mainly amongst people over the age of 45 years.

Suicide research shows that severe physical suffering is often reported as an important factor contributing to suicide. In some cases it could be the decisive one. An important question that arises is whether the recent changes in the law and professional practice regarding euthanasia and assisted suicide influenced the incidence of suicide.

In order to explore the effect of the new legal and professional practice on suicide we analysed data on self-determined death in the city of The Hague. This is the only data available in the Netherlands for suicide, euthanasia and assisted suicide for a defined population. All cases of unnatural death must be notified to the Municipal

Health Officer (Medical Coroner) who personally views the body and pronounces his official verdict. To exclude alternative explanations the police officers are usually involved in all cases of suspected suicide. The euthanasia data were derived from the notification procedures we have described. Table 1 presents the data for residents of the Hague aged 55 years or more between 1993 and 1999.

Table 1. Registered cases of suicide* and euthanasia** in persons 55 years of age and older, The Hague 1993-1999

	Men & Women						
Year	**Inhabitants**	**Suicide**	**Euthanasia**	**Total**	**Suicide per 100,000**	**Euthanasia per 100,000**	**Total per 100,000**
1993	118,724	27	26	53	22.7	21.9	44.6
1994	116,985	19	39	58	16.2	33.3	49.6
1995	115,346	18	30	48	15.6	26.0	41.6
1996	113,480	21	27	48	18.5	23.8	42.3
1997	111,674	13	39	52	11.6	34.9	46.6
1998	110,115	12	37	49	10.9	33.6	44.5
1999	108,939	12	46	58	11.0	42.2	53.2

* Suicide: registration by Municipal Health Officer and Regional Police Authority, The Hague

** Euthanasia and physician-assisted suicide: registration by Municipal Health Officer, The Hague. Notification by responsible physician.

Discussion

Over the seven year period the combined rate of suicide and euthanasia amongst people over the age of 55 years has been stable. However, the suicide rate has tended to decrease whilst the euthanasia rate has tended to increase. This is consistent with the view that carefully controlled euthanasia has not resulted in additional deaths but has provided an alternative method of death.

Amongst the alternative explanations for the trends are that there have been changes in reporting rates of either suicide or euthanasia. Suicides are unlikely to be missed, as the register is fed from two sources, the police and doctors. There are no moral or legal pressures that might lead to either cases not being reported. There is some degree of under reporting of euthanasia and/or assisted suicide, but this is probably less that it was some years ago when only 40-50% of all euthanasia cases were reported to the authorities (van der Maas et al, 1996). We have no reason to suppose that the willingness to report has decreased since, as the prosecution of carefully acting and reporting doctors has become more and more rare in this country.

It is premature to draw firm conclusions from these findings, but they do not support the view (mostly expressed outside the country) that there has been a substantial increase of self-determined death in the Netherlands. More detailed research findings are necessary before any conclusion on these issues can be drawn.

References

Gevers S (1996). Euthanasia: law and practice in the Netherlands. *British Medical Bulletin 52,* 326-333.

Griffith J, Bood A, Weyers H (1998). *Euthanasia and law in the Netherlands.* Amsterdam: University Press.

Hoogenboezem J, Berg WC van den (2000). *Zelfdoding in Nederland (Suicide in the Netherlands).* Maandstatistiek van de bevolking, April 2000. Centraal Bureau voor de Statistiek, Heerlen/Voorburg.

Maas PJ van der, Wal G van der, Haverkate I et al (1996). Euthanasia, physician-assisted suicide and other medical practices involving the end of life in the Netherlands, 1990-1995. *New England Journal of Medicine* 335,1699-1705.

Ministerie van Volksgezondheid, Welzijn en Sport (2000). Regionale Toestingscommissies Euthanasie. Jaarverslag 1998/1999 (Annual Report) (DVC 00-088).

Netherlands Ministry of Foreign Affairs (1998). *Euthanasia:* A guide to Dutch policy on euthanasia and other medical decisions in the terminal stages of life.